Email from Ngeti

Email from Ngeti

AN ETHNOGRAPHY OF SORCERY, REDEMPTION, AND FRIENDSHIP IN GLOBAL AFRICA

James H. Smith and Ngeti Mwadime

UNIVERSITY OF CALIFORNIA PRESS

University of California Press, one of the most distinguished university presses in the United States, enriches lives around the world by advancing scholarship in the humanities, social sciences, and natural sciences. Its activities are supported by the UC Press Foundation and by philanthropic contributions from individuals and institutions. For more information, visit www.ucpress.edu.

University of California Press
Oakland, California

Library of Congress Cataloging-in-Publication Data

Smith, James H., 1970– author.
    Email from Ngeti : an ethnography of sorcery, redemption, and friendship in global Africa / James H. Smith and Ngeti Mwadime.
        pages   cm
    Includes bibliographical references.
    ISBN 978-0-520-28110-3 (cloth : alk. paper) — ISBN 978-0-520-28112-7 (pbk : alk. paper) — ISBN 978-0-520-95940-8 (ebook)
    1. Taita (African people)—Social life and customs.   2. Taita (African people)—Religious life.   3. Witchcraft—Kenya—Taita Hills.   4. Taita Hills (Kenya)—Social life and customs.   I. Mwadime, Ngeti, 1968– author. II. Title.
    DT433.545.T34S654 2014
    305.896'395—dc23   2014020612

Manufactured in the United States of America

23 22 21 20 19 18 17 16 15 14
10 9 8 7 6 5 4 3 2 1

In keeping with a commitment to support environmentally responsible and sustainable printing practices, UC Press has printed this book on Natures Natural, a fiber that contains 30% post-consumer waste and meets the minimum requirements of ANSI/NISO Z39.48-1992 (R 1997) (*Permanence of Paper*).

He emerges along with the world and he reflects the historical emergence of the world itself. . . . This transition is accomplished in him and through him. He is forced to become a new, unprecedented form of human being. *The organizing force of the future is therefore extremely great here.* . . . It is as though the very foundations of the world are changing, and man must change along with them. Understandably . . . problems of reality and man's potential, problems of freedom and necessity, and the problem of creative initiative rise to their full height.

MIKHAIL BAKHTIN, *on one type of Bildungsroman,*
the "realistic novel of emergence" (1986, 24; italics mine)

CONTENTS

ACKNOWLEDGMENTS

I would like to warmly thank the following people for their careful and generous readings of earlier versions of this manuscript: Donald Donham, Cristiana Giordano, Mariane Ferme, Jeffrey Mantz, Robert Blunt, Janet McIntosh, Paul Stoller, Christian Doll, Jane Saffitz, Laura Meek, Michelle Stewart, and Chris Kortright. I would also like to thank Michelle and Chris for donating their laptop to Ngeti back in 2003. The undergraduate students in my winter 2013 East and Southern Africa class (140b) deserve special mention for reading and commenting on early drafts of the book. Thanks to Joubin Mirzadegan for his close readings and feedback during office hours. My former undergraduate student Naeta Rohr also deserves special thanks for having typed out most of Ngeti's emails so that I could select and arrange them more easily. Finally, without the hard work and tireless encouragement of Bekah Wilson, this book never would have been finished.

Our editor Reed Malcolm provided priceless and inexhaustible support and enthusiasm for the project, and a wealth of valuable suggestions without which this book would not have come to fruition. Stacy Eisenstark, our University of California Press editorial coordinator, has been extremely helpful and patient throughout this process. The fortuitously named Anne Canright was an exceptionally insightful copy editor.

James H. Smith

These are the people I would like to thank. First, the late Mr. Isuwiro, whose name literally means *hope* in the Taita language, my dramatic English teacher who taught me that English can grab you by the scruff of the neck and yank you to unbelievable levels of accomplishment. In short, he said English is a path that all erudite people must tread with unsullied pride. My wife, Jane Kang'ombe Ngumba, for being my comfort, and without whom life would suck big time. My father, Charles Mwadime, for his resilience in times of crisis and his hidden wisdom, and for letting me thumb through his hardcover copy of Michael West's dictionary, without which my English journey would never have come this far. My mother, Monica Shali Mwadime, for being such an enigmatic matriarch who taught us how to fight for our rights and strive to be autodidacts. My sisters, Linny Waleghwa Mwadime and her family; Amanda Eghwa Mwadime and her family; Praxedy Maghuwa Mwadime and her family. My father-in-law, Mr. Paul Ngumbao Yaa, for believing that lives and the world can be changed by education. Pancras Shete Mwakulomba and his entire family for being there for me. Tony Basil Maghanga "Zion" for being a tough guy whose story needs to be told. The Peace Corps volunteer Tracy Grant for teaching me how to make guacamole and rig together a biogas plant. The exchange student Colleen Osterhaus for teaching me to offer my shoulder for others to cry on. Scott Sweet for not pissing on me when he could have. And last but not least James H. Smith, my best friend and mentor, who makes sense out of nonsense, a man who can endure both physical and emotional pain and still talk about it over a glass of devil's piss.

Ngeti Mwadime

ONE

Emails from the Field

AN INTRODUCTION

IT IS 2009, AND Erastus Ngeti Mwadime, a man of forty years from the Taita Hills of Kenya, is resting on the stick bed beside me in a forest mining town in the North Kivu province of the eastern Democratic Republic of the Congo. We are staying in an impromptu lodge for artisanal miners and traders in a town that sprang up from nothing in the middle of the rainforest just a few years earlier, when trappers who live in the forest discovered bauxite and cassiterite here. A few weeks ago, the mine was seized by an armed group that some claim was the Forces for the Democratic Liberation of Rwanda (FDLR), a militia composed largely of former Hutu Interahamwe (those who kill together), some of whom participated in the Rwandan genocide back in 1994. Others claim it was a Congolese army battalion that took the mine and the town while pretending to be the Hutu FDLR, wanting to convince the Congolese government that their presence was necessary for security. Now, not far from here, the Congolese army—an agglomeration of reintegrated militarized groups, some of whose members were in a war with each other a few short months ago—is pushing back the FDLR in the forest. It is, in short, a situation characterized by uncertainty and rapid flux.

We are here conducting research on coltan mining and trade in the eastern DR Congo, observing how this work is organized and how it has affected people's lives in this region and beyond. Coltan, or colombite-tantalite, is an ore from which tantalum and niobium are derived. Tantalum is used in the manufacture of digital capacitors. During a tenfold global price hike brought about by the Christmas-season demand for the Sony Playstation in 2000 and subsequent on-line speculation, this mineral was at the center of Africa's "first world war." At its height, this war involved some fourteen foreign nations and multiple international corporate players. The ongoing conflicts in the region, whose "causes" have been complex and multiple, have resulted in around six million deaths, more than in any single conflict since World War II. Still, many families continue to depend on the extraction of minerals used in digital devices, and they directly experience the impacts of price fluctuations and shifts in demand for coltan and other "digital minerals" on the global market. The mines we have been visiting are controlled by overlapping networks of political authorities, including state officials, military figures, lineage heads, and cooperatives, and Ngeti and I must constantly renegotiate these competing claims to authority and the right to collect "tax" as we move from place to place. So Ngeti, who loves computer technology and the fast, "open" communication enabled by "the Internet" more than anyone I know, is witnessing first hand the unpredictable and often violent circumstances surrounding the extraction of the minerals that undergird the Digital Age.[1]

I have contracted malaria, and Ngeti is helping me by making sure that I have the water and medicine I need and by continuing to conduct research while I recuperate. Earlier today he went out while I slept, and ended up talking to a couple of female sex workers in town. They told him voluminous stories about their lives, focusing on their experiences as the concubines of Mai Mai militia generals.[2] I was impressed by the quality and quantity of this material and by the degree to which Ngeti understands what I am looking for. His presence is grounding and comforting to me in what I experience as an epistemically murky and potentially dangerous place. Right now, I am very glad that he is here.

But Ngeti is also a stranger here, far from his temperate, comparatively peaceful Kenyan home. He has never seen insects like the ones in this hot, wet, rainforest region. Yesterday we spent about an hour killing monstrous spiders that seemed to bother him more than they did me. The other day, too, he had a strange rash on his ass that he insisted I see for myself. And he was clearly upset during the plane flight from the lakeside city of Goma to the forest town of Walikale: he had to get himself drunk on banana gin just to board the cargo plane. We flew in, over miles of rainforest, on an old Russian Cessna with no seats, sitting on top of plastic jerry cans filled with palm oil, and we landed on a small strip of paved forest road as female banana sellers and male bicyclists scurried out of the way. By the time we disembarked, Ngeti was so out of it that he made a big scene in front of the demanding immigration and internal security officials who sat in shacks by the road. Ngeti's drunken anger ended up costing me an additional fifty dollars. At the time, I was outwardly irritated, but now I'm over it and feeling magnanimous.

"Ngeti, *unafanya nini sasa?*"—what are you doing now?—I ask in a half-asleep, drug-induced tone. The antimalaria cocktail they gave me at the rural clinic has psychotropic effects. Every time I hear a noise, I feel a paranoiac shock and am certain something terrible is happening just outside the door.

"Nothing," he responds in English, "just listening to the grasshoppers crepitating."

"What is 'crepitating'?" I ask.

"It's when grasshoppers rub their legs together and make that sound."

"Oh."

Sometimes Ngeti will use an English word that I claim doesn't exist. We will bet, and I will lose. This is very serious business for each of us. Perhaps it is embarrassing that Ngeti's English vocabulary is better than mine, considering that I once received a near perfect score on the verbal section of the GRE. Ngeti, in contrast, barely finished at an unprestigious rural Kenyan high school, and has never stepped foot inside a university. At some point in his early twenties, however, he got hold of an *Oxford English Dictionary* and memorized the entire thing from cover to cover—literally, the meaning of every single English word. And he has learned to interweave this abstract, static English with folk colloquialisms and profanity picked up from movies and fiction, all of which comes out of his mouth in a creative hodgepodge of living, often comic, profundity. In addition, Ngeti has learned several computer programming languages by illegally downloading courses on-line; lately, he has been able to sell his services to local companies in Mombasa, the Kenyan port city where he now spends most of his time. Aside from this unpredictable work and the occasional opportunities I give him, he doesn't have much of an income. So I have brought him to the eastern DR Congo to help him earn some money. But Ngeti is also here because we have grown accustomed to collaborating with each other, and we like it.

Ngeti and I have known each other since 1997, and this is not the first time we have traveled together to a new place to conduct "fieldwork." We have investigated conflicting interpretations of a returned python-ancestral spirit named Omieri in western Kenya, talked to victims of postelection ethnic violence in central Kenya, and spent many days interviewing members of a neotraditionalist vigilante group called Mungiki in Nairobi and central Kenya. Most recently, in 2009, he was my research assistant in the eastern DR Congo, after which he returned home to Kenya. Ngeti and I are now good friends who know each other perhaps a bit too well. We have helped each other and have overcome the few rifts our relationship has had. Ngeti has benefited from work and occasional gifts of money from me, as well as from regional foreign travel experiences that are very uncommon for Kenyans, and I have profited from his growing research and language capacities, his profound ethnographic insights, and his companionship. We have come to see each other as intellectual equals and collaborators, which is clear from the way we interact: we banter back and forth, and sometimes we get on each other's cases. But we are not equals, because I will go home to my university job, while he will return to Kenya, where he is currently spending months at a time trying, and failing, to blast gemstones out of the ground using dynamite. Twenty-five years ago, a Kenyan of his background and talents would have been securely ensconced in a government office job somewhere.

This book is a tapestry of email and in-person communications between myself and my Kenyan friend and collaborator, Erastus Ngeti Mwadime. Structurally and conceptually, it is built around Ngeti's lifelong odyssey to understand who has been behind his stunted progress in life, a journey that has taken him to "traditional" diviners, religious prophets, and healers and, ultimately, back home, where he confronted his own family and accused his parents of bewitching him. The book is partly Ngeti's effort to account for why he—a thoughtful, soft-spoken, affable young man who loved his mother, Monica, who passed away in 2005—also at one point felt that she may have been a witch, and that she may even have been bewitching him. If there is, in the end, no totally satisfying resolution to his quest, the outcome of his search yields a multitude of important truths and insights, and opens a rare window onto everyday life in postcolonial Africa.

Ngeti does not epitomize any of the real or represented extremes of Africa. He is not a Sudanese Lost Boy, like Dave Eggers's fictionalized Valentino Deng or the autobiographical figure John Bul Dau.[3] His life has not been filled with danger, uncertainty, and abuse like that of John Chernoff's migratory West African sex worker, Hawa.[4] Nor has he emerged from a newly liberated post-apartheid South Africa, bearing the full weight of its troubles and hopes upon his shoulders, like Adam Ashforth's Madumo.[5] Ngeti also does not represent the other end of the West's imaginative spectrum of understanding about Africa by serving as a living model of "nativist" knowledge, like Marcel Griaule's Ogotommêli, Victor Turner's Muchona the Hornet, or, in a somewhat different vein, Margorie Shostak's !Kung woman Nisa.[6] But Ngeti's experience of quiet frustration, banal tedium, endless waiting, and of feeling surrounded by a world of miraculous things he knows to exist but cannot enjoy, is probably more representative of the contemporary African situation than any other I can imagine.[7] So, in a way, is his narrative style, which communicates that he belongs nowhere and everywhere—a theme that is repeated throughout this book. Ngeti sits at an imaginative nexus that is not rooted in any particular territory (although Ngeti's physical body is very much rooted in territory, as he is all too aware). Rather, this space is composed of cross-currents of languages, things, and ideas.

These mobile things, often referred to collectively as globalization, are not merely forces that act on Ngeti. In his speech, thought, and practice, he appropriates, masters, and transforms the words, images, and ideas that come to him; in so doing, Ngeti is able to conceptually bracket these discursive threads, move between them, or blend them creatively for poetic and contrastive effect when he wants. Ngeti's remote cosmopolitanism and virtuoso mastery of multiple languages and "speech genres" are generic, especially for African youth, even if it is the case that Ngeti is especially good at what he does.[8] Although Ngeti has often felt stuck in a single place, unable to "develop" or move, he has managed to do quite a lot of imaginative traveling, sometimes piecing together various elements to develop unlikely and life-changing connections with others. Despite what I just wrote about Muchona the Hornet, Ngeti is also quite a bit like the anthropologist Victor Turner's mid-twentieth-century Ndembu collaborator, in that he is a local intellectual whose quixotic outsider status in his own society has encouraged him to think quite deeply and philosophically about the world he inhabits. They differ in that, unlike the senior Muchona, the "youth" Ngeti does not see himself as an expert on Taita "tradition," nor on anything really. But Ngeti is an expert on what it is like to try to collapse the boundaries that separate far-flung, distant worlds, and a philosopher who has experimented with the consequences of doing so, often by putting his body on the line, as we will see.

Although this book is composed mainly of email communications, it is not substantively "about" email and the Internet; even so, the story that is told here, and many of the events that have unfolded between Ngeti and me, would not have taken place in the way they have without the Internet. We have become collaborators because of this technology, which allowed us quick access despite our physical separation, and over the years we have created an ethnography out of our interactions in cyberspace, supplemented by my occasional return visits to Kenya. The Internet has also encouraged Ngeti to think of himself as a growing, changing subject whose life is an adventure filled with peaks and valleys that may be of interest to others.

In his email letters, Ngeti makes sense of things that are geographically and socially close to him—including the influence of his family on his prospects for success and failure. At the same time, Ngeti's very access to cyberspace was made possible in part by his most proximal relationships. Many of the emails in this volume were originally written by him by hand, when he was in the Taita Hills, and then passed on to a Mombasa-bound *matatu* (passenger minivan) driver, who in turn gave them to Ngeti's sister, who worked for a time at an Internet café. She then typed them into her company's computer, and off they went into cyberspace. Ngeti's experience of the Internet thus depended on some of the very social relationships that he has tried to transcend through the Internet. And so the mundane, social conditions of possibility for the Digital Age were not exactly new to him when he went to the DR Congo. It's just that, until he reached the DRC and found artisanal miners "midwifing the iPhone," as he later put it, he was never compelled to think about these connections so directly.

I first met Ngeti when I was in the Taita Hills of southeastern Kenya conducting the research for my doctoral dissertation. My first extended visit to the hills, in 1991, was indirectly brought about by my friendship with another young Kenyan man, a Luo college student at the University of Nairobi named Owidi mak Ogega Sila—but that friendship didn't end up nearly as well. I went to the hills after being expelled from the University of Nairobi because of my association with Owidi, who was accused of being a political dissident by the university administration during then-President Moi's chancellorship. I was an undergraduate exchange student, and the university administration and the Kenyan Special Branch were suspicious about my relationship with this Kenyan student, at a time when the United States, represented by the American ambassador Smith-Hempstone, was promoting political and media liberalization and other forms of "democratization" in Kenya. For three hours in a back room of the library, a committee of university and state officials questioned me about Owidi, to their mind unsuccessfully, and afterward they would not allow me to finish my year in the exchange program. So, on an American professor's recommendation, I traveled to the remote and relatively "cool" Taita Hills, where I spent four months teaching English and European history to high school students in exchange for room and board—an experience I was later allowed to convert into college credit.[9] Owidi was also expelled and briefly imprisoned for marijuana possession, which the university later claimed had been found in his room in an "American container, with an American dollar price tag" (meaning, in short, that he had allegedly bought it from me). I later tried to help Owidi by paying for his plane ticket so he could study law in Brazil, but he was returned to Kenya under mysterious circumstances. Owidi was active in the early opposition movement and, over the years, was repeatedly imprisoned and tortured in Kenya's infamous Nyayo House torture chambers until he was a shadow of his former self. The last I heard from him, he was bereft of shelter and most of his sanity on the streets of Nairobi. I have always regretted and felt somewhat responsible for what happened to Owidi, and since then have tried to ensure that my collaborations with Africans are as mutually rewarding as possible.

After that time in Kenya, I returned to the United States and to university life. Upon finishing college, I went on to pursue postgraduate study in anthropology, and after a couple of years it came time for me to pick an ethnographic field site. I ultimately decided, after some traveling around East Africa, to return to the Taita Hills. I did so in part because I had been there before and had enough experience to know that, unlike some other places in the region, people in Taita would be more than eager to share their stories and troubles with me. In Taita, "a guest is rain," as Wataita love to say (that's supposed to be a good thing). When I asked people there what my research should concern, many said something to the effect of, "The witches are making development impossible. Can you figure out why, and what can be done about it?" Ultimately I decided that their idea was a good one, and I ran with it. In the process, I tried to understand why these concepts, "witchcraft" and "development," and the practices associated with them, were important to people, what they meant, and why people perceived them as being in conflict with each other. Studying development and witchcraft, in the end, meant studying Taita people's ideas about where they had been, where they were going, and what was holding them back (after all, the root of the Kiswahili word for development, *maendeleo,* is "go"). It also meant studying Taita people's hopes for the future, as well as their understandings of the past, and how they mobilized or broke away from the past in their efforts to remake themselves.

It turns out that Taita hopes about the future and their thoughts about what development would look like are framed by their effective incarceration within Kenya's largest game park, Tsavo National Park. With overpopulation, deforestation, and general ecological collapse in the highlands, Tsavo is Wataita's main space for expansion and "development" for those who can't afford to own homes in the city. But Wataita are forbidden from entering the park, unless they shell out impossibly expensive park fees (they can be shot and killed if they are found in the park illegally). At the same time, Wataita receive no revenue from the funds generated by this land that they feel belongs to them, and so are effectively dispossessed by remote state actors who enrich themselves through tourist revenue at Taita's expense.

In late 1997, I made my way back to the Taita Hills, a seemingly remote place of near endless internal diversity. Wataita sometimes liken the hills, which seem small from a distance but turn out to be internally large and complex, to a coiled-up intestine: compact but huge and, of course, filled with shit (grudges, conflicts, concealed stories, etc.). If the hills are "like" intestines, intestines are also like the hills: diviners use goat intestines to communicate with ancestors because the intestines contain people's buried emotions and resentments and can be read like a text. Similarly, Taita has many nooks, each one saturated with the things that have happened before and inhabited by the shades of people and things that were once there. These invisible things and people jostle for space alongside the living and seek recognition from them, and the living differ about what all of this means and what they should do about it. The influence of the past, including the past's persistence in the present, is not something Wataita feel they can easily escape, even when they want to, as Ngeti often has. Living and instigative ancestors are a real part of the landscape, and they take on an active role in both helping and disciplining Taita people, even if they often do more harm than good.[10]

Shortly after my coming to Mgange, the town I had decided would be home, the chief, a poorly paid government administrator who supplemented his income with gifts from his neighbors, was introducing me at a town meeting. He informed everyone that I was a student who was going to be in Taita for some time, researching how Taita people lived and how their lives were changing. The crowd of mostly women that had gathered for the meeting seemed surprised and curious, and this curiosity about who I was and what I was doing persisted the whole time I lived there (had I come to buy land? did I want a Taita bride? was I CIA?). At the end of the meeting, the chief's assistant, Peter, accompanied me to look for a place where I could stay, and we ended up at a house near the church of this predominantly Catholic community. Peter had brought me to what he considered the best place in town, a relatively large house made of mud bricks, painted red in the style of European homes. It was the home of an absentee patriarch, a senior man named Valentine, who was then working as the head of security in a Mombasa tourist hotel. Valentine's wife, an older woman whom I came to know as Veronica, greeted us and, after a short conversation about rent and food, agreed that I could stay in the back room, adjacent to the sitting room.

And so I began the process of conducting fieldwork. In the mornings, I would wake up, drink sweetened milk tea courtesy of Veronica, and venture into town or down a trail to try to talk to people. Sometimes I would find myself wandering around like a witch in someone's maize field, and inevitably a concerned farmer would appear to escort me to a real trail. Communicating with a wide spectrum of people was tough work, and I didn't really have a clear idea of what I was supposed to be talking to them about. I didn't speak Kidawida (also called Kitaita, or Taita language), the language of the hills, but I did speak Kiswahili, so I paid a schoolteacher to help me with it, and I began writing hundreds of Taita words on index cards.[11] I would come back home in the evening with reams of material, some of it tape-recorded, none of which I understood much of. Each night I transcribed as much as I could, and afterward I would spend a little more time writing extemporaneously about various seemingly unimportant things that were happening to me in "the field."

In the evenings, there was always a handful of young people who were somehow related to Valentine hanging out in the sitting room watching ridiculous bootlegged action videos from Asia and the U.S. on a TV that ran on a car battery. The Vietnam War, corrupted martial arts competitions, and POW camps featured prominently, as did the directors' backyards. Looking back on it now, I realize that these films were suffused with themes of restriction, escape, and success achieved, finally, against impossible odds, and this was no doubt part of their appeal. But I remember being annoyed by the noise, and by the Taita youth, in whom I confess to having had very little interest. I preferred talking with older men because they seemed to want less and to have more interesting things to say. Plus, the youth who hung around Valentine's place while he was away spoke mostly in Swahili and avoided the Taita language, which I wanted to learn. So I mostly ignored them, though occasionally I tuned in for the better films, like when they came across a bootlegged VHS cassette of *The Rock,* which had just been released in the States and was yet to appear in Nairobi. One of the young men watching the movie was in his late twenties, just a couple of years older than me, of medium height, wearing horn-rimmed glasses and a long brown overcoat whose hood concealed most everything but his eyes. It was Ngeti, Valentine's sister's son, leaning in close and meticulously studying the film as if it contained a great secret. "I love American slang!" he said gleefully after one of the African American characters menacingly intoned, "I'm gonna enjoy guttin' you, boy!" to Nicolas Cage's lead character. I remember the line because it fascinated Ngeti and he repeated it often, for years.

One evening, I returned home drunk on homemade sugarcane beer that some senior men had given me, and found my Taita language index cards stacked neatly in a pile, covered in condemning red ink. Someone had taken the time not only to correct all of my many errors but also to supply alternative usages and examples in Kidawida; I soon realized it was Ngeti who had done all of this work. Our relationship evolved slowly: I taught him how to play chess, discovering that his English was better than I thought when I called him an ass-wipe under my breath. He introduced me to more people, and eventually we went to his home and ate, together with his parents and sisters. Through Ngeti, I became friendly with a whole network of people and learned a great deal about Taita and Taita language. And suddenly I was not alone at all. Ngeti had long been struggling with the issues that I was interested in, the conflict between what he described as "witchcraft" and "development" as these manifested in his own personal life and interactions, and he soon became one of my principal interlocutors.

Ngeti and I each approached the other as a gateway to another world that we desperately wanted to enter. He came across as an intellectually intense and wickedly humorous young man. At the time, he did not drink, and he would judgmentally call my beer "devil's piss"—which somehow made it taste even better. But he reveled in anything that was, as he put it, "salacious, scatological, or prurient" and couldn't get enough American profanity out of me. Like his mother and sisters, Ngeti was a saved Pentecostal Christian in a community composed almost entirely of Catholics, and many of our early conversations concerned the Bible, Christianity, and the practice of becoming "saved" or born again. I visited his Pentecostal church with him and was publicly shamed for being a typical American "devil worshiper" when I refused to be saved by the pastor. Many times we visited his best friend and guru, an early-forty-something Taita pastor-prophet named Patroba, who prayed for us and our success, usually over freshly slaughtered roast goat meat that I had paid for. Ngeti's relationship with Patroba is the subject of much of this book. My friendship with Ngeti grew out of long walks we took together, some of which lasted a few days, during which time we would camp out in a tent overnight in a faraway village and awake in the morning to ask questions of complete strangers.

Among the persons I had the pleasure of meeting through Ngeti was his mother, Monica, one of the most impressive individuals I have ever known. Much of Ngeti's narrative concerns his ambivalent relationship with his mother, which grew more tense as he got older. Monica was a powerful and magnetic woman who had a lot of strong opinions that she was not at all shy about communicating. Her jovial ebullience, to say nothing of her cooking, nourished me during many lonely, cold, and rainy days in the Taita Hills, and her smoky kitchen was a refuge for just about anyone looking for food, tea, and a place to sit and chat. Most men couldn't stay very long in that kitchen. They claimed that it was the smoke from the wood fire, but it was also because this was Monica's kingdom, a matricentric haven for women of all ages. From this kitchen, Monica slowly built a political career during the 1980s and early 1990s, eventually becoming the chairlady for Maendeleo ya Wanawake (The Development of Women), the state-sanctioned women's union that had long been involved in a reciprocal patron-client relationship with mostly incumbent male politicians, whom the women sometimes referred to as their "husbands."

Monica was a vocal leader in her community, and she represented Taita's interests to politicians who cared more about their friendships with political higher-ups, like President Moi, than they did about their constituents back home.[12] She verbally confronted powerful, even potentially violent, male politicians whom the men around her feared and placated. In the late 1990s, after state funding for Maendeleo ya Wanawake had long since disappeared, Monica was able to parlay her experience into important positions with Kenyan NGOs doing "development" and conservation work in Taita at a time when her once relatively successful husband, a former manager for a large private transport company, was unemployed and without savings or pension. She also became more invested in religious experience, developing her powers as a prophet who could communicate with God and pave the way for other people's projects on this terrestrial plane of existence.

But it is no good to simplify Monica by turning her into a feminist heroine. She was a complicated person who was, no doubt about it, fascinated by power, and she placed herself in contact with potent invisible forces. The few times that I slept at Ngeti's home, Monica would awake in the middle of the night and venture into the outside courtyard, where she entered into what sounded to me like a noisily passionate fit of explosive, incomprehensible babble. Her voice would reach me within my dreams and then surround me as I lay breathlessly awake. She was speaking in tongues, and when she did that she screamed herself hoarse, beseeching, commanding, and seemingly summoning some invisible force into our midst. She sounded angry and violent, and the fact that she was physically powerful and large made it all the more ominous. Ngeti said this was prayer, but it always unnerved me and made me wonder what exactly Monica was communicating with. God? Demons? Her own fractured self? Why, I wondered, did these communications happen involuntarily, and always at night?[13] I feel now that Monica was working to get in touch with a transcendent power that would change her and those around her, and as we will see, the power she channeled brought things and people into her life that she could not control—insidious rumors, corrupt pastors, unctuous politicians, treacherous in-laws. Ngeti has been puzzling over the consequences of his mother's power for some time, trying to understand, in his own way, what it all had to do with him. While he has always been impressed by her strength and courage, Monica has also often been a foil for Ngeti's accumulated feelings of inadequacy and failure.

Two things impressed me most about Ngeti. One was his thorough knowledge of American culture, idioms, and politics, all of which he garnered from his inconvenient vantage in the Taita Hills. The other was that, although he and his entire family were completely broke (his father had just lost his job at the company for which he had worked for nearly thirty years), his questions to me were rarely about money—at least at first. Rather, Ngeti was sincerely interested in what I can only call the meaning of life and wanted to know more about what was happening beyond the hills. At the time, he was particularly intrigued by the latest Mars probe and the U.S. government's UFO and alien conspiracy cover-up, which he had learned about from watching bad VHS cassette copies of *The X-Files* as if the show was a documentary. He also wanted to take in the things around him—the beauty of the Taita Hills and the largeness of the night sky—and would spend quite a bit of time memorizing and marveling over the many ingredients listed in my Power Bars, which he read aloud as if it was poetry. At the same time, there was a real angst and even a rancor about Ngeti: sometimes he would wave his hand in the air and, mimicking Sean Connery's Alcatraz prisoner character in *The Rock,* intone, "Gentlemen, welcome to the Rock!," and we'd laugh with bittersweet irony, because he was essentially saying that Taita was a prison in which he was destined to remain confined.

At times, Ngeti was more of a hindrance than a help. I remember on one occasion we tried to participate in a rainmaking ritual, and the organizer of the ritual informed us that if a white person were to be present, the ancestors would have to be appeased—which meant that I would need to contribute fifty dollars for a goat and beer. When news got out that I had in fact done so, rival rainmakers complained that the goat was supposed to have been a magnanimous gift from the rainmaker's homestead and accused the rainmaker of bewitching the ritual with his selfishness. When the day came, this turmoil entered into the divination proceedings, and Ngeti couldn't stand the hypocrisy. Like many young Taita men, he was ambivalent about Taita traditions and often disgusted by actual senior men, who he felt were sullying the past and probably ruining contemporary Wataita's relationships with the ancestors. He viewed these men as parochial and obsessed with money, in sharp contrast to what he understood to be the values of now deceased Taita people, who presumably embodied the ideals of reciprocity and openness that had made Taita hearts "cool" and "moist" like the disappearing forests. Ngeti, assuming that I was looking for the Truth about rainmaking and Taita culture, reasoned that I was not going to get it, or anything else of value, here, so we might as well go find some roast meat to eat somewhere else. "These guys are charlatans. Let's get out of here," he urged. Of course, I wouldn't leave. Instead I embraced the fact that there was contestation about the value and virtue of this and similar events (conflict meant, at the very least, that there would be more to write about).

Afterward, when I offered some of my own interpretations about what the rainmakers were doing, Ngeti expressed wonder for the discipline of anthropology, providing an insight that may well elude many professional anthropologists: "Anthropology is very interesting, bwana. It isn't about whether something is true or not. It's about understanding what things *mean*." From that moment on, Ngeti had no end of interpretations about the deep symbolic meanings of different Taita practices, and many of his ruminations were quite complexly anthropological indeed. I didn't realize it at the time, but he took to anthropology so readily because he was already trying to understand Americans and other Westerners, as well as his own society, as if he were an anthropologist. He was also coming to appreciate the ways in which all people were interconnected, as well as how and where they differed. A few years later, when I started sending him chapters of my thesis via email, he would respond with emails like this, which revealed, among other things, that he had found a way to read up on hermeneutics, or the art of interpretation (though he apparently still saw the senior men in his town as a "gang").

Allow me to say that your article was a very interesting reading, bwana. *Mimi sidhani kama iko na makosa yoyote* [I don't think there are any mistakes at all]. Frankly speaking, when you were doing your research, everything was very fuzzy, and for a guy with only a secondary school education you can't quite blame me so much, bwana. I think if there is gonna be another session of researching I'll pay more attention. You are an anthropologist with brain-hurting terminologies and a thorough knowledge of hermeneutics, both deep and suspicious. Mbatia and Mkula [rainmakers] will tell me that the rainmaking ritual at Ndolwa is gonna bring rain because fifty years ago it did bring tons upon tons of rain and because of blah blah blah rain is gonna come. Then you come in from thousands of miles from home, you engage in the hermeneutics of "surfaces" and "depths." You quietly sit with Mbatia and his gang and seek to articulate and explain the common meanings of the cultural practices via a sympathetic communion or participant-observer inquiry. Then you turn to "deep hermeneutics" and attempt (successfully) to dig beneath surface interpretation (beneath the hermeneutics of the everyday), because deep hermeneutics suspects that the Taita understanding and interpretations might in fact be quite distorted, partial, or deluded and might actually be motivated to hide the truth, to obscure or cover up deeper and more frightening truths. Then this hermeneutics of suspicion leads you to dig even deeper, a task which leads you to discover that the Taita have very little under-standing of the changes that are sweeping thru the globe, both eco-nomical, environmental, political, and spiritual. Terms like *El Niño* or *global warming*, structural adjustments, cannot be transliterated into Kitaita [Taita language]. The shifting world out there is all too magical and infested with diabolical beings that are threatening to blast the Taita asses to oblivion.[14]

Ngeti's email expressed his sympathy and love for a place that he has also seen as an obstacle to his personal progress. Indeed, he often thought about how he could harness the powerful forces emanating from outside Taita so that "Taita asses" might be saved, but his visions tended to be painfully impractical. In particular, I recall his idea that, one day, a ski lift would con-nect the Taita Hills with the tourist hotels in Tsavo's lowlands, enabling foreign tourists to visit the hills and interact with the people there while contributing to the local economy. At night he would go to sleep listening to movie dialogue on a Walkman I had lent him, surrounded by magazine advertisement images that smothered his mud brick walls: illustrious city-scapes; fast and furious sports cars; libidinous women clad only in bath bub-bles. In the morning he would awake to his tattered dreams on the wall, milk the one cow his family had, and make his way down to the maize fields to dig. But Ngeti remained patient, preparing himself, through these mediated glimpses of another world and through his mastery of its language, to enter into that parallel universe when the time was right. The problem was that he kept feeling himself drawn into another, more proximal world in which historical malevolence held sway over everything else.

Ngeti's situation was related to his being the descendant of a comparatively prosperous family that was now in decline. The family, and those around them, thought about their rise and decline in religious terms, because religion in Taita is a powerful social fact. When Christianity first started making headway in the Taita Hills in the 1920s, 1930s, and 1940s, it was not perceived as a religion in the modern Western sense of a "belief system." The first schools were mission schools, so Christianity and schooling went hand in hand, and with time they became the gateway for wage labor employment in cities. At first, many seniors resisted the spread of the new religion and the loss of their sons' labor to the mission schools, but young people saw opportunity in Christianity and education, and many used their schooling to curtail or evade the power of seniors and of what they saw as the past.[15] Conflict between youths and seniors was, and often still is, articulated in religious terms, as a conflict between Christianity and what some call Kidawida (hill ways) or Wutasi (after *kutasa,* the practice of unanimously spitting out beer in order to cleanse everyone's hearts of anger and demonstrate goodheartedness so that whatever is about to happen will be successful). Ironically, these seniors soon became dependent on their mostly male Christian children for wage remittances, which they argued should be handed over to them in the same way that captured livestock had been in earlier generations.[16] For their part, male youths worried about their elders' ability to "bewitch" them through cursing. And Christians, as they came to constitute a more affluent and somewhat withdrawn social class, worried that their less well off non-Christian neighbors might bewitch them out of jealousy. In those days, sustained interaction between Christian and non-Christian communities was limited: Christians were prevented from marrying non-Christians, and they were not allowed to participate in communitywide regenerative rituals like rainmaking and *fighi* (activated, weaponized forests) renewal (discussed later). As outward Christianity came to be equated with success, these public Kidawida rituals were effectively driven underground, becoming nocturnal activities that many equated with witchcraft. At the same time, the repressed non-Christian past continued to hold immense power. Wataita (including Ngeti's parents) regularly recount the various ways in which Taita magic has confounded, and continues to confound, colonial and postcolonial state authorities who work to punish or control Taita in one way or another.

Monica's father, Anthony Maghanga (born in 1913), was among the first people in their community to convert to Catholicism and the very first to be buried on church land. Most of Anthony's children were successful by local standards, having used their mission education to acquire full-time employment in Mombasa and to invest money in local land, businesses, and marriage and exchange partners. Ngeti's father's father, Boniface, converted later in life, and Boniface's son, Charles, used the income that Boniface had earned as a game poacher to marry up in status. Both of Ngeti's parents, Charles and Monica, grew up during the 1950s in a straight-lined row of houses near the Catholic church, set apart from neighboring, circular communities of "heathens" who practiced non-Christian, "traditional" Taita ritual.

By the 1990s, any "development" Ngeti's family had once acquired was purely symbolic, and the family's big house was, as Ngeti put it, an empty shell. Ngeti's parents blamed their family's economic decline on an invisible occult onslaught by people who were jealous of their Christian rectitude and the prosperity they had achieved as comparatively educated Christians. Ngeti and his family spun different explanations concerning why this decline was happening to them personally, focusing mostly on occult action by jealous kin and neighbors and at Charles's workplace. At the same time, many people in the neighborhood believed that Ngeti's family were the "biggest witches" and quietly suggested that they had camouflaged themselves in Christianity and used occult powers to "develop" while others "stayed behind." In the late 1980s, Monica was "saved" through Pentecostalism, explaining that the Catholic Church had long ago been taken over by Taita's witches, who now sat on the church council. Leaving the church and becoming saved was partly Monica's, and later her whole family's, way of responding to and protecting themselves both from decline and from the disturbing changes they saw taking place in their society.

As I grew more familiar with Ngeti's family, I came to understand their troubles and responsibilities and to feel that some of them were also my own. Over time, too, it became clear to me that Ngeti was indeed interested in making money with my help. It was simply that his imaginative ambitions were so vast that he had not wanted to chase me, and my investing potential, away with petty requests for small sums. By now I had been in Taita for well over a year, and in what he imagined, incorrectly, to be some of our final moments, Ngeti began to feel that he should secure my help before I disappeared, presumably forever. Slowly, he began introducing business ideas into our walks and games of chess, all the while making it clear that any business arrangement we entered into would have the protection of Divine Providence. He had spoken with his Pentecostal preacher friend Patroba, who had received word from God Himself that great things would happen to Ngeti and me, presuming that we pay a tithe to Patroba's church. Patroba wanted Ngeti to know that God was watching our emerging friendship and had a plan for both of us. "You know," Ngeti said one evening as we waited for his mother and sisters to prepare a dinner of stewed meat and *ugali* (maize meal) for us at his home, "business is not the kind of thing that you enter into with a large investment. You do not begin at Form Four [meaning, roughly, the senior year of high school], before going to Standard One [the first grade]. You work up from small things."

Ngeti unfurled a plan: his father's father, Boniface, had been a famous poacher during the 1950s and had been the first African in the Taita Hills to own a car. This man had a son by another wife who now had a rhino horn that he had kept in his possession for many years. Might I be able to find a foreign buyer for this illegal item—perhaps in Dubai, if smuggling a whole rhino horn into the United States was too difficult? Or, he suggested, it could be broken down into smaller units, which could easily be concealed. He had done enough homework to know that rhino horn, with its special medicinal uses, especially as an aphrodisiac, is more valuable than gold and can sell for over $1,000 per ounce on the right market.

I refused. "Ngeti, I am not going to smuggle a rhino horn."

"Why?" he demanded.

"Because it's illegal and unethical—rhinos are an endangered species," I offered weakly. Anyway, I continued, the horn had been sitting around for some time. Would it even still be valuable?

Ngeti persisted: "But I have already talked to Patroba about this, and God says it's a good idea and it will work."

"I don't care what Patroba says God says," I retorted, redrawing the disappearing boundary that separated Patroba from God. "There's just no way."

Ngeti concealed his frustration, waited about a week, and switched his approach to gemstones. The plains around Tsavo are rich in green garnet, rubies, and other precious stones, and many Wataita dream of becoming rich from these resources, which they feel belong to them, since they lie within Taita-Taveta District. Many Wataita are angered by the "foreign" Kenyan Kikuyu entrepreneurs, mostly women, who make a small fortune off Taita's wealth, from which Wataita are excluded. Wataita simply don't have the money to get started in this trade—though those who work in the mostly foreign-owned mines will often surreptitiously pocket some stones, then sell them to non-Taita middlemen in the back rooms of bars and other businesses, like hair salons.

Eventually, I relented. I felt indebted to Ngeti for the help he had given me in the field and for work he had done, much of which had been uncompensated, carried out under the rubric of friendship. I agreed to look into it, and we ended up spending a whole Saturday buying gemstones in the semiarid lowland Taita town of Mwatate. As we sat in a room in the back of a bar, shady dealers came out of the woodwork with their materials wrapped in old newspaper shards. We listened to their stories and gazed at their little stones for hours, picking and sorting. We drew some men close and shooed others away. In the end, I probably spent a couple hundred dollars on a small plastic bag filled with stones. It was only about a week prior to my planned departure for the States, so Ngeti and I went together to Nairobi immediately to look for potential buyers. There, we booked a room at a cheap hotel in a bad part of town and visited several Indian and South African jewelry stores. The stones were worthless: too dull, too many cracks, too many bubbles. I could see all of Ngeti's dreams of fast wealth disappear in an instant when one jeweler did us a favor by smashing the stones into dust before our eyes. Ngeti's horrified shock vanished under a dark cloud of depression. He returned to Mgange to milk the cow and dig in his *shamba* (field).

I returned home and, over the course of two years, wrote my dissertation, then, after much searching, landed a job. Ngeti and I lost touch, until one day in 2002 he managed to email me:

> Mzungu! [White man!] Where in Zeus's butt-hole are you?!!!! [This is a paraphrase of a line from *The Rock*.] Hope you're well! Have been trying to contact you! Get in touch, Ngeti.

I responded with an email that I no longer have, and we exchanged a few more emails back and forth. Eventually, I told him that I had an old laptop computer that I would pass on to him, and that a school friend and aspiring anthropologist named Robert Blunt, who was visiting Kenya, would soon give him some money from me. Ngeti responded, in his characteristic amalgam of Swahili, English, and even Spanish and French. I have edited some of the emails that appear later in this book for readability, but here I have retained the original to provide a sense of Ngeti's capacity to move back and forth between languages and speech genres, containing all of them within himself while also merging them to create something new. In this way we are able to glimpse, through him, a world that is not divided by cultural and linguistic exclusivity, but which exists as a creative dialogic synthesis that, in turn, tells us a great deal about who Ngeti is. It is worth taking in:

Pole sana ati huku pata huu ujumbe, sasa nina tuma tena, bwana. Nilipata e-mail moja kutoka kwa some fuck head *anaitwa daemon yuko* pale@midway.kitu fulani. *Cheka chaeka!!!!* [I'm sorry you didn't get my messages, and I'm attaching them again. I got an email from some fuckhead named "daemon" there at there@midway.something. LOL!]

Just for light moments sake, I have been thinking about migrating to Canada and beginning a generation of Taitas there. The present Negroes were dragged there by force, this time I wanna make a voluntary trip there. That's my dream, that's my joke. But you know, however, when there is no way, then make one.

So tell me mon ami, what is new apart from other things that we are familiar with? Tell you what, remember I told you I was seeing some girl? This is this twenty something lady that I have been seeing. Man, she is something. When I'm okay, financially okay, I will scan her photo and send it to you. Man, I have been lonely but I think with time things are gonna be fine for me. There is so much that we have to say but right now my mind is in a foment. So please write Rob and tell him he can give me a call on 433724. Let him ask for Ngeti and the password will be "The Eagle Has Landed." I'll try writing him again and seeing what happens. Thanks once again buddy and wait for my call. Take care. Love, Ngeti.

Then came the earlier email, which he had failed to send successfully at first:

Vipi amerikanski! [What's up, American! *(Ngeti has picked up the Russian term from Cold War-era American movies)*],

Sasa mimi niko Mombasa bwana [Right now, I'm in Mombasa, man]. By the way, Happy Independence Day. It also happens to be my birthday. *Mimi nilikuandikia through Amanda lakini inaonekana kuwa wewe labda hukupata hii kitu* [I have written to you through Amanda *(mean-*

ing he had written me letters by hand, which he then gave to his sister, who worked at a cybercafé, to send to me by email), but it seems you haven't received them]. *Habari ya mambo ya kule marekani? Sasa niko Mombasa, nilifika huku jana 4th of July, ninajaribu kutafuta mambo kidogo kidogo lakini sijui itakua vipi, lakini ninafikiri mambo yatakua sawa* [How are things in America? Right now I am in Mombasa, and arrived on the 4th of July, and I'm trying to look for something small small *(meaning a job)*, but I don't know how it's going to turn out]. Tell you what bwana, *hebu niambiye mambo ya ile* laptop [tell me about the laptop], what is it able to do, apart from exploring the Net? *Unajua hiyo kitu nina weza kupata nayo kitu kidogo kidogo. Sijui una mpango gani wakuifikisha hapa* [You know, with this thing I can get something small small *(meaning some money)*. I don't know what plan you have to get it here]. Tell me *mambo mazuri mazuri bwana, hapa mimi nimeboeka sana* [Tell me something good man, I'm bored stiff here].

Tell me, can you get those crazy books on hacking, and more on UFOs? For some crazy reasons, I do not believe we are alone in this freaking universe. There are multicolored guys out there waiting for the earthlings to wake up from their religious slumber and realize that God is not a small timer, and he thinks big, and his thinking does not end with human beings.

Write me man, and tell me something. I miss you mucho grande. In the mean time, take care my friend.   Ngeti

After a week or two, Ngeti got a couple of hundred dollars from me, through Rob, and I think I did manage to send him some books. Over the years, most of my emails to Ngeti centered around journeys I was making for work: a trip across country in a beater car to an adjunct professor job in Santa Cruz, another trip in the opposite direction to a post-doc in northeastern Indiana, yet another trip in a pickup truck to a tenure-track position in Atlanta. Each relocation brought romantic troubles, and Ngeti would express his sympathy, sometimes even offering to get a "witchdoctor" to help me appease a lover's heart. I was busy during this time, and now I feel guilty to admit that he wrote me more often than I wrote him, and a number of his emails went unanswered.

In his email letters, Ngeti told me about some of his recent problems. He had suffered a falling out with his parents, which culminated in his father cursing him—at least, that was Ngeti's interpretation of his father's words. The story involved a dispute about whom his younger sister should be marrying. Ngeti did not approve of his sister's fiancé, but his parents were receiving bridewealth payments from him, which Ngeti believed clouded their judgment. Ngeti confronted the potential groom and ended up alienating himself from both his sisters and his parents, who went to the chief and persuaded him to write a letter insisting that Ngeti remove himself from these affairs. The chief, who controlled the police and was considered a spokesperson for customary law (a form of law inherited from colonial times), potentially had the ability to put Ngeti in jail. In the midst of all this, Ngeti wrote me the following email:

> Vipi mzungu, this is the guy who wrote you a couple of weeks ago to inform you that the goods have been received and the S.O.B. is fucking grateful.
> Right now, Jim, my parents think I'm an asshole or something. The situation is not good. Tell you what, I will forward you the letter, which I assume you did not get. Actually, this is what I did some time back. As I was surfing the net, I entered the porno world and I, like an idiot, subscribed to one of them magazines. From that day on there has been no end to naked women in my mail, man. So much spam, it's fucking nuts! So, use my virgin address, which has known no man, and let the old whore be fucked. Tell you what, on Monday I saw "Star Wars: The Attack of the Clones." Tell me about Uncle Sam and what you are up to in the meantime.

Ngeti went on to explain that he had a story he wanted to tell me that would "knock my socks off," which concerned his parents and his family. He said that when I was done reading it, "the hermeneutics of suspicion would set in." His decision to write about this was partly cathartic and partly counter-cultural, because Taita families do not ordinarily tell their secrets. It is for this reason, Ngeti believes, that these families, and Wataita as a whole, never truly move beyond historic grudges, which end up manifesting as witchcraft attacks and accusations in the present. So Ngeti was breaking with the past, and with tradition, in a way that he hoped would be productive and that was in keeping with some of his earlier experiments, including his interest in Pentecostalism. Initially, Ngeti probably also wanted to shame his parents, and so revenge was no doubt a partial motive. Ngeti's feelings about and interpretations of the events described in this book have changed since he began writing them down several years ago, a change that has much to do with the death of his mother. This event traumatized Ngeti, causing him to feel sorrow and regret. These days, writing about his past has helped him to forgive and understand himself as much as the people around him.

Ngeti's subsequent email laid the foundation for his new witchcraft story. Some parts of it were in Swahili, but I have translated the entirety into English:

What's up, white man, how's America? I believe you received my email of a few days ago. Now I'm going to give you one very crazy story, but after this story is over I think you'll have a different picture about Taita families. It's a long story, and it's going to take a while to write it. It is gonna come in bits and pieces.

It is conventional knowledge that my maternal grandparents were superwitches. Before I proceed, you are wondering why there is this story now and not when you were around. Well, for the last two years I have been going through some bad shit and so I started doing research on my entire family. I came up with some pretty amazing stuff. As you know, this witchcraft thing is a very hush hush thing among the Taita and the only time you hear people talking about it is when there is a witch hunter in town or when someone dies in mysterious circumstances, and even then people will be like, "Well, you did not hear this from me."

Well, my maternal grandfather, as is common knowledge among those in the age bracket of forty up to a hundred years, was a staunch Catholic. This is attested to by the unusual fact that, when he died, he was interred in the church compound at the Mgange Catholic church. The circumstances surrounding his death are bizarre, in that he collapsed in the witness box while being cross examined in a land case in which he was the defendant. The story has it that, when he collapsed, he was quickly taken to Wesu hospital, where he died several hours later. People say he was losing the case and that he had used witchcraft to try and get the case decided in his favor. His sudden collapse in the witness box is attributed by many to the fact that he had been sworn to tell the truth with the Bible. Anyway, the guy left behind a grieving family whose dark side was deliberately overlooked by men and women in whose minds the fear of coming out and pointing a finger at a known witch reigned supreme.

I can as a Taita add that 90% of Taita families have witchcraft. I give the 10% the benefit of the doubt, though I wouldn't put medium consultation past them. I'm sure you're aware of the user-friendly terms that are used to describe and defend the practice, terms like *fighi* and *milimu*, these being to defend against dangerous neighbors.[17] But remember, all are lethal despite their various applications. When people talk about using such things for defense, they are just villains claiming to be victims. My maternal grandparents were what I will call "upper-class witches" or "holy witches." By this term I mean those witches who at the time of the introduction of Catholicism were the first to embrace it and were ardent teachers and defenders of its doctrines . . .

[In the original email, which I can no longer find, Ngeti offered a story about his grandmother, who allegedly killed some children by issuing incantations over some food. Ngeti referred to this as

"transubstantiation" and went on to explain, anthropologically, "but here the effect is not the renewal of the soul but its demise."]

One fact that we should be aware of is that witches are scared silly of death and being found out that they are witches. Their lives are spent in perpetual rituals of secrecy and covering their tracks. They spend a great deal of energy being likable; you find them in the church council, village committees, school committees, etc. Another fact is witchcraft has 2 distinct forms—for good, that is defending the land against aliens (fighi); and for evil, destroying the progress or retarding the development of those that it sometimes defends. Both are passed on from generation to generation, and their potency is dependent upon the sacrifices that its practitioners are prepared to make, which ranges from animal to human sacrifice.

Well, mon ami, this is just the beginning of the saga. This is Ngeti your friend signing out, take care of yourself. God bless.

As his emails began to accumulate in my inbox, it became clear to me that, with my help, Ngeti and I might have a coauthored book here, and that it would be a moving personal account of postcolonial African life, told in a first-person English whose verisimilitude would be unique and moving to an American audience. I also hoped that, by publishing Ngeti's emails and giving him any royalties that might accrue from these writings, our ongoing collaboration would finally benefit him in a substantial way without my having to smuggle a rhino horn. When Ngeti became aware, at my suggestion, that his emails could someday be read by a wider audience, if he was so inclined, he was very enthusiastic. Later, he gave me part of his diary, which I also include here, and we had a couple of long interview discussions about these events as well, which I have turned into chapters.

As Ngeti started writing more explicitly for an audience, his writing style shifted away from heteroglossic "Swa-English" toward "pure" English, with his new public in mind. Even as this happened, his writing continued to shift among different genres, evoking, at different points, magical realism, American pulp horror fiction, ethnography, explorer narratives, and the Beats. Over time, I have become ever more taken in by this story and by Ngeti's powers of authorship and narration. I am now convinced that his is the voice of a whole generation of young men in the Global South, who are trying to find a way to improve their lives by using the conceptual and cultural resources that are available to them, from places near and far away.

I say "men" because his is a particularly gendered story, and his hopes and actions are shaped by the comparative "wiggle room" his gender has conferred upon him. Here and in what follows I have included all of his language, from ruminations on theology to descriptions of fungal towels soaked in the semen of unknown men, and I have embraced and echoed his profanity, because I see this carnivalesque collapsing of hierarchies as fertile and generative. It speaks to Ngeti's knowledge of, and confidence in, multiple worlds, in which he goes traveling. I want to close now with a few contextualizing remarks that I feel are important for fully appreciating Ngeti and his narrative.

SOME BIG IDEAS

Some of the issues that emerge from the story we are telling include youth subjectivity in Africa; the cultural politics of language; the politicization of gender and generation; the influence of technology, media, and the Internet; changing understandings of "development"; the growth of new religious movements like Pentecostalism; and the continuing importance of what anthropologists have long glossed as "kinship" (or what Marshall Sahlins refers to as "the mutuality of belonging").[18] I want to draw attention to three overarching Big Themes that frame all of these others before turning back to Ngeti's story. The first has to do with political economy and African futures, the second with subjectivity and globalization, and the third with ethnographic practice.

The first major theme concerns what has been variously called neoliberalism or post-Fordism, referring to the transnationalization of a political-economic system formerly framed by national territorial borders, in which the state figured prominently as the symbol and generator of "development." The collapse and reconfiguration of this system is part of the reason why Ngeti feels bewitched in the first place. Although the shift from a Fordist to a post-Fordist economy has played out differently in Kenya than it has in the United States, it is nonetheless a global phenomenon.[19] Ngeti's narrative gives us a sense of how people are experiencing and acting on this structural transformation in locally idiomatic repertoires that are also broadly relevant to people the world over. While Ngeti's biography has been shaped by these global and national events, in this book he does not dwell on them at all, so a brief history is in order.

Postcolonial Kenya began as a nation mainly in name, its sovereignty compromised by the "debt" that it allegedly owed to its colonizing invaders.[20] Kenya's people achieved independence from the British in 1963, after a protracted anticolonial and civil war in which approximately fifteen thousand Africans were killed. Afterward, Kenyans inherited a number of enduring problems, including foreign debt, dependence on foreign inputs and aid, and structural inequality that would only worsen over time. Nonetheless, until the late 1980s Kenya was, for many, the model modernizing African nation state because of its strong export-driven economy based mostly on coffee, its vibrant Indian Ocean port of Mombasa, its internationally renowned wildlife tourism, and its relatively peaceful political environment. During this time, the Kenyan state was at the center of the nation's "development," the government was the main employer, and high school–educated men could look forward to long-term government jobs that often came with pensions.[2] Schooling and health care were largely subsidized, and people strongly demanded education, viewing it as a mechanism for acquiring employment and connecting to a larger world. In Taita, many men went to school, secured jobs in the city of Mombasa, and sent part of their wages home to their wives in Taita, who used these funds to send their children to school, thus renewing the whole cyclical process. In the meantime, women and children grew crops at home, and villages developed relationships with male politicians (most of whom had also made their money in Mombasa), many of whom funneled development resources from the state to Taita. This is not to say that everything was wonderful in the 1970s and 1980s—there was a great deal of inequality and political oppression on the part of a clique of people who tried to control the state for their own interests. But there was at least a kind of recognizable system, and a relationship between means and ends, which would later seem to come undone.

This postcolonial model of development, which was structurally and ideologically dependent on male labor, male state figures, and a state cast as male, changed fundamentally throughout the 1990s. It started when the national economy was hit hard by a decline in the global price of coffee, Kenya's main export, in the 1980s. Under President Daniel arap T. Moi, Kenya began taking out structural adjustment loans (also referred to as structural adjustment programs, or SAPS), which were tied to "conditionalities" deemed necessary by the banks because the Kenyan government couldn't pay its so-called debt. About a quarter of the Kenyan budget continues to go to servicing the interest from this debt. During the post–Cold War 1990s, when Kenya was no longer usable as a bulwark against Soviet communism, aid was cut dramatically, and the World Bank and the IMF (International Monetary Fund) increasingly tied loans to what they now called "good governance."

Kenyan state actors responded to the decline of aid and the new "conditionalities" attached to loans by enacting the model of "free market capitalism" that the economic developers were peddling.[22] Kenyan state officials like then–Minister of Finance Mudavadi rapidly lifted price controls, floated the Kenyan shilling, removed restrictions on imports, privatized all public industries, and dramatically downsized the civil service. All of this produced massive unemployment and inflation, while also transforming the state. State figures and politicians continued to hang on, of course, but often they could no longer rely on their salaries or state resources and so became increasingly "corrupt," the very thing that structural adjustment reforms were intended to eradicate. At the same time, foreign NGOs (nongovernmental organizations), working on everything from "development" to human rights and civil society education, became visibly powerful in Kenyan political and economic life. Their influence came to eclipse that of the state, so much so that, in Ngeti's town, an international NGO called Plan International completely took over development work from the chiefs and politicians, building projects and subsidizing children's school fees. These NGOs fed local social change by actively recruiting women and young men to work for them, awarding salaries that were much better than the government could offer.

An explosion of new media matched the apparent decline of the state, as presses became liberalized and foreign bootlegged films from the United States, South Asia, and Nigeria quickly materialized in local markets. By the beginning of the twenty-first century these changes were coupled with the rise of cybercafés, which became magnets for youth and supercharged incubators of youth consciousness.[23] They also became points of immersion in an imaginary alternative universe where, for the first time in history, African youth could study, say, the sexual practices of white people in the same way that white anthropologists had been doing with respect to Africans for decades. In the course of this study, they became familiar with Wazungu (whites/Europeans) in a way that was revolutionary and destabilizing and that has not been even close to fully appreciated. Pornography was not the only, or even the main, thing that came out of the rise of Internet culture, but its cultural and political importance is easily overlooked by those who would be inclined to see it as embarrassing.

Ngeti was coming of age in the midst of this crisis and transformation, but all of the people presented in this book were coming to terms with these changes in their own way: Ngeti's father, Charles, lost his job and his pension; his mother, Monica, moved from involvement in state-centered politics to immersion in new religious movements; his friend Patroba used his religious practice to teach people what kinds of subjects they should be in the new economy. And so on. What was happening was that old structures were disintegrating and people were reimagining what the future would look like in various ways.[24] Some of these involved breaking with the past completely, while others involved recuperating and engaging with the past in imaginative ways. In practice, even breaking with the past entailed conjuring it up in a new guise. Always, there was a sense that reality as lived in Africa was somehow "fake" or substandard in relation to other places, and this was confirmed by pervasive media and, for some, Internet exposure.[25] Ngeti wanted to break through from his world to another, largely imaginary one, and he used various instruments to do this, including language, technology, books, religion, and eventually, anthropology. He took these things and changed them, and he was also changed by them.

Making a new future means reinventing oneself, and Ngeti is quite palpably engaged in a project of self-remaking—which brings us to our second theme: subjectivity. Ngeti has often tried to transcend local, parochial relationships and entanglements in order to access what he perceives as more meaningful and universal connections. He attempts to do this by "untying" himself from people who are related to him through descent and territory.[26] His first effort in this direction is through language, and later through his travels into the repressed and hidden aspects of daily life, like the worlds of "witchdoctors" and sex workers. Eventually, he tried to reinvent himself and the future through Pentecostal religion. He has often felt that others people's histories, emotions, and interests hold him back, and that living in the countryside both produces this situation and is the outcome of it—he is home because he has been tied, and he knows he has been tied because he is at home. Ngeti imagines another world in which people are free of history and move into the future fueled by their own free will, a fantasy that has been nurtured by the books he reads, the films he watches, the music he listens to, and the particular relationship to God that he has tried to cultivate. Ngeti's project of self-actualization puts him in good company, for he is joined by a host of young people in the Global South who re-create themselves in testimonials about their life struggles in churches, radio shows, and, of course, Facebook. But Ngeti, and others like him, are also trying to create something greater than the autonomous self, by forging new patterns of kinship and new forms of belonging with others who are not connected to them by virtue of some shared connection to territory.

I believe that all of this is quite important and sheds a great deal of light not only on African subjectivity, but on subjectivity in general.[27] There is a grand metanarrative concerning the individualized person in Africa and the West that runs something like this: In the modern West, a diverse set of things happened to make it seem as if we are bounded individual subjects.[28] Crawford Macpherson famously called it the philosophy of possessive individualism, highlighting the coimplication of modern Western notions of property (a bounded thing, as opposed to the fluid materialization of social relationships) and the idea of a rights-bearing person that owns his or her characteristics as property.[29] Thanks to Raymond Williams, we know that the term *individual* wasn't applied to people until the eighteenth century, which was also the time when modernist notions of individually owned, completely commodified property became fully elaborated.[30] In direct and telling contrast, African subjectivity has been portrayed as open, relational, and incomplete, as if African notions of the person had not yet evolved toward a single, known telos.[31]

Africanist anthropology has done much work to show the diversity of African understandings and enactments of the person, in the process challenging simple Western notions of African subjectivity as "open" and unbounded.[32] John and Jean Comaroff, for example, have argued that "postmodern" Western understandings of fractal, shifting personhood actually resemble certain African (specifically Tswana) understandings of the person as "becoming" rather than "being," citing this as evidence for Europe's belated "evolution" toward Africa.[33] This is certainly true of Taita, where, well into colonial times, men became individuated subjects by expanding themselves, across space and over time, through exchange networks. They became "big" persons through the exchange of things like livestock, which generated the expanding social networks that the objects themselves also symbolized. Over the course of their lives, men were "called" to positions of ever-expanding authority by everyday objects that were also materializations of ancestors. These agentive objects (a cow bell, a medicine bag, and a sitting stool, acquired in stages throughout one's life) represented and enabled men to enter into relations of mutual indebtedness: keeping and trading livestock (bell), healing and protecting communities with medicine (bag), and sitting on the council of elders (stool).[34] The spatial-temporal expansion of the male self continued after death, with his ongoing participation in daily life as an ancestor whose skull, similarly agentive, was likely to be placed in a nearby cave, while his lineage descendants carried on his name and personality. This process of expanding the self through communication and exchange with others was always threatened by *usabi,* or what Ngeti glosses as witchcraft. Witchcraft, directed at men and women by enemies, subverted the process of progressive self-expansion through others.[35]

Over the course of the colonial and postcolonial periods, elites often adopted more outwardly Western understandings of individualism, and sometimes used Western idioms to complain about Taita kinship as a form of dependency synonymous with witchcraft, or being "tied." In a similar vein, Ngeti is trying to become an autonomous subject, in part by communicating with and connecting to something foreign that is outside of him. Through autobiographical narration and email communication, he is also baring his soul and releasing pain and resentment. This seemingly "modern" compulsion to communicate through technology also reflects the main purpose of Taita ritual action, which is aimed at releasing anger through symbolically loaded acts like kutasa as a prelude to building communities based on trust.[36] Ngeti's actions thus reflect long-standing Taita understandings of self-making, an active and explicitly social process that one brings about by contacting and communicating with relatively distant others through objects and media. This thing he wants to connect with shifts: sometimes it exists in a geographical location, and sometimes it is rooted in a transcendent Divine.

As Ngeti persistently fails to make the connections he wants to make, or to communicate effectively with Truth, he is drawn deeper into geographically immediate histories and comes to the realization, over and over again, that his body and life are not really his own. In other words, discovering the fact that he has been penetrated by others comes as the result of trying to communicate with a different, foreign Other. This means that Ngeti's witchcraft "beliefs" don't make sense in terms of a local, bounded cosmology, or ontology, but must be seen as the product of a thwarted relationship with an imaginary outside world through which he struggles to realize himself as an autonomous being.

We could put this in a somewhat different vein and say simply that Ngeti is bored. His boredom, I contend, is produced by his practice of withdrawal from the people and routines around him. This makes him feel suspended, held in limbo, a state which Heidegger saw as a chief characteristic of what he called "profound boredom." Heidegger viewed the withdrawal from lived temporality and the corresponding extension of time (also known as boredom) as a peculiarly "modern" condition. As the philosopher David Hoy paraphrases, "This boredom permeates 'modern man' generally and is the mood or attunement of the present age."[37] For Ngeti, withdrawal goes hand in hand with his knowledge of another temporality from which he is excluded—one that is presumably faster and more interesting, broken down into countless yet-to-be-experienced experiences that have the effect of compressing time. The more Ngeti withdraws from the temporality of daily life, the more anxious he becomes about being pulled back into it, feeling the power of past events on his life. These past experiences, many of which were not actually his own, constrain his desire to free himself from one lived, experiential temporality and to enter into another, imaginary one. And so throughout the following text Ngeti alternates between boredom and anxiety, always acutely aware that he is running out of time. His humor and talent help him to get loose from this suspended state.

In trying to understand other people's affects, which (we will see) reside inside him as objects, Ngeti ends up being drawn to some very classical anthropological subject matters, including kinship, ritual, and witchcraft. All of which leads us to the third and final theme. In recent years, considerable effort has been given to analyzing and attempting to accomplish collaborative ethnography.[38] All ethnography has always been collaborative to some degree, but for most of its history anthropologists defined the agenda for research as they encountered people who had little if any idea of what the anthropological project was. Only rare individuals, like Victor Turner's Muchona the Hornet and Marcel Griaule's Ogotommêli, seemed to think of their own culture anthropologically, and typically they did so as guardians of secret, esoteric knowledges and traditions. Recently, George Marcus and others have used the terms *para-ethnography* and *para-site* to describe fieldwork among people who are already thinking ethnographically and anthropologically about their actions and about their social situations.[39] These anthropologists typically have in mind fieldwork among experts (say, lawyers or journalists) who are also doing a kind of ethnographic fieldwork in a particular institutional setting, like a laboratory or corporation.[40]

But increasingly anthropologists are doing para-ethnographic work even in seemingly remote settings that are actually as "globalized" as any other.[41] In fact, as a result of trying to understand the world beyond Taita, Ngeti has come to identify more closely with that world and to feel kinship with it, a process that has made him feel estranged from his geographical home. Ngeti's experience of disconnection from home is quintessentially anthropological. After all, many anthropologists routinely describe the purpose of their discipline as "making the strange familiar, and the familiar strange," especially to their first-year undergraduates. There is no doubt a major difference in our anthropological missions: Ngeti's is an effort to identify and manage the social forces that are operating on him, and he is compelled to take these forces seriously as "facts" rather than as metaphors or signs of something else.

This is methodologically frustrating for the anthropologist who wants to engage Ngeti the anthropologist, because his actions and statements do signify in ways that he is not always aware of and which require interpretation. And the verisimilitude that characterizes Ngeti's statements and actions, as well as our relationship, covers over a great deal of important difference. No two people who watch a movie are watching the same movie, but the way in which my *The Rock* differs from Ngeti's *The Rock* reveals a complicated, mutually imbricated cultural history that is also a global history.

To cite one particularly relevant example: Ngeti uses English terms like *witchcraft* to describe his experiences, but this does not mean that what he is referencing is the same as the European understanding of witchcraft that emerged in the 1500s. It also doesn't mean that we should throw away the English term *witchcraft* and look for a more "Taita" term, because some of the implications of the English term (e.g., an absolute evil that is synonymous with Satan) are part of what Ngeti is trying to get across and, indeed, are among the meanings buried in this dialogic utterance. In general, Ngeti's speech and practice resemble his use of the term *witchcraft:* the things he says and does look so familiar to us because they are designed to, but that does not make them the same, and it does not make what Ngeti calls an interpretive "hermeneutics of suspicion" any less necessary or relevant. At the same time, we would not understand Ngeti any better by resorting completely to Taita terms and idioms. So, Ngeti challenges us as anthropologists to think about how to engage a world in which people move self-consciously between different epistemic frames, at times stepping completely into the language of their interlocutors while simultaneously acknowledging that there are things (like witchcraft) that cannot be reduced to a universal language or rationality. Moreover, Ngeti offers an ethnographic window into a potential utopian future, providing insights into what a citizen in a borderless world might look like. For this emergent subject, "identity" and "subjectivity" are not static things, or inherited histories, but practices of movement back and forth and of translation that is never finished, because naturally there is always something left unsaid.

This book is divided into eight chapters, each of which contains multiple essays by Ngeti and commentary written by me. Chapter 2, "English Makes You See Far," concerns Ngeti's lifelong love affair with the English language. His essays in this chapter touch on a stubborn weed, a sociopathic missionary, an angry school prefect, a creative teacher, an Irish nun, and pornographic magazines. Taken together, these email letters, and my comments, make an argument about what his fluency means and what it has enabled him to do. Chapter 3, "God Helps Those That Help Themselves," focuses on the efforts of Ngeti's family to ascertain who was bewitching him so that he "hated books." Here Ngeti describes his adolescent experiences of being "tied" so that other people's anger would not enter him. His writings capture the exotic mystery of these rituals, and my commentary contextualizes them with essays about Taita's colonial history and the current postcolonial situation. In chapter 4, "Good Ants, Bad Milk, and Ugly Deeds," Ngeti pulls back, at my suggestion, and provides some backdrop to witchcraft in Taita and to his anxieties about being bewitched. His essays dwell on the insect world of the past, a sick cow, a family brawl, and a magic cat. They also move us from rural Taita to the city of Mombasa, the setting for chapters 5 and 6.

In chapter 5, "The Power of Prayer," Ngeti writes about his decision to take a cue from his mother and leave his life of marijuana, reggae, and brothels behind to become "saved" in a major Pentecostal church. He describes the excitement of public salvation, how it felt to speak in tongues, and his early interactions with the preacher-prophet Patroba, who would become a significant figure in his life. The chapter is filled with other anecdotes, including an adolescent run-in with the police, a fight with a demonic avocado, and an encounter with hungry demons on the beach. Chapter 6, "Works and Days," comprises a diary that Ngeti wrote for a year while he was living with Patroba in Mombasa and struggling, with another saved friend, to put together a business with the Lord's blessing. This chapter marks the beginning of Ngeti's disillusionment with Pentecostalism. It is filled with pithy, tantalizing narratives about a fateful accident, a case of plastic teeth, and God's favorite cell phone, among other things. Chapter 7, "A Confrontation," emerges from oral discussions I had with Ngeti when I returned to Taita in 2003. In this chapter, Ngeti brings me up to speed about his recent conflicts with his parents, and together we work to arrive at a solution. Chapter 8, "Reflections," is also based on an interview with Ngeti, this one at the end of 2010, and includes Ngeti's more recent interpretations of the events depicted in the book, following on the deaths of Patroba and his mother. In this chapter, I also offer insights into Ngeti's story and, in the spirit of dialogic anthropology, suggest the impact that it has had on my own life.

TWO

English Makes You See Far

Sasa rafiki [What's up man],

Bado niko Mombasa kwa siku chache [I'm still in Mombasa for a few days].

   Sasa [now] let me ask you, why did Osama bin Laden have to wait until a week before the American elections to send that message? [Ngeti is referring to a 2004 Aljazeera broadcast of a message from Osama bin Laden to the American public, explaining his motivation for the "9/11" hijackings.] Now the whole of America is fearing fear itself, and this has in some way influenced the way you guys have ended up choosing your president [referring to the Bush vs. Gore election]. And this electoral college shit, why the fuck do you keep using it? It is stupid, so much so you guys trying to explain it makes you look more stupid. I think America should stop preaching about democracy. Why are you people so scared of Osama? The guy is not there. America is afraid of its own bullish shadow. I know *wewe si mmarekani lakini pia ninajua ni afadhali kua mmarekani mjinga kuliko miraqi mwerevu au vipi? Sema kitu rafiki yangu hii si yako* [I know you are not an American, but I also know it's better to be a stupid American than a clever Iraqi, or what do you say? Say something, my friend; this is not yours].

NGETI, *in an email he sent me following*
the American presidential election of 2004

AS OUR CORRESPONDENCE CONTINUED, it became clear to me that Ngeti wanted to use the opportunity that his knowing me presented to communicate his story to a larger, global community, and perhaps even to profit from the often puzzling and at times traumatic events that he had experienced. Over the course of telling me this story via email communications and in person, Ngeti's circumstances and his feelings about the events described in this book have changed, but he has always seen this as his story, which he, an existing, coherent (if not exactly autonomous) subject, is telling. It would be fair to say that narration is a technique through which Ngeti works to become an autonomous subject—a person who is exercising control over the course of events, and over his fate. In this way, the act of writing his personal narratives exemplifies the longer process that Ngeti describes, in which he struggles to break free from the shackles of the past by seeking out people— human conduits—who claim to have access to miraculous, often divine, power. These people are able to reveal the concealed and the unspoken, that which exceeds so-called "rational" communication, as Ngeti tells us time and time again.

Because I believe that to tell his story unencumbered is at least part of what Ngeti wants, and because I know that he has scant opportunities to feel like a person in control, I have chosen not to intervene too much in his narration. Friendship is among the complex ties that bind us, and it sometimes makes me resist analytical deconstruction of Ngeti's narratives. I also don't want this to be my book about him—rather, it is our book about what it is like to be him. But in the course of assembling his piecemeal writings and beginning to share them with others in classes and lectures, I realized that something was not quite sitting right, at least for a North American audience. That is why this chapter is structured differently than later ones: whereas in subsequent chapters I mostly step aside and allow Ngeti to tell his own story with relatively minimal interventions on my part, here I actively interject myself in his narrative, to try to eke out some additional meanings and interpretations.

As I began to publicly read Ngeti's letters, I found that one major issue for my audiences had to do with Ngeti's mastery of English, specifically American English—not just the words (he knows them all), but the idioms and references that would appear to be "insider" knowledge, which only an American would know. I have always been very impressed by Ngeti and have seen his virtuoso multiplicity—his ability to move among and master different speech genres without being subsumed by any of them—as eminently cosmopolitan. I have been intrigued by his ability to acquire this cosmopolitanism despite the fact that he has lived most of his life in a geographically remote rural place in Africa. For me, it has said something about our popular, and even academic, prejudices concerning where we should locate the "cosmopolitan" or the "modern" in the first place. That location would not be in the Taita Hills, and yet this place may be more cosmopolitan than many in the United States, partly because people there look outward to a world beyond limited territorial confines. That world may exist for them as an idea, or perhaps a dream, partly mediated by imagery garnered from CNN or *Kung Fu Panda* or Stephen King, but it has substance nonetheless.

[Ngeti is able to connect conceptually and linguistically to the world beyond the territory that is the Taita Hills] even as the decline of meaningful employment brought about by structural adjustment programs (an example of the deregulation that economists and other American pundits glibly call "globalization") has rendered him more disconnected from these global "flows" than his parents were. This reflects the fact that globalization is a complicated and multidimensional process, as Arjun Appadurai long ago pointed out in his description of the axes along which this process unfolds, in divergent and irreducible "scapes" (financescapes, ideoscapes, mediascapes, etc.).[1] One consequence of the disconnect between Ngeti's fluent knowledge of an imaginary world outside Africa and his perceived exclusion from it is that Ngeti epitomizes the condition of "abjection" that James Ferguson argues is characteristic of contemporary Africa.[2] This somewhat pathologizing term, however, does not begin to do justice to Ngeti's ability to create, invent, and improvise. Such terminology also gives short shrift to the "Taita" practice of conjuring up social collectivities through collaborative speech acts (or what Wataita call "chewing tongue meat").

Many of the anti-imperialist American students who heard Ngeti's English did not interpret it the way I did, as being replete with emancipatory meanings. Rather than see Ngeti's linguistic competence as a sign of his empowerment, or at least his mastery of something foreign and powerful, they often viewed it as a sign that he was dispossessed, alienated from a more authentic African self. In this view, Ngeti was cursed to feel a sense of belonging to a world that would not let him in, while he remained an incompetent in the world to which he actually belonged, the territory of the Taita Hills. When, for example, I presented his letters to a small audience of students at Spelman College, a historically black women's college in Atlanta, the reaction of some surprised and even annoyed me. At least one student commented that Ngeti sounded like a child parroting the words of more adult others, and she expressed pity for this person who should be learning to be more like what he was—a Taita man.[3]

Later, I received somewhat similar comments from other people, including senior academics at large research universities. Some wondered whether I had translated or even written Ngeti's letters myself, and if they were in fact authentic. The writings, they said, sounded too familiar, too close to "us." Ultimately, I realized that I was confronting an underlying philosophical assumption in these talks: mainly, that there is an autochthonous African essence that Africans should embrace because it stands as a cultural and political alternative to Western hegemony—even though every essentializing notion of African ontology, however positive it may be, is some version of a Western fantasy projected back onto the Other.[4]

I knew that I had to find a way to show others that Ngeti's knowledge was not only impressive, but also based on as authentic an experience as any other—that the purified "Tradition" many of these people seemed to want Ngeti to embrace was at least as oppressive to Ngeti and his aspirations as the ostensibly "foreign" language of English. I wanted people to see that his knowledge of English signaled something greater than his oppression in the face of a racist and unequal world that views African languages and ways of being as inferior. Indeed, it was essential for people to appreciate this if they were to understand anything else about Ngeti and what he was doing—his visits to "witchdoctors," his conversion to Pentecostalism, and so forth. All of these actions are driven by a similar kind of motivation, or urge, on Ngeti's part.

So I wrote to Ngeti and told him about the doubt that I was picking up from some interlocutors. I asked him if he could perhaps write an essay or a letter recounting his experiences with English and why he came to love this language in the way that I knew he did.

Ngeti's response was quick and comically angry:

Vipi rafiki [What's up, buddy?],

Now who the fuck thinks a Taita guy cannot come up with a story like mine? What is wrong with the story? Why would I pretend to be a Taita in the first place? If you're not a Taita, you can write about other stuff rather than visiting witches and prophets. What do they expect of a guy who reads the dictionary like some holy book? My mind is saturated with the language. I think in English. I dream in English, for fuck's sake. If I was over there I would probably have a PhD in English up my black ass by now. Or they think I am still evolving into a human being? They think I still have a long, hairy tail, a furry coat, and I eat berries and nuts and goddamn roots ... eeeehhhh ... (laugh). Anyways we gotta do what we gotta do. I hope you are well, my friend.

The response is meant to be funny, while also conveying a sense of Ngeti's accomplishment in the face of seemingly impossible obstacles. Ngeti is in effect saying that, had he been born in the States, he would be the intellectual equal, if not the superior, of my academic colleagues. He is also making it clear that he does not possess this language like a piece of secondhand cloth-ing. Ngeti owns the real deal, and it does not hang foolishly on his shoulders. He dreams in English, goddamnit.

But there is something else in this statement that is potentially more embarrassing to a reflexively anti-imperialist anthropologist: Ngeti sees English as sacred—he reads the dictionary like a Holy Book—and he seems to suggest that African languages, and perhaps by extension Africa itself, are at an earlier stage of evolution or "development." Africans are compelled to tell stories about going to witchdoctors, rather than doing more liberating, exciting, and universally relevant things, like visiting aquariums, something Ngeti wrote about in one of his high school English essays. He even seems, if only in jest, to equate ignorance of English with living in a tree and eating nuts, like a monkey. In other words, one possible interpretation of this pas-sage is that Ngeti sees English as civilization and "the real," and Africa as synonymous with old, petty entanglements and destructive illusions. All of this seems to evoke some of the most fundamental and racist European imagery about the dark continent—such as Georg Hegel's famous statement that Africans are outside of "World History" because they identify com-pletely with nature and have yet to conceptualize a universal standard that might serve as a moral measure for their actions.[5]

Ngeti's email calls to mind Frantz Fanon's well-known writings on language and colonial domination. Fanon argued that colonialism led the colonized to want to identify with the colonizer to acquire personal power and mastery. For the colonized, acquisition of the colonial power's language granted access to a civilization and way of being that was assumed to be superior. However, this relationship to the language (whether one mastered it or not) was psychologi-cally destructive. The colonized could never truly accept the dominant lan-guage as actually belonging to them because of the real processes of material exclusion that were fundamental to colonialism. The result was self-hate on a global scale. As Fanon put it in "The Negro and Language," "I ascribe a basic importance to the phenomenon of language. . . . Every colonized people—in other words, every people in whose soul an inferiority complex has been cre-ated by the death and burial of its local cultural originality—finds itself face to face with the language of the civilizing nation; that is, with the culture of the mother country. The colonized is elevated above his jungle status in proportion to his adoption of the mother country's cultural standards."[6]

Fanon saw language as the distilled essence of colonial power, and the colonized's identification with it as productive of psychosis. Ironically,

Kenyan colonial administrators of British extraction would have agreed with him. Like him, they would have worried about whether Ngeti's simultaneous connection to and disconnection from global flows of power and knowledge was healthy—for Ngeti *and* for the Kenyan body politic. For colonial officials, whose political order was predicated on an imagined stable tradition vested in the African elders through which they governed, knowing one's place, in space and time, was psychologically healthy. A so-called hybrid being like Ngeti was pathologically out of place. Kenyan colonial state officials relied on certain kinds of anthropology and psychology to articulate their knee-jerk anxiety about Africans' mimicry of European ways. Like Fanon, they viewed the trauma of being betwixt and between as a disease that especially affected African elites, and they were genuinely concerned about the potential consequences of what they called the "detribalized" African male—the being whose education and travels had made him neither African nor European, but something else.[7] Colonial administrators argued that these allegedly disturbed individuals, like the late president and cultural anthropologist Jomo Kenyatta, were the main impetus for mass anticolonial rebellions like Mau Mau. In turn, they tended to view the Mau Mau insurrection not as a direct reaction to colonial expropriation of land and resources, but as a symptom of cultural atrophy combined with the subconscious desire to go feral, so as to return to the savage past.

Postcolonial Kenyan thinkers tended to accept the idea of a pure African identity as the foundation of nationalist politics and identity. They responded to colonialism by reversing the polarity of values that colonialism had thrust upon them, often accepting their radical ontological separateness. To take one powerful example, the world-famous Kenyan playwright and novelist Ngugi wa Thiongo has long viewed Kenyans' sacralization of English to be synonymous with the colonization of their consciousness.[8] For him, the hegemony of the English language and, by association, culture created a submissive neocolonial African subject prone to compliance in the face of the cunning and self-interested schemes of former colonial masters. He argued that slavishness toward the master language had vanquished the promise of "development" in Kenya by creating cultural conditions that legitimated the Kenyan elite's compulsive "eating" of the working peasants.

Ngugi's ideas were shaped in part by his own childhood experience of being beaten by one of his teachers for speaking Gikuyu on the school grounds. In the 1970s, Ngugi famously renounced English altogether and began writing almost exclusively in Swahili and his first language, Gikuyu.

Ngugi embraced vernacular languages and committed himself to liberating art from the Kenyan bourgeoisie by producing popular theater critical of elite culture and political economy. This landed Ngugi in a Kenyan jail without trial, where he languished until he became a cause célèbre of Amnesty International. Ngugi's extolling of an autochthonous identity made him recognizable and sympathetic to an international community, whereas Ngeti's cosmopolitan multidimensionality can confuse and even embarrass Westerners.

Ngeti's embrace of English seems to some like a disavowal of self, even if we do live in a globalized world that has rendered the borders between the global North and the global South ever more porous—conceptually, if not economically. As James Ferguson, in accounting for the "embarrassment" engendered in anthropologists by "African mimicry," has posed the question, "How does one deal with the object of alterity who refuses to be other and who deliberately aims to spoil his or her own 'authenticity'? What does one do with the cultural other who 'wants to become like you'?"[9]

Ferguson goes on to point out that anthropology has dealt with this issue by claiming that Africans (and other non-Europeans) have adopted European ways and practices either as a form of resistance to oppression or in order to become more like themselves, a process that can also be figured as resistance. In the latter version of anthropology's efforts to make sense of mimesis, that which appears familiar at first ("They are becoming like us!") turns out to be quite different after all (thankfully, from the point of view of the liberal relativist anthropologist). Thus, a new religious movement is shown to revitalize older African cultural forms, or a foreign language is shown to intermingle with vernacular languages to create a hybrid that is neither African nor European (say, the multilingual text message). Or, to use Ngeti as an example, a young man's interest in email and English expresses a historically entrenched strategy of building social worlds by voicing pain and resentment while forging speech communities composed of people who understand and love each other.

Ferguson sees such arguments as limited and circular and urges us to instead take seriously the structural inequality from which people like Ngeti want to escape. According to Ferguson, we should view practices like Ngeti's as attempts to create solidarity with a global North that systematically expropriates and excludes Africa. And Ferguson is right: Ngeti desires mastery of English (as well as technology and other things he associates with the West) because he wants to liberate himself from the "abjection" he experiences as a postcolonial subject—specifically, his experience of feeling stuck. He seeks avenues of direct communication with the world outside and with powers at once secular and divine, whether through English, Pentecostalism, or digital technology. And this desire for unfettered communication is as much "Taita" as it is, say, "Digital Modern."[10]

Nonetheless, I suggest we focus our attention less on the object of Ngeti's actions—say, English, which we often assume to be synonymous with white people and European civilization—and more on the symbolically constituted action itself. That is, not to foreground the fetish object English and the social structures in which the language is enmeshed, but to address the way Ngeti's creativity collapses boundaries and redirects words and ideas so they end up in places they would not seem to belong. Ngeti is propelled by his desire to be transformed by something transcendent, and this desire incites him to find new things to do, new strategies for living. It is this creativity that distinguishes him, and others like him, at a time when the structures that organize the world seem to be immune to our efforts to change them, and the planet seems to barrel toward an apocalyptic climax that sometimes appears inevitable.

In a similar vein, Achille Mbembe, in "African Modes of Self-Writing," writes "against the arguments of critics who have equated [African] identity with race and geography."[11] Mbembe lays out the limitations of what he claims to be the two main academic modes of African self-knowledge, one "Marxist-nationalist" and the other "nativist." The former asserts that African ontology only emerges from political resistance to colonial and post-colonial structures of power. The latter has it that there is a "true" African essence that comes to life in a vanquished "tradition" from which Africans have been exiled. After criticizing each of these efforts to "hypostasize African identity," Mbembe goes on to argue that the "imaginative and social practices of African agents show that other orders of reality are being established," even if African and Western academics are not paying attention.[12] I like to think that Ngeti is a case study of what Mbembe is writing about here.

Let's take Mbembe's cue to pay attention, and leave these musings behind, so as to better hear what Ngeti has to say. Again, I had asked Ngeti to account, in writing, for his specific relationship to English—both his knowledge of the language and his passion for it. I was intrigued to find that Ngeti's first essay in response concerned his desire to use English to eradicate a stubborn and resilient weed that had formerly been managed through cooperative work and the kind of "local knowledge" that has to be learned the hard way. And it turned out that Ngeti was speaking English before he even knew a word of it. Here is his first essay.

The Childhood of the Man from the Hills

One day, and this was back in the 70's and I think I was about five or six years old, my parents and I were in the garden, digging. My father was on leave from the bus company in Mombasa and the three of us were preparing the land for the season's planting. Now, this place that we were digging in was infested with couch grass (*lusangari* in Kidawida). The agriculturists will tell you that this kind of grass, or weed, is the worst that can invade your garden. Its roots go pretty deep into the ground and take up a lot of food from the soil, thus preventing the useful crops, like maize and beans, from giving their full and expected yield. On this day, I watched as my father attacked this weed with his *jembe* (hoe), making sure that he followed the roots of this weed as deep as they went into the ground, and this could be up to two or three feet. There was so much of this damn weed in our *shamba* (plot). I recall coming behind my parents with my baby jembe, collecting this weed, which looked like abnormally long worms, in small heaps ready for burning.

By the way, people did not joke around when dealing with this weed: a successful harvest of beans and maize and any other food crops hinged upon its successful extermination and the savage energy a farmer used to destroy it. Lusangari sent chills down the spines of farmers, so much so that they were ready to pay extra money to anyone who was skilled in digging it up. People, both men and women, who were skilled in digging up lusangari usually joined themselves into groups of two, three, or four people and hired themselves out to others. I recall people saying, and even now they still do, *"Oh mwana ndeuchi kufunya lusangari, icho onilimia aha ukalu dumbua na mapemba ghapo ghikazama, ndeuwuya unilimie sena"* ("So and so does not know how to uproot couch grass; the other season he dug for me and cut the couch grass carelessly, and my maize was spoilt"). If, say, I invited you to come dig with me and my land has this weed, I would mark where you were digging, and I would check to see if this weed would rear its ugly head before I harvested my maize or beans. If it did, then I would write you off the list of guys whom I would invite next season to come dig. But if this weed did not spring up again, then I would give you a portion of my harvest and I would not hesitate to sing your accolades to other people. Digging careers, and friendships, were made or destroyed by this weed.

Anyways, on this day, my father picked himself up from his bent position, sweating profusely, and asked no one in particular, *"Lakini ghoko wughanga ghwa lusangari?"* ("Isn't there medicine/pesticide for couch grass?"). I remember my mother saying that there was none, but I blurted, *"He ghoko, ghwadawangwa Gazil kwa kizungu"* ("Yes there is, and it is called Gazil in English"). Of course, I had made this up, but in the process had somehow convinced myself that it was true. My parents saw right through me and burst out laughing, and it made me feel good to see them laugh. I did not care whether there was a herbicide in Kenya or the world going by that name or not. All I knew was that I was happy I had uttered what I believed to be an English word for some fucking herbicide that might give me a break from collecting lusangari. But unconsciously I was developing a soft spot for this *language.*

And so Taita is a place with stubborn weeds that most people fail to uproot, even though everyone wants to. This is a good metaphor for Ngeti's whole attitude toward Taita and his family—conflicts and grudges, other people's problems, surround him and keep him from planting something that he can harvest and "eat." Ngeti imagines that there is something powerful out there that can save him from this, and tries to conjure it into existence by inventing the "English" language, which comes to stand for this powerful outside and serves as the main means for achieving it. This orientation would frame Ngeti's whole approach to the world and his problems.

I couldn't help but be struck by the fact that Ngeti was writing about a rhizomatic plant and English in the same breath. These days in my world I never stop hearing about philosophical rhizomes, so I enjoyed the coincidence. In botany, rhizomes are root systems that exist just below the surface of the ground and that grow horizontally, forming networks and clusters of connectedness that intermingle with the rhizomes of other plants, which may be of different species. Social theorists influenced by the French philosophers Gilles Deleuze and Félix Guattari have made the rhizome into a philosophical concept, contrasting a rhizomatic theory of culture to a more classical "arboreal," or treelike, theory of culture that they see as old-fashioned.[13]

Arboreal roots are centralized and singular, originating from a known source, and arborescent knowledge (a term typically used by Deleuzians to refer to modernist Western thought) focuses on origins, hierarchies, and dualistic categories: something is either African or it is European, for example. In contrast, rhizomes draw attention to trans-species connections, heterogeneity, nonstructure, and multiplicity; they render a search for origins absurd, for it is impossible to tell where the rhizome begins and ends. Although I know that this is not what Ngeti had in mind, the concept of the rhizome, and Ngeti's unwitting evocation of it, does suggest for me Ngeti's lifelong orientation to the English language. Ngeti will take this language that exists for him as a foreign tree with deep roots that don't seem to connect with his own roots at all, and cause this entrenched and awesome thing to lose its already fictive origins and become entwined with his own history. His strategy begins with mimicry bereft of knowledge.

Ngeti's essay continues from here, going on to discuss his understandings of how people in his village first came to know English. Again, we find more plant stories, this time involving contagious bananas.

I first heard about the white humans from my parents. My mother used to tell us a story about a colonialist or a priest who would come to our village, at the invitation of the area chief of course, to tell people about some new thing that was happening in the world. This mzungu [white person, European] would come along with his family or friends and they would eat bananas and just throw the banana peels away carelessly, but the people in the village would scramble for the peels—not because they wanted to eat them, but because they wanted to touch them. They believed that if they touched something touched by an mzungu then some of the mzungu "whiteness" would rub off on them. The kids who managed to put as much as a finger to the peel by some sheer miracle would boast to their peers saying, "Nawada ikanda zha irughu zhawadwa ni mzungu" ("I have touched a banana peel that has been touched by a white man"). Some would keep these peels as proof to whoever might challenge the veracity of their claim.

According to my mother, this one mzungu, his name was Verby, had some powers, which he often used to the consternation of the villagers. The story goes that this guy would inflict various afflictions on the villagers who had gone for the meeting, and this might be any ailment from flu to scabies to jiggers. According to the story, after talking to the villagers about whatever it was that he was talking about on that day (things like getting them to buy new maize or bean seeds from the market, or trying to cajole people to do some communal work, like carrying stones or sand for the church under construction), he would then ask them in English, "Do you want to get flu and scabies?" The people, who wanted anything this guy and all other wazungu had to offer, would roar back in unison, "Yes, Yes!!!!!!!!!!" And he would wave his hand like a magic wand over the crowd, and everybody thought they were being blessed. But for the whole of that week the people would have running noses and would be scratching themselves nuts. If these people knew what this white man was asking them, they would not have responded in the affirmative. Later the people came to know the meaning of scabies and flu, and every time this motherfucker asked them whether they wanted flu or jiggers they all would roar back with a reverberating "No!!!" Of course, they came to learn that knowing English was pretty important.

Ngeti's story highlights how central miscommunication was to the colonial encounter, and even now we are left wondering about the true nature of the missionary Verby's words and actions. Did Verby really ask Wataita if they wanted flu and scabies, and if so was he in fact invoking the well-rehearsed figure of a diseased Africa, perhaps to scare people into building hospitals and cattle dips? Or did Taita people simply discern the true, sinister intention underpinning the White Man's Burden, embodied in Verby, who wanted to bring disease and chaos where there had been none? Certainly then-Chief Mengo was suspicious of Verby's project: around 1915, he beat Verby in front of the whole village of Mwanda, very close to where Ngeti would later be born, and paid for this action with a lifelong prison sentence on the island of Lamu.

In a similar vein, African stories about the origin of the names of the places they inhabit often dwell on the silly accidents, follies that can no longer be fixed, that surrounded the colonial encounter. In my experience, these narrated memories of a fatal confusion that prefigured violent expropriation are more common than stories about actual violence and expropriation. So Kenya got it's name because, when the Wazungu visited Gikuyu territory and asked their Maasai guides the name of Mt. Kirinyaga, they didn't realize the Maasai language had no r's and g's. Taita, a Swahili word for the place, became an administrative category under colonialism. The eastern Congolese city of Bukavu, where I'm writing this now, got its name because the Africans that the Belgian surveyors just happened to meet mistakenly thought they were asking about the local cattle rather than the name for the place. Such confusions carried over into postcolonial times, as when Mobutu sese Seko tried to Africanize the Congo by giving it the name Zaire, which, it turns out, is derived from Portuguese. It is often hard to tell if these stories are literally true, or if the main takeaway is that the current trajectory of African social life—its past, present, and future—is forever marred by an Original Incoherence that any emancipatory practice must first address.

The story of Verby suggests that the English language held power over Africans because they did not speak it and that only whites felt there was something dangerous about Africans learning English. For Ngeti's mother, Monica, who told him this story, English belonged exclusively to Wazungu like Verby and was synonymous with their power, and with the power of the colonial state, as the imprisonment of Chief Mengo made clear. God, the English language, and whiteness were united in a fiery dynamo that created and destroyed. Ngeti wanted to break from his mother's relationship to English and to make the language his own, and as he grew older his desire for connection through this language became inseparable from other erotic desires. Ngeti continues:

When I came of age to go to school I remember my favorite subject was English. I had the desire to master the language. I knew all the English words for the different parts of the human body before I went to grade one. As I progressed to higher classes and started reading storybooks, I was particularly fascinated by the Cinderella and Snow White stories. Then some kids started coming to school with fashion magazines that had the most beautiful white women I had ever seen. I was old enough to appreciate a good-looking woman. Some of these women were so beautiful we joked with my friends that, if these women did indeed shit, then they shat nothing but chocolate and cookies and other goodies. And if they did fart, then it was definitely some perfume by Nina Ricci, Armani Armani, or Chanel. For me, these women had ethereal beauty that elicited a Latin phrase I had picked up somehow, and I remember saying it to my peers aloud: "Sic oculos, sic ille manus, sic ora ferebat" (Such eyes, such hands, such looks). I wanted to learn English and get to talk to these white girls. I wanted to become a doctor, or a pilot or a movie star, careers that would bring me into constant contact with the white race in general. I even toyed with the idea of getting married to a white woman so I could speak this language at breakfast, lunch, dinner, and bedtime. I do not remember whether I was particularly good at it, but I remember an incident when we were in class seven, the final year of our primary education, that made me vow that I would not stumble my way through the English language my whole life.

We had this class prefect who was too big for his age to be in our class. In all fairness, he was supposed to be in Form Three. On the day in question, this prefect was assigned the duty of handing off a wooden block, called a monitor, with words that said, "I cannot speak English because I am a fool," to any unlucky pupil whom he found speaking Kidawida. Now, everyone was speaking Kidawida in the classroom, and the prefect was in a quandary as to whom he was gonna give the monitor to. Out of frustration and anger and the desire to prove to us that he was both the oldest in the class and more eloquent in the English language, he decided to curse us in English. He shot up from his desk and glared at us, nostrils flaring like a mustang running against the prairies' wind, and screamed, "You are all marvelous! Very marvelous!" A sudden silence fell upon the class, as if the guy had just passed a death sentence on us all. This guy had just used the most abusive word we had ever heard. See, the first four letters of the word marvelous sounded like the Kiswahili word *mavi*, which means feces. We thought he had said we were full of shit. We were so livid with rage that all of us felt like skinning the bombastic prefect alive. One by one, we all called him marvelous as a rejoinder to his insult. This incident masturbated my desire to know the language thoroughly.

My efforts were given a boost by the compositions that we used to write. I remember I wrote a composition in which the teacher gave me 42 points out of 50. When I look at the composition today I can't help laughing at my mixture of tenses and spelling mistakes, but it also gives me reason to be proud of myself for how much I have achieved. I have my primary school teacher to thank for the good grounding that he had given me. This teacher had his own unique style of teaching, though at the time we thought he was fucking cuckoo. If no one in the class had reached the pass mark that he had set for an English paper, he would stand on the table and tell us to sit in a circle on the floor. Then he would ask us if we could see the grass outside and all that he was seeing through the window. Of course we couldn't, so we would say, "No," and he would respond, "It is because you do not know English. If you knew English you would see what I am seeing now. English makes you see far, it makes you see things other people cannot see. It makes you tall." We did not know what the fuck the guy was saying, but now I see what he meant.

When I left primary and went to secondary school, I was lucky to get into a seminary school where the English teacher was not a Kenyan, but an Irish nun. This was the first time I was coming into contact with a white person and had an opportunity to speak English to them. What I learned was that our Kenyan teachers didn't know shit about English. They hadn't known how to pronounce the simplest words. Our bad English appalled our Irish nun. All that we saw at the seminary was the Bible and prayer books and the rosary and a myriad of other religious paraphernalia, and if we read storybooks, then they were about some English knight in medieval Europe rescuing some princess from some nefarious witch, or some Roman god, or some fabulous story about some Greek deity. The first two years at the seminary were boring in every sense of the word. We lived a controlled life; we lived by a timetable that drove some of us who had come into contact with the ways of the world up the fucking wall. But I think I'm getting ahead of myself.

Because of the nun, I managed to get pen pals through an Irish pen pal organization. I had one pen pal from the United States, one in Trinidad and Tobago, and another one in India. I kept in touch with all of them for a while, and they would all comment about my good English. They said they did not know that there were people in Africa who could write English so fluently. This gave me a lot of satisfaction and egged me on to learn more and become fluent. Unfortunately, my communication with them came to an end because of the cost of mailing letters to them. And it took like three months for a letter from me to reach these guys and vice versa, and so eventually there was a total breakdown in our communication. There was no Internet then and the idea of email I think had not even entered the Western mind. This was in the early eighties. I believe that if I had been communicating with them through the net, I would probably still be in touch with them.

Instead, I took to reading novels, and my favorites were James Hadley Chase whodunit novels and more mushy stuff like Mills and Boons. The latter type of novels dealt mostly with romance and love. I loved the slang that Chase used. My reading preferences gradually became what I can call eclectic, in that as the years passed I read everything that I could get my hands on. But what really made me want to learn all English, all of its possible permutations, the high and the low of it, was Bob Marley—I worshipped him and his music and I wanted to understand every single word that came out of that saint's mouth. He was a radical revolutionary of the people, but still the music was so mellow and relaxed—great for smoking bhang, or pot, which by now I was doing plenty of.

But my sources of inspiration weren't all so inspirational. Like, I remember there was a kid who used to come to school with a very graphic porn magazine. I think it must have been *Hustler* or *Gallery*. Where that kid got the mag we did not know, and he did not tell us. But I remember the kid making some money out of it. One had to pay ten cents to see just a page of nude men and women humping each other. The boy would allow us just a few seconds of very worried furtive peeks at these glossy pages of white women's thighs and bushy crotches getting poked by the biggest tools we had ever seen. Not every kid was allowed to look at these pictures. It was just a select few who could come up with the required fee of around ten cents per page. This was a damn lot of money for kids like us back then.

More next time, buddy. Ngeti

Ngeti's elementary school teacher had instructed him that language determined the kind of reality he would inhabit. Ngeti could either choose to "see far" and to know the world as it was, or be compelled to sit in a circle (suggesting tautological information that goes nowhere in particular) with other "fools" for the rest of his life, literally recirculating their blind and uninformed opinions. One thing was certain: choosing the latter meant boredom, because there was nothing worth knowing through this vernacular language spoken from "on the ground." It is when he decided to enter the seminary, with the plan of eventually becoming a Catholic priest, that Ngeti came to really know English by coming into contact with its authentic speakers and through them other students in the African diaspora. Only then did Ngeti come to believe that everyone back home in Taita, even the professional guardians of this powerful language, was scarcely better than he had been as a small child, back when he impulsively mimed an English word for a nonexistent herbicide. They were mimics, each and all.

But the problem with the seminary and the Irish nun, above and beyond the regimentation, was that learning this language through his teachers meant inhabiting histories and fantasies that really did not to belong to him. These Catholic nuns offered access not to the global citizenship Ngeti hoped for, but to something historically particular and even archaic. If anything, they wanted to keep Ngeti locked in their own outmoded fantasies of Greek pantheons and medieval courts. Ngeti would spend the rest of his life trying to extricate this powerful language, English, from the oppressive colonial structures and histories to which it has been bound—the "bombastic" prefects who humiliated African kids for speaking their native languages, and the capricious missionaries who forced people to inhabit their vision of reality. But for a while, Ngeti was left standing alone, genitals in hand, with his erotic desire for another reality, and with his instrument he masturbated over the memory of picture copies that he didn't have the wherewithal to actually own. As Ngeti says, it was the music of Bob Marley, who had taken English and turned it into something radical and unassuming all at once, that gave Ngeti hope that he could make this language—and all of the foreign things that came with it—his own without having to completely inhabit the worlds and assumptions of distant others.

After sending me these writings, Ngeti asked me if I would like to see some of his school essays from childhood. Apparently, he had been holding on to them, keeping track of the progress he was making in English. I've included parts of them here because I think they show how his affair with English combined with other aspirations, which developed alongside his mastery of the language. Some were written when he was very young and had to do with things that were quite close to him—how important water is, hunting antelopes in the Taita lowlands. Later essays reached out to larger spheres of belonging and became more imaginative. One that struck me concerned the national Kenyan Independence Day, Madaraka, when Kenya obtained what the thirteen-year-old Ngeti mistakenly, but suggestively, calls "Eternal [read Internal] Self Government." In it, Ngeti looks forward to the country becoming the city for just one day, and expresses an unmistakable admiration for the functioning, independent Kenyan state, whose future decline would parallel Ngeti's ascent into adulthood.

15th June 1981

HOW I M GOING TO SPENT MY MADARAKA DAY

Madaraka is the day which *Kenya* Celebrated on the 1st June. And it is Celebrated in whole because it remainds us that Kenya got its Eternal Self Government. The day I am going to spend it I will be very happy because I will go to Wundanyi with my friends. And that day is the most day of our Government. And that day the people go to Wundanyi to hear the new Burget of 1981 to 1982. And that day the District Commitioner reads the Burget. And after that dancer will start dancing to invite people which have came from different places of our Government and the Wananchi. And that day I will go to Wundanyi to hear the new Burget of Governement of Kenya. And that day Wundanyi will be decorated and it will look like Nairobi. And some polices will be there to look every thing is going goodly.

When I first read this piece, I wondered if perhaps the child Ngeti had a less than fully conscious presentiment that his own subjective freedom was connected to the sovereignty of the Kenyan state, which was supposed to nurture and protect his emergent self. If so, later he would drop any such nationalist sentiments in favor of other paths to self-actualization, like Pentecostalism. In later essays, Ngeti showed that he already conceptually inhabited an imaginary urban milieu that was somehow more real than the place in which his body remained stuck. One essay concerns a fictive friend's wedding; an excerpt of it reads:

> After dressing him we walked out to meet his wife to be. The bride was a fantastic woman, elegant and immaculate in her snow white wedding dress. The maids were also dressed in white. The whole scene was glorious. . . . At around 10.30 a.m., the couple was carried to the church by a brand new Porsche, which moved at a walking pace. They were accompanied by people singing traditional wedding songs. . . . Everything in the church was heavenly. . . . [A] television crew used every minute of every event that was being performed, the priest delivered a sermon concerning the happiness of marriage and the purpose of creation.

In another essay, Ngeti goes on a date to visit a "magnificent aquarium" complete with underground floodlit rooms, miraculous marble walls, and free information booklets. Although it feels like he is recounting a dream, the passage evokes a solid and monolithic reality that is more real than real and whose grandiosity matches Ngeti's now very developed literary imagination:

> The pavements were so crowded that it was impossible to see a few meters ahead, but fortunately Emmah managed to catch a glimpse of a guide post, which read "VISIT THE MAGNIFICENT AQUARIUM." In less than ten minutes, a gigantic building stood erect before us, its glittering marble walls. . . . No sooner had we got in than a current of cool scented air invited us into this paradise. Everything in this aquarium had a good taste to the eye. I was feasting my surprised eyes on the marble walls when suddenly Emmah gave me a jerk on my arm; ahead of us a blood cuddling croc stared at us, its mouth agape, revealing its dagger-like teeth. On the other side the hippos bobbed their colossal bodies in the water. They looked peaceful from afar. After seeing the terrific crocs, we decided to go and see the fishes. The room in which they were was underground and was floodlit. They swam gaily in front

of us, showing some curiosity to our presence. We asked the aquarium guide a few questions concerning the aquatic animals they reared and he gave us books teaching the ways of life of the aquatic animals.

Ngeti used English to conjure up a miraculous world that he believed existed elsewhere, and perhaps to escape from his own reality (there are no such aquariums in Kenya). But as "magnificent" as this world was, it was also transparent and straightforward—the imaginary aquariums had guides that could answer questions about the aquatic animals, and Ngeti imagined he owned the relationships depicted in his school essays because he chose these imaginary girlfriends and bridegrooms. The world that English enables one to inhabit is fantastic, but it is also manifestly visible, at least in theory. As Ngeti once put it to me, "English allows you to get from point A to point B." It comes to fruition in concrete (or marble) forms, and it is only a mystery, and a potential bane, for those who do not know it, as it was back in the days of the missionary, Verby. In the chapter that follows, Ngeti discusses a spatially proximal world that is equally miraculous but in a way that frightens him. Here he begins to tell us about the witches who lived close to home, and who held on to grudges from the past.

So where does all of this leave us? Has Ngeti been empowered by the English language, or is it the instrument of his dispossession? Does it enable him to speak more effectively and directly with people from afar, or is it the very thing that makes it impossible for him to speak at all?[14] Ngeti's short email about Osama bin Laden and the 2004 presidential election, with which I began this chapter, offers some additional clues about what Ngeti is doing with language and how what Mikhail Bakhtin might have referred to as his "speech plan" is related to his overall strategy for being in the world.[15] The email's manifest message is, straightforwardly, a Kenyan's reflection on American politics and foreign policy. While the content may seem transgressive, there is nothing especially controversial or even atypical about it. Ngeti is suggesting that the American concern with "terrorism" is exaggerated and that political leaders have used this inflated anxiety to win elections. All of this is standard fare and reflects popular understandings of American culture and politics in many parts of Kenya and the rest of the world.

What is transgressive, I would argue, is the dialogic and multigeneric form in which Ngeti communicates this commonly held idea. First, the overall email is written in a casual, intimate style, expressing a convivial identification and equality with the addressee, me. He begins with the urban slang version of Swahili, an African language we both speak well and a lingua franca for an entire region. Then Ngeti launches into a playful, but clearly exasperated, discussion of the war on terrorism, which frames American foreign policy as a misdirected dialogue based on a misunderstanding. Osama has made an utterance, perhaps expecting to be understood, and the American public has responded by electing the wrong guy, or allowing the guy who was not elected to become the president illegitimately. Then Ngeti drops the interrogative (Can you explain this to me? Why is this happening? Why did Osama do this?), taking on the voice of a fraternally judgmental, but ultimately friendly and equal, interlocutor speaking to someone (here an entire nation) who could use a little well-intentioned advice: "Why the fuck do you guys keep doing such a stupid thing and then make yourselves look more stupid by trying to explain it?" But later he separates me from them, saying that I am not an American and that "this [action] is not mine."

Ngeti goes on to tell his friend, America, what its actions really mean. Americans may think they are acting bravely, but they are acting out of fear, and the fear is also misplaced, because there is nothing to be afraid of, and ultimately America is fearing the repercussions of its own powerful, bullish actions. Americans believe they know something, but they have been duped because of their own ignorance. In contrast, he and other non-Americans in the Global South are watching Americans and see them clearly, even when Americans cannot see *them*. They know about our foreign policy, and our elections, and even about relatively arcane electoral procedures. And they want us to know that they know that our politics are not to be emulated, and we have no business giving unsolicited advice. All of this is communicated in language style as much as it is in direct words; the shift to English and then back to Swahili alone communicates these concepts effectively: *I see you well. Yes, I'd love to let you see me too. Now watch as I disappear again into obscurity.*

All of the code and genre switching helps to articulate another meaning: mainly, *You and I are not limited by a specific set of national or territorial codes. We transcend these limitations because we are not afraid, and we are not afraid because we transcend these limitations and territorial boundaries. My language use, which mocks territorial borders, exemplifies this fluency.* As Ngeti once put it to me, "I like to mix it up, the high and the low, the motherfuckers and the corpus delectis!" Ngeti's language use collapses the barriers that separate the high from the low, the sublime from the scabrous, the terrestrial from the subterranean—as well as "us" from "him." He equalizes them all, us all, and he sets about creating a new world that is fecund with the marriage of the beautiful and the disgusting, from which to begin afresh.

But, in engaging Fanon and Ngugi, and in trying to draw attention to Ngeti's implicit strategy for life, I have ended up dwelling far too much on politics, partly because I do see all of this as having political implications. We should take Ngeti at his word when he says that he "loves English." This loves conquers all and knows no bounds. English is not just a means of communication for Ngeti; it is not principally a tool. Nor is it a sign for something else, like moral rectitude, social mobility, cosmopolitan "development," or whatever. Ngeti has always had wanderlust, and language is a window into another world, plain and simple. His imagination, and the freedom of his desire, takes Ngeti to places that he can't actually visit, and this is what he loves about English. His is not the deliberately imperious English of someone who admires a language from afar, as if it were a centerfold in a sought-after porn magazine. Ngeti's easy, nuanced familiarity with the language is exactly the kind of nonpompous usage you would expect from a long-term lover who has merged himself with the object of his affections.

Unfortunately, as Plato put it, love is also a serious mental illness. Ngeti associated English with traveling and transcending boundaries, but his high school life in the Catholic seminary was extremely restrictive. In fact, Ngeti was expelled from the seminary because he and a friend grew tired of the terrible food and the carbonara-eating priests, and one night snuck out to town to buy bread and cookies. The more disaffected Ngeti became with the regimentation at the school, not to mention the English usages he was being exposed to, the more earnestly he went about learning English on his own. He divorced his study of English from schooling so that he could sojourn as he saw fit. But his family responded to his failure in school by thinking there was something deeply wrong with Ngeti and that he had in fact gone mad. It was this that started his family on the road to therapy, seeking out diviners and healers who could help their only son, who supposedly "hated books" so much.

THREE

God Helps Those That Help Themselves

This story was as we would say in Latin mirabile dictu, it
was wonderful to tell. It probably reads like a blockbuster
movie script, or like the mad rumblings of a disjointed
personality. But I wanted to help the reader get sucked
into the maelstrom of the plot. You teach at a university,
an institution of higher learning whose sole purpose
is to seek knowledge. This story is also about human
knowledge and experience. I am trying to render asunder
the diaphanous veil that prevents us from exploring the
unknown. When the reader confronts this story a whole
new vista of possibilities emerges from the everyday.

NGETI *in a 2013 email to me, reflecting on
the emails he wrote me in 2002*

IN THIS CHAPTER I HAVE grouped together a series of emails that Ngeti
wrote to me in 2002, recounting his adolescent visits to *waghanga,* or what
Ngeti refers to, in English, as "witchdoctors" and "bush doctors."[1] In these
emails, Ngeti narrates the beginning of a personal odyssey that is at once a
physical journey and, as Ngeti puts it, a trip into the "twilight zone of the
unconscious" where "reason plays second fiddle to the intricacies of the subconscious mind." In his visits to witchdoctors, Ngeti was now finally traveling,
although not to the places he had hoped, read about in novels, or described in
his imaginative school essays. In trying to understand what was happening to
him, Ngeti found that his seemingly simple rural home was a complicated
vortex of multiple, layered dimensions that he had to move through and grap-
ple with if he wanted to have some degree of control over the outcome of his
actions. Throughout, Ngeti conveys his deeply personal concern with the
power and consequences of ritual, and his existential struggle to understand
the secret, coded meanings that permeate ritual performance.

Vipi, mzungu, mambo vipi? [What's up, white man, how are things?].
This is the man from the hills. The Man with a Mission. Many will not

like the mission, but the mission has to be accomplished. I hope you are doing fine, man. So we continue this story from where we left it. In this story, which is a true life experience, I'll try to recount with the sober mind of an active player, as well as an active observer, what I went through at the hands of the famous *waghanga*, or witchdoctors. I underwent these experiences when I was a mere boy who did not know the difference between his right elbow and his arse. As a boy I grew up in a very Catholic family, where we were taught to pray for everything from the food we ate to the *chofi*, or homemade sugarcane beer, that the grown-ups binged on. We went through all the motions of being the most Godly family, jostling for a closer position to God with the other families, by learning the rosary and the litany so thoroughly it was possible to recite them backwards.

At the same time, we received another kind of teaching from our parents, especially my mother, which was that we were supposed to avoid certain folks at all costs. We were to make sure that their kids didn't sit with us at school lest some of their wickedness rub off on us. They were not supposed to touch our books and pens lest we become unable to put two and two together and started forgetting the simplest English words. We were not supposed to receive any food articles from the bad grown-ups. By calling them bad the connotation was straightforward—these guys were believed, by those in the know, to be witches.

I recall incidents in which we would hear running outside our compound at night, and this would leave us all coiled up in bed like croissants in fear,[2] forgetting to invoke the name of the God that the family had learnt to worship by rote so fervently. I'm sure this must have left our supposedly vigilant guardian angels with egg streaming down their cherubic faces. I vividly recall one night when the family was sitting together in the kitchen waffling about this and that, ping-ponging from one topic to another. Suddenly we heard someone try to open the door to the sitting room. This sudden, audacious, and intrusive action by whoever it was momentarily suspended all lively animation and brutally froze everyone in the midst of what they were doing and saying. Then, suddenly, an avalanche of raw and furious adrenalin drenched and reanimated the vocal chords, the parched tongues, and the fossilized limbs of the adults, and a flurry of obscenities and imprecations was hurled at the callous intruder whom we all believed was a witch.

Cautiously, the adults, still under the influence of adrenalin mixed in fear and anger, inched their way slowly into the dark night outside to see which neighbor was paying us a rude visit, the flashlight that the family owned peeling away the covers of silky darkness, which harbored and concealed nefarious and abhorrent nocturnal creatures. The flashlight did not reveal the intruder, but the night was alive with the lullaby of the wind whistling thru the branches of the vegetation. But the following morning our worst fears were confirmed: There was a dead mole at the site on which the family was planning to put up a bigger house. It could have been some sicko playing pranks on us, but in this society you do not assume that people are out to just scare you or make you pee in your pants. In this society there is room for self-defense and alternative means of protection that God cannot readily afford; therefore, the best way to deal with fire is with fire.

This fragment of an essay communicates a great deal. First, Ngeti expresses his strong ambivalence regarding the reality of what he is about to narrate in his emails. On the one hand, his parents fed him stories about witchcraft, and so Ngeti suggests that a lot of his fears could be the product of social conditioning or discourse. And yet there *was* a dead mole, people *did* knock on the door, the night *was* thick with invisible enemies, and, as we will see from subsequent emails, a number of strange, coinciding events *did* happen to Ngeti's family and to their property. Ngeti's current uncertainty complicates him, and it also complicates the ontological status of witchcraft, as Ngeti himself remains unsure about what was real and what was not, and about which reality trumped the other, and at what point. As Ngeti later puts it, there is "no terra firma" with respect to witchcraft, no firm ontological ground, but rather a big doughy mass that offers its defiant dirty finger to any attempt to understand or control it.

Second, Ngeti suggests that to understand the story he is telling we need to know that he was born into a world that has a particular history, and that his self-actualization has meant coming to terms with that history in one way or another. The historic past played itself out in his own personal life, and he powerfully felt is weight on his shoulders, ever more so because he wanted to live in the future. His family was Catholic and was suspicious of other families whose relationship to Catholic Christianity was uncertain, or perhaps false. These families may have had access to secret, inherited knowledge that could be used to destroy him, and so, to be safe, Ngeti had to be wary of others and to make sure that his personal things, like pens and paper, remained firmly in his possession and not circulate far from his body. He had to work to bound himself off from others, to be a coherent individuated self, and the price of failure was high. He could be made to forget English, the currency of articulation with the world outside Taita and of connection to what Ngeti saw as a more real reality than the substandard or false reality in which he lived. But what exactly was the nature of the threat that concerned his parents? Did they only fear the neighbors who might be jealous of Ngeti's potential to progress, to jump over barriers to class mobility? Or was there something else, something even more powerful, that concerned Ngeti's family—something that they feared they might have disrespected or disavowed at great personal risk? What, in short, was the "fire" that could only be fought with fire?

When Chief Mwangeka led an army of Taita warriors against the forces of the British Imperial East Africa Company in the 1890s, he confronted them with magic in which was combined the power of the forests, the power of ancestors, and the power of inherited local knowledge. He successfully evaded and defeated these technologically superior forces, these vicious butterflies who wanted to force Taita men into the dangerous work of building the railway across the lion-infested Tsavo to Nairobi and beyond.[3] Mwangeka turned their bullets into water and made himself invisible. But he was eventually defeated, not by the power of European military technology, but by a jealous political rival who used magic to do him in. It was the passions of Mwangeka's now forgotten enemy that brought down the early Taita resistance to armed imperialism and that paved the way for an era of progressively declining regional autonomy in the face of state control. Today, Mwangeka's memory is recorded in the names of two powerful, seemingly incompatible things that symbolize conflicting modes of knowledge and authority: the hairy goatskin medicine bags that some old men carry over their backs, and one of the best high schools in the Taita Hills. What these seemingly irreconcilable forms of knowledge and power have in common is that these days they are both perceived as being in decline.

Many times the power of Taita landscape and history, instrumentalized in magic, was vindicated against the visible power of European colonialism. One particularly memorable incident was the violent defeat of the mad cannibal Mtula Ngeti (of no known relation to our Ngeti) in the 1950s. Mtula terrorized and stole from homes near Ngeti's village and was said to sell the flesh of his dead victims to butchers in the Taita Hills under the pretense that it was unusually salty beef. Wataita blamed the colonial administration for the rise of Mtula, because it was the colonial government that had put down Mwangeka and outlawed the warrior grades while implementing a new system of governance based on state-appointed chiefs. And the growing importance of schooling and wage labor in Mombasa had drawn youth away from the control of their seniors and into the hands of missionaries and government. Meanwhile, the collapse of the Taita army had allowed their historic enemies, the Maasai, to gain an unprecedented foothold in the area, and now it was encouraging the proliferation of gangsters like Mtula. Worst of all was the fact that the colonial administrative police proved incapable of finding and capturing Mtula, who used magic to evade them. Eventually, the police enlisted the help of a local healer and ritual specialist, who took Mtula's footprint from the ground and spoke to it, commanding Mtula to freeze in his tracks and to call out for his pursuers to find him. When Mtula began screaming his whereabouts to the police from the top of a giant hilltop rock, the police shot him down, and they dragged his body behind their truck by a rope all the way to Wundanyi, the seat of the colonial administration in Taita. But the police never would have been able to unleash this spectacle of state sovereignty on the body of Mtula without the cooperation and secret knowledge of Taita seniors and ancestors.

The decline of Taita's military power did not leave it totally unprotected, but it did mean that warfare became increasingly virtual. In particular, Taita people now depended on fighi forest shrines for their security. These forests, which once served mainly as barriers between potentially hostile villages, increasingly came to be seen as protecting an emerging and embattled Taita ethnic identity against foreign threats, particularly Maasai cattle raiders, but also "foreign" merchants and interlopers. Fighi (the word means stopper or cork) are indigenous forests that have been programmed by ritual specialists to protect a neighborhood and its "resources" from outside enemies while enforcing "traditional values" within the community. Fighi forests are sentient and seeing entities that were empowered by the ancestors to attack foreign enemies. The problem is that they were programmed so long ago, and today's elders have a tenuous grasp of the knowledge needed to maintain them. And so fighi often go berserk, mistaking ordinary Wataita for enemies because their spoken language, dress, and food differ so much from those of the ancestors who programmed them.

It's not that Taita people somehow forgot about the power of Taita locality and ancestors, as if through some collective amnesia. By the 1940s, many of the mission-educated Christians who were becoming the commercial and political leaders of Taita were waging an all out war against Taita tradition in an attempt to bring Taita reeling into a "modern," global community. These mostly educated young men were also resisting the power of their fathers and seniors, many of whom demanded that they hand over their hard-earned wages to them, just as youths had once handed over to seniors the cattle they had plundered from the Maasai. These young men named the first Taita political association the Taita Fighi Union, claiming that education would protect Taita from foreign threats in the same way that fighi once had. And in the early postcolonial period, the 1960s, Taita Christian state officials built a library on top of what used to be a fighi shrine, hoping to supplant what they saw as the pagan past with their vision of a future in which Western education would protect and develop Taita.

The most visible and dramatic Taita attack on the power of Taita tradition came through land reform, or "land consolidation," from the 1960s through the 1990s. Land consolidation was a joint attempt by Kenyan state authorities and educated Taita Christians to improve the productivity of Taita land in the face of massive land expropriation by settlers, sisal plantations, and the state's largest game park, Tsavo National Park. Land consolidation involved the privatization and grouping together of dispersed family land holdings into a single place, which would then be owned by an individual male house-hold head with legal title to that land.[4] The process of land consolidation, which took decades to complete and in some places was never finished, involved measuring all of the land units possessed by a household; the result-ing combined areal extent was then mapped onto another place, which could never match the diversity of the sum's parts. Villages that had once consisted of male-headed households organized in concentric circles were now frag-mented and dispersed. Square houses aligned in rows on square plots replaced the old circular houses, with junior households on the periphery and seniors at the center.

But land consolidation was not a success, by any standard. Taita agricul-tural strategy depended on people acquiring access to different kinds of land in diverse locations through the mobilization of networks of friends and dependents. There were just too many different kinds of soil and wind for planners to possibly give people what they had before. Moreover, Taita land ownership was complex. Like other East Africans, Taita people did not own homogenous land units as individuals in perpetuity; rather, people enjoyed overlapping and bundled claims to land and its products, and the status of these claims changed over time, as did all relationships.[5] Finally, the govern-ment's extension officers favored the relatively prosperous, providing them with high-quality land for growing commercial crops, while marginal fami-lies often found themselves on rocky cliffs without access to good soil.[6]

When people in Taita remember land consolidation, they go beyond this material description of the failures of a "high-modernist" development project.[7] They narrate a moral drama in which the powerful occult knowledge that had made possible the likes of Mwangeka and built the powerful fighi force fields was transformed into something socially destructive. People found themselves in strange neighborhoods or on privatized land; neighborhood councils of elders ceased to hold sway; and the formerly public fighi and *ngomenyi*, or ancestral skull caves, were confined to private parcels. And so these newly atomized individuals began to use their inherited occult knowledge to bewitch and destroy others, or to enrich themselves. To top it all off, there was no longer any ritual authority strong enough to prevent them from doing so. In other words, land privatization led to an analogous privatization of occult knowledge, turning inherited, generative memories and knowledge into fodder for deadly nocturnal warfare in an era of ever growing inequalities.

Sigmund Freud, in his essay "The Uncanny," suggests that the feeling of the uncanny—the unsettling, eerie supernatural—happens when one encounters the "repressed familiar."[8] For Freud, the uncanny consists in the discomfiting return of repressed memories, which grow more powerful for all the work that is put into repressing them. And in Taita, those steamrollered places and practices that never actually went away are indeed surrounded by the powerful aura of a repressed past that continues to stand as an alternative to what sometimes gets glossed as "modernity" by Westerners and Africans alike. A walk around the Taita Hills can be like a tour of this repressed imagined past, when Taita was dominated by a different kind of social and political order that people alternately romanticize and demonize. Over there is a fighi forest that once protected people, but which now has "gone mad." It is killing the ancestors' living children because it has not been cared for properly or because it mistakes the people it should protect for enemies. On that guy's shamba, or small farm, is an ngomenyi cave that once held the skulls of all the deceased male members of a lineage. It has been destroyed because kids from the mission schools have been throwing rocks at it for years, and now the ancestors are striking back with sickness and drought. This market was once a magical forest that made people invisible to unwanted tax collectors, but now the uphill shop owners use magic to shore up the water supply for their own profit, while everyone else goes without water. The examples multiply.

Ngeti's parents were among those who tried to forget the past and move into a future unencumbered, sometimes turning their backs on people they imagined to be "heathens" as they went about "developing" themselves through Christianity, schooling, formal employment, and occasional relocation to the city. Ngeti's family cut itself off from others, first when Ngeti's grandparents converted to Catholicism and moved to a Christian village near the church, and later when Charles built his square home on land he purchased from Ngeti's mother's father, Anthony Maghanga, in defiance of the norms of patrilocal residence. When the events that Ngeti narrates below took place, his family was not only relatively prosperous, but was also well known for its staunch Catholicism. They seemed to have succeeded in leaving behind the dirty past of Watasi, those who spit beer out of their mouths in the act of kutasa, or libation to ancestors. But the uncanny presence of these forsaken others kept returning, sometimes in the form of disgruntled family and neighbors who allegedly knocked on the door at night, then disappeared. Ngeti's family tried in vain to break away from the entangled past, and in the events narrated in this chapter circumstances compel them to leave behind their outward Christian rectitude and enter into a non-Christian realm that Ngeti represents as alien and otherworldly. To Ngeti, it seems to belong to another dimension.

Ngeti continues:

Well, these nocturnal events by the witches led the family to seek the help of a bush doctor from Mwanda [a village close to Mgange, which Mgange residents believe to be more "traditional"]. The bush doctor instructed the family to get a black sheep and a couple liters of *mbangara*, a local sugarcane beer that the Taitas credit themselves as being the original brewers of. The family was to take these things to the bush doctor so he could use them to immunize us against the powers of the night-runners [people who come to one's door at night, often in the nude, and knock on it or leave something behind]. Then he told the whole of us to go to the *mghanga* (witchdoctor) to get us immunized against the powers of the night-runners. I recall the bush doctor jamming a long stick coated with very black stuff down the throat of this ram and uttering some incantations and instructions to the choking and shocked sheep. The instructions were something like this:

You, ram, shall protect this man and his family from every kind of evil, from the night-runner to anyone who might be envious of him and his family, including his property. Even those close to him (next of kin) should they wish this man or his family harm, then let their lives be poured out (ended) like your blood, which is going to be the seal of this covenant. Let death be the recompense of their enemies.

And the poor thing was slaughtered and its blood mixed with herbs and sprinkled upon us a little. Its meat was also cooked in a hodgepodge of some herbs, and we ate portions of it and scattered some around our compound. Some of this medicine was placed at the gate of the compound (entry and exit). Practically everything was touched with this medicine, including the chickens, the sheep, and the cow that we had. After the "anointing" there followed the ordeal of getting lacerated with a razor blade to get more medicine into our bodies, and after it was over my body itched like hell.

After three days the bush doctor came to our place to perform more rituals. He had more herbs and more of the sheep's meat, which had remained from the previous meeting, and he scattered this around the whole compound again. Another ritual followed, and in this ritual the bush doctor stood by the door of the kitchen. There was a calabash full of more of this guy's concoction raised above his head against the lintel of the door, and he made us go in and out of the kitchen myriad times, all the while emptying the contents of the calabash (*chofi* [beer] mixed with herbs) on us. And you know what, this guy had put a container full of chofi in the house and another container outside. Every time that we went in we would sip a little chofi from the container, and go out and, once outside, we would sip from the container and utter some shit like "God help us, protect us," and stuff. That was, I think, the first time that I drank chofi with the old folks without their disapproving of it. While this was going on, the compound was packed with people, wondering what the fuck had come over us. Some people were rolling in the aisles, and some were downright disgusted.

After this, the night-running in the compound did not stop, as had been expected. We continued calling upon the name of God, who helped those that helped themselves. All the while, the old folks continued shopping for a better, more powerful bush doctor, preferably from a tribe that had the reputation of bringing up committed, no-nonsense bush doctors, like the Kambas, Digos, and the masters of them all, the Tanzanians.[9] Here are professed Catholics doing exactly what the Bible forbade them to do, that is, consulting mediums and witches, etc. This was inculcated into the adherents of the faith day and night, but those that came to witness weren't at all surprised, for their surprise was pure pretense, coz deep down they knew they did the same things that they were witnessing.

I recall the first time that we went to this bush doctor. We left at like three in the morning, for fear of being seen by the villagers. If these very acts were to be reenacted today, for whatever reasons, with the new-found faith of the family, this born-again thing [Pentecostalism], it would be ostracized straight away. The "filthy practice" would have to be repudiated and a prayer of penance said over the family. Yet when I think of it, I realize this is what it means to be "a little Catholic." During this time, my mother was actually a big lady in these prayer groups. These groups name themselves after some saints of yore, and she was in this group that called itself Saint Anna.

After these events, we continued being the "good Catholics" that we were expected to be. We went to church, and I served as an altar boy. I swung the thurible with such expertise that I felt I deserved to drink from the Eucharistic chalice, and we prayed the rosary so many times we probably deserved to be canonized while still alive! I went to the seminary, and this act was construed to mean that we were the most worthy Catholics in the area. We received the sacraments regularly. In short, we were the Catholics that my grandfather (mother's side) would have been proud of. Yet this did not stop the family from taking recourse to the bush doctors.

The story continues next time. We are getting to the interesting part of it, so keep your fingers crossed and your mind open to the craziness of the Taitas. Tell me mambo mapya [something new], bwana, you're so quiet. Take care buddy.

At first, Ngeti's parents allowed non-Christian ritual practitioners into their home, inviting much ridicule from their neighbors. These rituals, though meant to be traditional, invoked and reiterated Catholicism (the sacrifice of the lamb, the sealing of the covenant, the anointing of the believers), while also standing as an alternative to it. This is because Taita tradition, as powerful as it was, never existed as a stable or discrete ontological Other, but changed in conversation with other sources of power, including Catholicism. Nonetheless, all of this "heathen" activity must have seemed very strange and even comical to those who had long been led to believe that Ngeti's family had "developed" beyond visiting local healers and diviners. When this ritual failed, Ngeti's parents became more creative and peripatetic in their search, and they began to feel that the jealousy and resentment that were holding Ngeti back ran deeper than they had expected. As they searched for salvation, Ngeti witnessed people interacting with an invisible world that seemed more real than the world of appearances because it determined the visible world in which people were acting and effecting change. Let's follow Ngeti the prodigal son on the run from school as he bonds with his father in an "emergency room" on the frontline of the visible and the invisible.

Hello *mzungu, habari ya leo, bado* story *yetu inaendelea* [Hello, white man. How's the day? Still our story continues].

I will fast-forward to the time when I was around 14 or 15 years old. At this time I had gone to the seminary for two years and quit coz the idea of becoming a priest was not up my street. Actually, this is not the reason that I gave my old folks, but the seminary bailed me out of the hassle of telling them. The rector at the time wrote my parish priest and told him that I was not fit for the priesthood. I had done a couple of crazy things with a couple of my friends when we were there—things like sneaking out of the school compound and going to the market to get us some nice food, like bread, butter, and juice. The diet at the school sucked, and we spent the whole time drooling while the Italian priest and his buddies ate carbonara.

After this incident, I went to Nakuru [in central Kenya, between Nairobi and Kisumu, so far from home] to continue with my Form Three [roughly junior year of high school]. At the time, I had an uncle on my father's side who was staying in town. I was enrolled in this school *ya wahindi* [Indian school] and stayed there for one year before I felt like quitting, which I did and went back to Mombasa [on the coast, over a hundred miles from Taita]. The old folks suggested that I enroll at St. John's [a low-status Harambee (or "pull together") school that receives no funding from the government, located in their home village of Mgange], but deep down I resented the idea. They paid the school fees, but on the day that I was supposed to report to class, I went to the headmaster and demanded my money back. I took off with a friend of mine to Voi [a lowland railway and truckstop town in Taita district], where we drank and fucked bar maids until the money was finished.

I decided to go to Mombasa, and when I got there was greeted by a father who looked at me as if I had come back from the moon, because I was supposed to be at school in Mgange. For two or three days we said nothing to each other. After deciding that I was not gonna talk to him, he decided to break the ice by asking me how was school, and I told him school was fine. "How are the guys at home?" he asked. I said they were fine: in fact, they sent their greetings. I think this little performance on my part convinced the old man that there was something wrong with this son of his.

The next thing I know, the old man is telling me that God helps those that help themselves. He briefed me on how he and his brothers had decided to deal with my apparently abnormal behavior "spiritually," and by this he meant by consulting a bush doctor. He told me how he had visited the doc and he was told that my not feeling like going to school was due to some evil forces whose root cause was his stepmother. His stepmother, who was now living with his father, was on a nefarious mission to finish the offspring of the first wife (that is, my father's mother, who, we were told, was killed by this woman long before my old man was married).

This woman, Elizabeth Katuga, was married to my grandfather Boniface when he was in Tanzania, and during that time my father, Charles, and his brothers went to school in Tanzania. Boniface was a very wealthy man by then. Several years later he settled in a place called Bachuma, a small town on your way to Voi town. According to the bush doc, this stepmother, Elizabeth, had several filthy aces up her wicked sleeve. The bush doctor said the old woman was not gonna rest until she had done her job of wrecking the lives of those that belonged to the first wife, Eliza Samba, but the doc was gonna help these guys put an end to this woman's evil plans. I listened to this story from my father with a lot of rapt fascination.

The day came and the old man and I went to see this "messiah." She lived in a Swahili house in a place called "Chaani," in Mombasa. When we got there we found other Christians and Muslims who believe in the adage that God helps those that help themselves. It was like walking into an emergency room: guys with a multiplicity of facial expressions, crazy body postures, a guy drooling here and a woman sobbing there, another one in a xenoglossic exchange with an unseen being in a corner. There was a couple reassuring each other that, after they drank whatever "baby medicine" that the doc was gonna throw at them, they would fuck so hard until the baby that they had been looking for was conceived that night.

Man, it was crazy! It was like walking into a world that was permanently drifting in and out of a thick pea soup, no terra firma, just gently undulating dough under your feet. Imagine the dough to be grayish in color, a fucking large expanse of it, and if you looked real hard at it you would catch a glimpse of a winking eye and an obscene fat finger with a pouting red mouth at the end of it sticking up at you saying, "Fuck you, with knots on, A-hole!!" It was pure zombieland, where reason plays second fiddle to the intricacies of the unconscious.

Three separate but interconnecting realities are coming into focus in these essays. First is the visible world that Ngeti inhabits every day. Then there is the imaginary, but nonetheless real, world of English-speaking white ladies, skyscrapers, and pilots that Ngeti wants to access, and that shapes his hopes and behavior in the visible world, which seems somehow less real than his imaginative reality. And then there is the exceptionally real invisible world in which people's repressed emotions hold sway over everything else. This reality mocks, and ultimately has dominion over, visible reality. Coming to terms with the invisible reality was the only way Ngeti could hope to succeed in everyday visible reality and in the hoped-for reality of another world in which he had long traveled in his imagination. But he was soon to find that this invisible world wasn't just "out there," but inside of him. Who knows how long ago that world had set up shop in his bones and skull?

Hi Rafiki, this is the man from the hills. How's the going, bwana? Like I told you, the story picks up from where we left off the last time we communicated: where the conscious mind plays second fiddle to the convolutions of the subconscious mind.

Then our turn came to enter the bush doctor's *sanctum sanctorum*. The first thing that I encountered was the light that streamed in through the small window in the wall in front. This disoriented me, and before I knew what was going on, a croaky voice invited me to sit on a bench that was leaning against the wall. No sooner had I sat myself down uneasily than a whiff of sweet-smelling perfume brushed against my nostrils, which were trying very hard, but unsuccessfully, to make sense of the myriad of scents that was swirling around me, threatening to flood me in its crazy eddy. That scent was so real one could embrace it and probably make love to it, talk to it, and do all kinds of things that one could imagine. It was actually tangible, but its coming and going was so quick that the whole thing could have been the product of the imagination. This woman was sitting on a mat covered with a blue cloth, and to her right was an earthen pot, and leaning against a wall was a one-stringed musical instrument. The neck of the instrument was wood and its body was made out of a calabash.

The walls of the room were of mud festooned with countless bits of small stones. Several calendars, five to ten years old, were plastered on it, along with a framed picture of [President] Moi hanging askew next to a framed practicing license [to perform traditional healing] issued by the Ministry of Culture that looked like it could use a cleaning. Then the woman spoke: *"Kijana yangu usiogope, karibu hapa. Sasa, wacha tuzungumze na wazee tena tusikie watatuambia nini leo"* [My son, don't be afraid, come here. Now, let's talk to the old folks again so we can hear what they'll tell us today]. By "old folks" she meant her medium spirits [ancestors] that these people use to get arcane and esoteric messages from the world beyond, and which are revered by their keepers and those that have recourse to them like we were doing. Everything they say is believed to come from the seat of authority *ex cathedra*.

The woman reached for her petite musical instrument, and pluck, pluck, pluck went the strings, which oscillated like the heartbeat waves on a cardiograph. Yet this action managed to wring out a tune at once discordant and hypnotic from the poor thing. The woman swayed from side to side like a storm-tossed seafaring vessel, and the messages started trickling in from the underworld: *"Huyu kijana anarogwa na mama yako ya kambo"* [This youth is being bewitched by your mother on the other side]—meaning, my grandfather's second wife from Tanzania. She interspersed her messages with Kamba lyrics and more half-assed violin playing.[10] The messages from the netherland kept streaming up to our ears: *"Huyu mama amemtia huyu kijana vitu ndani ya mwili wake"* [This old woman has placed things inside of this boy's body]. That is why I did not feel like going to school. *"Ameweka vitu ndani ya kichwa chake pia"* [She's put things inside his head, too]. The woman continued with her ejaculations of abstruse revelations. Then the music and messages stopped, and what followed was a briefing from the lady on the plan of action as directed by the *wazees* [ancestors], which was to get these things out of my body and head, which was "hating books so much."

My mind reeled at the thought of undergoing an operation on my head and body at the hands of a Kamba woman who didn't know the first thing about writing her own fucking name, let along neurosurgery. As I was pondering this madness, the woman was instructing me to remove my clothes and join her on the floor. The mud walls seemed to move in on me, grimy hands reaching out to grab me and suck me into the walls, where I would become a permanent spectator to the goings-on of this loony bin. Reality became warped, time slowed down, a portal seemed to be opened into a world where everything was unnaturally married to everything else. A crazy moment of mysterious symbiosis ensued. That is, my standing up seemed to agree with my belly wanting to unbutton my shirt and my whole body wanting to literally cascade down to the floor and join the woman and sweep her with me into the walls, out of the house, and into the streets. My eyes saw the activities as one fluid movement, no pauses, no gaps, no fits and starts. I floated to the floor like a fucking feather and planted myself between the woman's legs, my back to her.

The woman reached into the earthen pot and drew something with a container and took this to her mouth, sipped, then spat on the floor. Then she reached for my head and took it in her hands and she brought her mouth on my head and the next thing that I knew I felt her teeth sink into my scalp, and she bit a fair chunk of my cranium and pulled her mouth away. Then she took a can and spat into it and something went plonk plonk, and whatever it was this thing was supposed to be coming out of my head. She repeated the procedure several times, and more things went plonk plonk. And after she was done eating my head she instructed me to lie on my back coz she had to get more of these things out of my heart and stomach. She sipped more water and bit into me, and she kept coming up with things. I just lay there praying that she was not going to come up with some live shit like a snake or a frog. I was fucking scared and yet at the same time filled with admiration for this woman who could reach into me and come out with stuff that I didn't even know existed.

After the oral op, she emptied the can on the floor, and there they were, the things that made me hate school: there was a dik-dik horn, several cowrie shells, manila strings with different numbers of knots. There were bones of snakes and some small animals. It was crazy, but it was all there for the world to see. After feasting our eyes on the stuff, she prescribed some herbal medicines, and some she cut into my body with a razor. I was to drink some and bathe with some, and I was not to approach a woman during the time of my cleansing. That is, no fucking, bwana. She told me that she had secured me against any witchcraft, that whoever tried to bewitch me would die. We swallowed the bull—head, horns, body, and tail. After this visit I had nightmares and I generally felt like a piece of fried shit. The story continues next time with a visit by Father with his brothers to their father and step-mother and the confrontation that followed between them.

Sasa leta mambo mapya mapya, bwana [Now tell me something new, man]. How is work? I hope you're having fun. Take care, buddy, till next time, God bless.

Ngeti had found that the resentments of a woman he didn't even know were very much alive (not literally so, fortunately) in his young body and that it was these reminders from other people's pasts that kept him from wanting to go to school. According to the stories that Ngeti and I had been told about his father's side of the family, his paternal grandfather Boniface had gone across the border to Tanzania during the 1950s to work as a game ranger. At the time, Boniface had been married to Eliza, the mother of Charles, Ngeti's father, but he met a Tanzanian woman, Elizabeth, whose family were poachers. Ngeti used to say that his grandfather got "sucked into the dark side" by his second wife's family, and became such an amazing game poacher that the Tanzanian government employed him as an informant. But, according to the rumor, Boniface's poacher compatriots found him out, so he came back to Kenya with Elizabeth after his first wife, Charles's mother, had died. Even while he was living in Tanzania, Boniface made frequent trips to Taita to be with his Taita family, fathering five children with Eliza, his Taita wife, and eleven with Elizabeth, his Tanzanian wife. Now the families were about to engage in a showdown.

The Confrontation with the Enemy

Our story continues from where we left last time and I believe this was at the visit with the bush doctor.

After this, my father, together with his brother Venant, decided to face their father, Boniface, and stepmother, Elizabeth, with the dark truth of what they had been told by the doctors. Venant was also having troubles of his own in his life. He had suffered several road accidents, one of which left him hospitalized for several months. Prior to this, he said he had been receiving visits from *kanzu*-clad Swahili guys.[11] He said they were responsible for the accidents that he had, because these guys would materialize on the road in front of him, and as he tried to avoid them they would disappear just as suddenly, but not before making sure that this guy had either ended up in a ditch or hit a tree or overturned. This prompted him to visit a doctor, who told him that what he saw on the road as people were nothing else but jinn spirits sent to him by his stepmother who he said was not happy with the way this guy was making progress in life. The doctor told him that the next time he saw anyone clad in white or the black robe that Swahili women wear *(buibui)*, he should just go ahead and run them over.

And believe it or not, one day Venant actually ran over someone dressed in white. He said that this jinni materialized not far from the "black spot" where they usually materialized. My uncle said he was ready to be accused of running someone over, that he didn't care.

One thing to be noted here is that these jinnis usually materialized in the uninhabited stretch between Taru and Voi, which is semiarid. On the material day, Venant had been driving from Voi to Mombasa. He was with a friend who happened to be descended from a family that reared jinnis. It was at night when, suddenly, they saw a guy in white crossing the road in the middle of this wilderness. They looked at each other and both shouted, *"Hili ni jinni!"* [That's a jinni!], and Venant stepped on the gas harder, and they hit this man with the full fury of the car and their anger. But there was no thudding sound, as would be expected when someone hit something. The guy turned the car around to inspect any damage but there was nothing, only the sound of crepitating insects.

Ngeti probably meant this brief interlude about jinnis, or jinn spirits (*majini* in Kidawida), on the road to be an amusing detour on the way to the real story, but it does reveal something interesting about what is going on in these events. The "herding" of jinn spirits is seen as being a different kind of witchcraft than the "traditional" witchcraft of Taita families. In many Muslim societies, jinn are ambivalent spirits that inhabit another dimension, and their social order is organized in a way that resembles human societies. These spirits can choose to interact with humans with good or evil intent, and often take on the role of tricksters in human affairs. Taita people are mostly Christian, and many have suspicious attitudes about Swahili Muslims that go back to the Arab slave trade and more recent experiences with Swahili neighbors, colleagues, and employers in Mombasa, the "go-to" city for Taita people seeking a job. Taita attitudes about jinn spirits reflect this suspicion and prejudice about coastal Swahili people.

Wataita people hold that Taita migrant laborers sometimes purchase jinn spirits from Swahili merchants when they go to Mombasa and other coastal towns. These spirits, which are seductive shape-shifters that appear as handsome men or beautiful women, promise their fictive "owners" gifts of cash and luxury goods in exchange for regular blood sacrifice. According to Taita people, jinn spirits crave blood, animal and human, and they interact with humans so they can satisfy this need. At first, a jinni may ask that its regular gifts of cash be compensated with an occasional chicken, but later, as the value of the gifts increase, the jinni will begin going after the cows and, finally, the children and loved ones of the family. The "blood," or substance, of these people will be consumed invisibly and not exactly literally: the jinni's "eating" of a victim may cause that person to become mentally disabled, for example. In the same way, the goods that the jinni bestows are not exactly "real"—jinn play with visible reality, perhaps transforming a boulder into what looks like a passenger minivan. When the blood sacrifices stop, the minivan will return to being a boulder. As a result, removing majini from a house, business, or town can be a risky business, leaving people with nothing, and even abruptly destroying local commerce—like an IMF "sharp shock" structural adjustment program.

In addition to providing gifts, these spirits can also be used to attack enemies on the road or in the marketplace, as well as to defend households. As Ngeti writes, they often appear in desolate, liminal zones of passage that are neither rural nor urban, but wild, and they can prevent people who are traveling from the countryside from getting what they want in the city, like money or a job. More typically, jinn spirits stand in for insufficient male migrant labor by "helping out" female-headed rural households, which take on incrementally accruing risk as part of the bargain. These spirits thereby encourage people to sacrifice enduring household resources. For these reasons, jinn spirits represent the dangers of the city and capitalism for Wataita: they come from the city, are purchased with money, and, like money, enable the conversion of one kind of thing into another kind of thing without regard for social consequences.[12] Fears about majini reflect the fact that Wataita are often seduced into selling off social resources for private wealth at the same time as they are lured, by the city and its temptations, into leaving their loved ones back home behind. None of this is meant to imply that majini are not also real.

For Ngeti and his parents, the idea that his grandfather's Tanzanian wife might be bewitching them with jinn spirits reflected the fact that she was foreign and that her family was involved in illegal commerce. It made sense to them that Elizabeth would have the contacts and connections as well as the moral lassitude required to engage in the buying and selling of malevolent spirits. This foreign, urban magic had been brought home to Taita, a place that had few traditional defenses against this threat. And so Ngeti's family and neighbors were about to opt for a surprisingly direct approach to combating witchcraft, egged on by Ngeti, the truth seeker.

Anyway, this day when my father and his brother decided to hit the roof was like any other day. Guys had gone to work and I was at home, coz I had dropped out of school and I can't tell whether this was having an effect on me or not. It was at around 9 o'clock in the evening and I was in my room doing something I can't remember and the adults were in another room watching TV. Suddenly a heavy feeling of melancholia descended on me and I stormed out of the room and went to the sitting room, where these guys were watching TV. Suddenly I started crying uncontrollably, asking why this woman, meaning my dad's stepmother, was bewitching us and why these guys were doing nothing about it, meaning facing this woman with the truth about her witchcraft. This caught the big guys with their pants down. When it comes to matters of witchcraft, no one in their right mind would face a witch with the truth of what they knew for fear of incurring the witch's wrath. They are satisfied with the "protection" that the bush doctors give them. They wait to see if the witch will die for tampering with them. The witch never dies, and the trips to the doctors never end.

After some calm had been restored in me, the guys decided to go face their parents with the dark secrets of what they had been told by the bush doctors. We got a few neighbors together, got into my uncle's company pick-up, and drove all the way to my grandfather's place in Bachuma. Before going there, my father had gotten this long machete with which to finish his parents. The guy had vowed he was going to kill somebody that night. When we were almost there, my uncle turned off the light of the car coz they wanted to take the neighborhood by surprise: no survivors. The car was parked right outside my granddad's house, and my father got out all mad, raging like a bull that had been shown a red rag. He went to the door and started pounding on it with his fists and the machete, all the while screaming stuff like, *"Leo tumekuja kuua wachawi hapa! Toke nje tuwaue ama tuwachome na moto. Wewe mama toka inje!"* [Today we've come to kill the witches here! Come outside so we can kill them or so we can burn them with fire. You, mother, come outside!]. The guy had gone practically nuts. Those who had known him as a mellow guy could not believe their eyes. I recall my grandfather responding from inside the house, *"Nini kinaendelea hapo inje mbona mnaleta fujo hapa kwani kuna nini Charles?"* [What's going on out there? Why are you bringing chaos here? Why, what's up, Charles?]. The neighbors were streaming into Granddad's compound; a couple of guys had to restrain Dad from using his machete in case Granddad happened to open the door.

We were told that the stepmother, Elizabeth, had given birth that day, and most of the neighbors that came thought that something had happened to the baby. After some calm had been restored, my grandfather Boniface opened the door, and he was confronted by a group of very angry guys from Mombasa who had the audacity to interrupt his sleep and even wake up the whole fucking neighborhood. The boys did not mince words with their father but went straight to the point. They told him that they had come to deal with their step-mother, who they said was bewitching the sons and grandchildren of his first wife, and that they had the evidence with them and that the evidence was me: I had dropped out of school for no apparent reason. When this was said, the neighbors turned their eyes to see the scholar who had started hating books, not that they cared really, but people like seeing for themselves the victims of witchcraft to see whether they've mutated. Elizabeth was there cuddling her kid to her breast wearing a face of pity, but the boys did not give a damn if she had given birth to eleven babies and was on the verge of dying. The boys narrated their story about how they had gone to an *mghanga* [witch-doctor] and what had prompted them to do it and what they had found out. There were "*aahhhs!*," "*eehs!*," "*hiyo kalis,*" "*aah maskini kwanini huyu mama anafanya hivi sasa?*" [There were "aahs," "eehs," "That's seriouses," "Ahh, unfortunate. Why is this mother doing this now?"]. Some of the neighbors did not trust the woman and were saying quietly that they had had their own share of the woman's evil and were hoping that someday someone was gonna deal with her like this.

After the short meeting, chaired by one of the residents of that place, it was decided that the only solution to the problem was the taking of an oath to get the truth about who was bewitching whom. I was surprised by the amount of knowledge that people had concerning these cases. The worldview in which this drama was taking place called for everyone to be versed in these matters, since having your finger on the pulse of witchcraft and counter-witchcraft is what makes the difference between life and death. The parents had denied that they had any evil designs upon their kids, but the kids, my father and his brothers, were not buying that.

A doctor was picked to administer this oath. The oath administrator they had chosen was the best in those days, but he's dead now. He was a Kamba, and he traveled all over the country like Maji Marefu hunting down witches.[13] There is this story that one day he went to Kambaland to get rid of some witches who had been stopping the rain from falling. When he got there these witches had turned their compounds into swampy forests to avoid detection. But the guy turned himself into a bush of reeds and just swam across this forest and when he was in the middle of it said, "Abracadabra!" and everything turned back to normal—the witch and his household were standing in front of this super-witchdoctor.

Anyway, a couple of guys from my granddad's neighborhood were asked to come with us to be witnesses to what was about to transpire. We went to this oath administrator and arrived there at around three in the morning. Unfortunately, the doctor was not there, so his wife attended to us. She was not surprised by our being there in the middle of the night. If anything, she was happy, coz that proved to her that they were the best of the best, and we were neither the first nor the last ones to call upon them at the hour of the witch. Dad explained why we were there, all the while the woman giving him and his stepmother dirty looks as Dad told his story of how he had gone to the bush doctor, and how he was told that his stepmother was behind the woes that they were experiencing in their family. Without saying a word, the woman got up and went to a pot that at first glance looked like a hunched-up old guy waiting to divine. She fetched something out of the pot with a ladle made out of a coconut shell, took three cups, and gave one to my father, one to Elizabeth, and one to Grandpa Boniface.

It's worth remembering that all of these confrontational rituals were undertaken because Ngeti didn't want to go to school, and they were intended to place his desires in line with this taken-for-granted mechanism for achieving success and becoming a "developed" person. It's easy to read these passages and get caught up in the story of witchcraft and possession, asking questions like, "Why do they believe that witchcraft is the cause of his disinterest in school?" or "Why does he think that it's possible for a frog to be placed in his body even if the perpetrator is nowhere near the scene?" The anthropology of witchcraft has often been dominated by this line of inquiry, with anthropologists seeing it as their job to demonstrate the "rationality" of witchcraft beliefs and practices to skeptical Western audiences committed to a secular worldview. It's at least equally productive, however, to ask another question that is rarely posed: specifically, why would people be so enchanted with the concept and practice of schooling that they worry not only that other people might try to keep them from getting it, but that they would go to amazing lengths to do so? And why go back "home" to resolve this problem? The answer, I think, is complex and ironic. Education is potentially very powerful, but alone it is not enough. For schooling to work on Ngeti in the way that it ought, Ngeti's family felt they needed to depend on marginalized people with little or no schooling at all, by all accounts "lesser" people who nonetheless had the power to see the invisible reality of other people's emotions and intentions. The ritual they were performing required them to acknowledge the limitations of schooling, as well as the necessity of respecting the power that was already there, in Taita, if one was to make any progress in life.

Ngeti continues:

She said she did not yet know who the real witch was, coz she had seen cases of people who had wrongly accused others of witchcraft, when in reality they were the ones who were bewitching those they had accused. This water that they were drinking was to prevent them from practicing any witchcraft while they waited for the oath to be administered. She informed us that her husband had traveled to Kambaland to deal with witches who were terrifying other people by causing thunder and lightning, which smote people and their cattle. She told us that she was going to hand us over to one of her husband's associates, who was an expert in administering oaths.

We waited until daybreak, at which point we were sent off to this guy who was to give the oath. At this guy's place the story was repeated again, to this Swahili guy dressed in a white kanzu and a white Swahili hat. He looked at our group and said, *"Ni nani mchawi hapa? Nyinyi nyote labda ni wachawi. Lakini tutajua kweli leo!"* [Who is the witch here? Maybe all of you are witches. But we will know the truth today!]. He looked at my father and said to him, *"Wewe ndio unaroga mama yako?"* [You, are you really bewitching your mother?]. Then he turned to the stepmother and asked her, *"Mama wewe ni mchawi, una roga watoto wa watu, hata hutaki wasome?"* [Mother, are you a witch? Are you bewitching people's children—you don't even want them to study?].

We were all gathered outside this guy's place, and a small crowd had gathered as well to witness the little drama that was about to unfold. The oath was going to be given to my father, representing his brothers, and the stepmother, who represented her family. Before the doc started his business, he informed the recipients that if any of them was "caught" by the oath, they would have to be cleansed from the inevitable death that would follow. Everyone was suddenly filled with fear, but the boys said they didn't care—they were prepared for anything.

The doctor told us that there were two kinds of oath on his menu on that day. The first oath was what I will call a "rice grain oath." In this oath, two grains of rice are used, and this is what happens: some shit is uttered over these grains, and thereafter these are given to the complainants. Now, if this grain sticks in the throat of any of them, then he/she is a witch. The grain actually starts to swell, choking the life out of the witch. The second type of oath was what I call a "red-hot machete oath." And this is the oath that the folks picked to decide this case.

The bush doctor set about his business by first lighting a fire, and he made the complainants sit with him around this fire. He took some herbs, chewed them, and spat on the palms of the recipients. He repeated the action like three times. He also gave them some herbs to chew themselves. When the fire was ready, this guy took a machete and stuck it into the fire. He kept talking in xenoglossia, took out the machete and stuck it in water, then returned it into the fire. We all watched in amazement as this guy continued chewing herbs and spitting into the fire. He turned his cold eyes on these guys that were sitting around the fire and croaked, *"Tutaanza na nani, wewe mama ama wewe mzee?"* [Who will we begin with—you, mother, or you, father?]. My old man was like, "Start with me!"

The doc took out the red-hot machete, grabbed my father's hand, and brought down the machete on his palm. He slid the machete up and down on his palm until the thing had cooled down. All of us were gawking at the spectacle, not believing our eyes at all. The guy stuck the machete back into the fire and looked at the woman, who was now trembling. Some of the people who had witnessed this before were like, *"Huyo mzee ni msafi, hana neno, wacha tungojee tuone kama huyo mama ataepuka hiyo panga"* [The old man is clean, he has no word/issue; let's wait and see if this mother will escape this machete].

The doctor took the machete out of the fire and stuck it into the water again, then returned it into the fire. He continued chanting, in Greek of all things, while we waited to see what would happen. The guy grabbed the red-hot *panga* again, grabbed the woman's hand, and brought it on the palm of her hand. No sooner had the machete touched her palm than she jumped up screaming with pain and horror. Her entire palm skin had come off with the machete and was smoking away on the blade. The doctor clung to her with all his might, forced her back into the seat, stood up, and lifted the machete above his head. "Do you still want more!?" he roared. All at once, the woman admitted she was a witch in front of the whole crowd. She was reminded again that she did not have long to live unless she was cleansed from the curse of the oath. She was cleansed, and I recall the whole operation cost around nine hundred shillings, which was a lot of money back then. Nothing much was said between the sons and the parents; there was this silence that engulfed everyone. They traveled back to their home the same day. You could see there was no love lost between them. There was not much communication between them for several years, until one day they decide to get together at Granddad's place and bury the hatchet of this day.

Ngeti was probably expecting to find something traditionally "Taita" when he left Mombasa to return to his grandfather's place with his father, but what he found was a diviner who spoke Greek! For these Taita Catholics, Greek was synonymous with esoteric Western ancestral power, which they were now channeling. The diviner was tapping into a foreign, original, and "indigenous" power, transcending the limits of locality to poach from different places and times, just as Ngeti does. Their "recombinative" practice reveals a broad-based strategy that characterizes much social, political, and economic life in postcolonial Africa.

Locating a stable ground from which to act and make statements is a major part of Kenyan social and political life. After all, as Achille Mbembe puts it, "the postcolony is chaotically pluralistic," a loud cacophony of competing times and places and powers, none of which have unchallenged hegemony over the other.[14] In Taita, we have so far identified at least three of these realities, and their tense coexistence sometimes makes it difficult to locate a clear foundation for speaking and acting in pursuit of particular goals. The search for a stable ground becomes even more challenging when taken-for-granted mechanisms for separating truth from falsehood, and for making one's way in life, come undone: when schools cease to operate in the way they should, when money no longer holds its value, and when state officials are no longer visible sources of patronage. At these moments of crisis, signs are unleashed from referents, and things no longer seem to mean what they're supposed to mean. People start talking about the "corruption" of things that they imagine to be stable in other places and times.

In contemporary Kenya, religious leaders, state officials, computer programmers, and World Bank representatives all claim to have special techniques for stabilizing reality and establishing truth. Depending on their backgrounds and orientations, they may try to create a foundation for transparent action by, for example, rooting believers' behavior in biblical texts or imagined ethnic traditions, reforming the constitution, digitally mapping the slums, or devaluing the currency and privatizing public utilities. But what made this particular episode so interesting was that persons who would have ordinarily been looked down upon, or even despised, held in their hands the future of these relatively educated cultural elites who had tried in vain to flee from Taita's past. What must Ngeti, who had spent so much of his time mastering English in the hopes of escape, thought of the awesome power of these forgotten nobodies who knew no English but had apparently mastered Greek?

Whatever happened on that day may have actually been effective, because Ngeti did return to school. But he had not seen the last of diviners, for this episode proved to the family that people were trying to bewitch their, and Ngeti's, development. As Ngeti reached the threshold of his release from school and into the world, it was time for him to be sent somewhere far away so he could be protected from those who would turn development backward with their witchcraft. Two years had passed since "the confrontation with the enemy," and Ngeti was itching to make it in the world.

Enter Another Kamba Woman

After this event I went back to school and did my O levels and was ready for the job market. My parents were not ready to take any chances with their only son. They had been bitten once and they were gonna be twice shy. It is a dog-eat-dog world, where God helps those that help themselves. This time round, the family, and here I'm referring to my dad and mother, sought the help of another Kamba woman. They had heard stories that this woman was an expert in "tying people" so that anyone who tried to bewitch them would die, no screwing around. They went there wanting to know the truth about those people that had evil designs on their lives. As usual, the woman had something to say. She said there was this woman neighbor at home (in Taita) who had taken to the habit of dancing in our compound at night and was planting witchcraft there. She suggested that the homestead had to be "stoppered" (or *figikwa*, from the word *fighi*—that is, to support and protect it with magical powers, most likely jinnis).[15] As the first born in the family, I was to be "tied" (*kufungwa*); this means that I would undergo some rituals that would make me immune to all forms of witchcraft used against me. Again, I was fed fairy tales about how those who try to bewitch those that have been "tied" are cursed by their own witchcraft. Again, the family swallowed this tale of invincibility.

At the behest of my parents I went to visit this woman and went through the motions of sitting on the floor listening to another tune-less song accompanied by the sound of another badly played one-string guitar, receiving abstruse messages from the nether world, licked this powder and washed with another and had some more cut into my body. I recall being told that there was someone who did not wish me well but they were not going to succeed. I remember my first assignment was to go to Taita and catch some of those witches that had turned our compound into a playing field for their nocturnal games. This woman cut some medicine into my eyebrows, and she said that in doing so she was lifting the veil that prevented us from seeing the invisible world. She told me that when I went to Taita I would be able to see the witches in their various metamorphosed states: i.e., as dogs, cats, lizards, etc. I was very excited.

I went to Taita confident that I was gonna catch them witches, beat the demons out of them, and probably fuck the fuckable ones before killing them. I remember sitting up late at night waiting for these buggers. I would smoke weed and sit there, door ajar so as not to make any noise when the time came for me to storm out and grab the guys. Four nights went by without any action, and I was almost giving up when, on the fifth night at around midnight, I heard what I took to be footsteps. I was stoned on *bhang* [pot], and I wanted to hear footsteps, as I was spoiling for a fight. I pricked up my ears like a cat, listened carefully to make sure I was not making a mistake, and tightened my grip on a club that was given to us by a great-grandfa-ther—we were told that it had come crashing on the heads of many of his foes. Without hesitating further, after establishing the direction from which the sound came, I stormed out like a jet and headed in the direction from which I thought the sound had come. This was toward the cow pen. I thought, "Now they are bewitching the milk in the cow!" I followed the beam of my flashlight, which I swung around furiously, all the while fighting hard to keep my tongue in my mouth, which had swollen exponentially.

I brought the beam of the flashlight smack on a dog that was as surprised to see me as I was to see it. Only I did not look at it as a dog at that moment. The thought that this poor dog could be a witch triggered a violent stream of imprecations, which I had spent some time rehearsing; stuff like, "Your witchcraft will not work on me! If you want me to die, then you will die yourself! I have seen you in your dog state and you can't scare me!" I was scared as shit, though. Fear and disbelief overwhelmed me; the *rungu*-club just hung by my side limply.

I just did not know what to do, just continued raving at the dog/witch, which/who finally yelped/cried at this sudden cacophony of incomprehensible tirades, tucked its/his/her tail between its/his/her legs, and off it/he/she went. It was when it/he/she was disappearing round the corner that I came to my senses, lifted the club above my head, and let go at the dog/witch. I only managed to graze its/his/her back. That woman had told me that I would be able to see all the witchcraft buried in the ground, but I did not see any.

I went back to Mombasa and narrated to the woman what had taken place, and she told me that what I had seen was not a dog but a witch. She said that they were not going to succeed, that I had disrupted their working plans and they were not going to dare step in our compound again. The next step was to get the men of the family, that is Dad and me, "tied" so that no witchcraft would work on us. This "tying" was going to be performed in Lunga-Lunga, a border town between Kenya and Tanzania.[16] This woman had a shamba there and stories abounded, still do, that those who are taken to be "tied" there are invincible: no witchcraft works on them. Most *waghanga* have plots in this town and most of them live there. Arrangements were made, and I left for the border town with this woman. This was in 1988.

Before we left, the woman had instructed me to buy some foodstuffs for the *wazee* [ancestral spirits] who were going to minister to me at Lunga-Lunga. I bought stuff like rice, green grams, onions, garlic, spices for pilau, and a full-grown chicken. I remember I was also told to buy a blue *kaniki,* or cloth, whose purpose was not fully clear; it was something to do with the wazee. We left Mombasa one afternoon, and before we left (it was only the two of us), this woman told me that the success of our trip depended on our not meeting any woman within a hundred meters of her house on our way to the bus. This woman gave me a small sisal work-basket, which she said I should not let go of. Whatever happened, I was to hang on to it. She even joked and said that even if the *matatu* [minibus] overturned, I was to make sure that nothing happened to the basket. She told me the wazee were in the basket and I should give some respect to them by carrying them on my lap.

We arrived at this border town late in the evening, so the woman told me that she was going to work on me early in the morning of the following day.

The following day, at around six in the morning, the woman summoned me into her sitting room and told me that the work of "tying" me against any future witchcraft was to begin. She ordered me to strip down to my shorts and told me to sit on the floor, which she had covered with a red kaniki. She blindfolded me and told me to relax. I could hear the woman placing her paraphernalia on the floor. Then she started playing a tuneless song that could easily confuse the metronome. She circled me as she chanted in a mixture of Kamba and xenoglossia. Then she started touching my body with unidentifiable objects that felt real cold and slimy against my skin. She knocked some metallic objects on the soles of feet, my ankles, hips, the base of my spine, right up to the top of my head, my hands, and my stomach. She sang some more tunes as she removed the blindfold. Whatever she had used to touch me was nowhere to be seen! She must have hidden it in the basket that stood on one side of the room. She pulled out a razor blade from the small basket that I'd carried the previous day and started making small cuts on the parts that she had touched with the metal objects, after which she rubbed some black stuff into them. I still have those marks from that day. She told me that no one was gonna succeed in bewitching me and that I was gonna be a very successful guy. Music to my ears! I spent the day feeling the medicine burn into my body.

The next day I underwent another ritual, whose purpose, according to the woman, was to "open my ways in life," that is stuff like money, family, etc. The ritual was carried out outside the house under a not-so-tall tree whose branches had spread out to form a beautiful canopy. Under this tree was a tiny hut about a foot in diameter; in this hut was a small earthen pot and other stuff that I could not identify. The hut was made out of sticks and had a thatched roof. Before the ritual began, I was told to strip down to my shorts. The woman took a twenty-shilling bill (Kenyatta bill) and placed it on the ground near the entrance of this midget hut and told me to sit on the money with my back to the hut. More xenoglossic chanting, followed by a good full-body rubdown with herbs. A bit of my hair was cut off and mixed with herbs and other stuff I didn't know, and two talismans were made for me—one for protection from the envy of fellow men and another for good luck. More razor-blade cuts and more medicine. After that, the woman gave me ten-cent coins and told me to put them in the pot that was in the hut; this was my thanksgiving offering to the wazee for the protection that they were going to give me and the wealth that would accompany that.

After the "tying" of my life and opening of its ways, I went back to Mombasa confident that I was invincible and that I was gonna be burying those that messed with me—again. A couple of days later the old man, my father, also went with this woman to the same town and had the same rituals performed, only he did not sit on the money like I did.[17] Instead he was given some wooden pegs that he was told to go plant in our compound in Taita. These pegs had holes in one end of them and in these holes was what looked like nettles and more black stuff. He was told that these would freeze all the witches that ventured into the compound. These pegs were to be planted at the entrances and exits of the compound, and the instructions were to be followed to the letter, no fucking around.

When I first read the above email, I laughed out loud at the thought of a stoned Ngeti crouching in the night, convinced that the neighbor's dog was no dog at all. I remember thinking of Nabokov's line about how only one letter separates the cosmic from the comic. But I also knew that a lot of important work was happening through these rituals. They taught Ngeti that reality was not what was visible and that certain rather fundamental things he had been taught in school were not true at all. "Nature," in the form of an animal bone, was not separate from "culture," or from the knowledge of a witch or ritual specialist, and one's body was not really separate from the world outside of it. And life was not separable from death, because the world of the living was largely determined by the world of the dead. Later on, all of these rituals would take on a new and very different significance, when Ngeti converted to Pentecostalism.

When Ngeti describes his otherworldly interaction with a Kamba diviner in which "everything seemed to be unnaturally married to everything else," it is almost as if he is channeling Victor Turner, the late doyen of ritual studies in anthropology. Following Arnold van Gennep, in the second half of the twentieth century Victor Turner extensively theorized the symbolic and experiential dimension of rites de passage that are somewhat like the ones Ngeti describes.[18] Turner, who worked with the Ndembu people in what is now Zambia, focused on liminal moments in ritual, spaces and times in which the structure of society was temporarily suspended, allowing people to reflect critically on their ordinary social roles and to perceive alternative ways of being and doing.[19] In liminal space-times, social structure is stripped down, just as Ngeti is stripped down before the Kamba diviner, and the social rules loosen their grip in a way that Turner described as being both dangerous and necessary for society. In rites of passage, liminality occurs in the middle of the performance, when initiates "stand at the threshold" of becoming new selves, with new statuses in society. In these often surreal events, mundane things such as trees become transcendentally powerful, and unrelated "significata" are recombined in ways that are jarringly poetic to the initiates. Everything explodes with significance, and the boundaries that separate seemingly discrete things and people in everyday life disappear, revealing hidden webs of interconnectivity.[20]

Unlike "traditional" anthropologists, Ngeti is not so interested in describing an abstract social structure, real or imaginary, to which ritual relates, or in understanding ritual as a mechanism for reproducing or resisting that imaginary social structure. Rather, he is focused on the personal emotional and experiential impacts of ritual, and in what these dramatic events allowed him to see for the first time. For Ngeti, these concealed interconnections, which transcend space and time to materialize in a body that, he learns, belongs more to others than to him, are frightening and hypnotizing. Discovering them also makes Ngeti angry and maybe even a little psychotic, as he sees people in dogs and dogs in people and fantasizes about committing acts of violence. These dramatic experiences do not "function" in some recognizable sociological way, but rather make Ngeti more convinced than he ever was of the absolute necessity of divorcing himself from the affects and machinations of those close to him. These things that were found in his body—the snake skeleton and the bones of small animals—and that were holding him back are opposed to all the high-minded dreams that Ngeti had when he envisioned himself as a pilot, or having sex with white women, or just going to the magnificent aquarium. These were the mostly cast-away parts of dead, lowly animals that Wataita don't even eat, all of which are beyond the social pale, such that their being inside Ngeti's body is consummately taboo. And they were revealed to him by a woman who "couldn't even write her own fucking name," on whom Ngeti is compelled to depend. But Ngeti takes heart in the fact that they are dead and not alive, and goes away feeling initiated into an invisible world in which he can see when people materialize their raw emotions as dangerous animals like wayward dogs, beyond social control.

These rituals, taken together, were designed to integrate Ngeti into a larger social system, although one that was more imaginary than "real," and at the same time more Real than actual everyday life. Like a liminal initiate in a rite of passage, Ngeti stood at the threshold of radical transformation, and his parents used ritual in their efforts to change Ngeti 's life for the better. But Ngeti and his family were not trying to reproduce a "traditional" Taita past, and the rituals he engaged in were not meant to integrate him into some imaginary traditional Taita society. Rather, his parents wanted to make him successful in a type of capitalist system that Wataita had lately come to accept as traditional. In this system, Taita males first acquired schooling (usually in mission schools), then went to the city (usually Mombasa) to find work, and ultimately sent wage remittances home to their families in the countryside (sometimes using jinn spirits to help them out when necessary).

For Ngeti's parents' generation, schooling was the accepted mechanism for achieving positive personal and social transformation—not just income and jobs, but cosmopolitan respectability and moral rectitude in general. But Ngeti interpreted actual schooling as something rather backward, enmired in colonial traditions that he saw as specifically local. Remember the colonial institution of the head boy that Ngeti discussed in an earlier email, for example, as well as the demeaning practices of the Irish nuns. Ngeti wanted authentic communication and connection with another world, and he saw that English language as a purer medium for this than schooling in general. This search for an unadulterated mechanism for communicating Truth prefigured his later interest in Pentecostalism, whose practitioners seek direct communication with the Divine. As Ngeti grew into adulthood, his desire to produce his own future shorn of the interference of kin grew ever stronger. At first he immersed himself in sensual stimulations like sex, drugs, and reggae. But eventually he returned to the world of rituals himself, looking for a communication technology that would grant him unadulterated access to the True and the Divine—to Reality. It was Ngeti's mother, engaged in her own search for autonomous truth and power in a male-dominated society, who turned Ngeti on to the possibility of salvation through her Pentecostal mentor, Patroba. In subsequent email communications, Ngeti discusses his experiences with Pentecostalism—but before he could continue, I wanted to ask him some questions of my own.

FOUR

Good Ants, Bad Milk, and Ugly Deeds

"NGETI, PLEASE, SLOW DOWN!"

I wrote him this in an email in 2003. Ngeti was caught up in his story about how he had been forever cursed by these rituals, but I felt there was more that needed to be accounted for, so I asked him to write additional background. Why had his parents assumed that his decision to drop out of the seminary was caused by other people's witchcraft? Why were they so quick to believe "witchdoctors" *(waghanga)* who told them that a dead co-wife was bewitching him? And could he write more background to these family conflicts? I was surprised that so far his stories had concerned only his father's side of the family (specifically his paternal grandfather's second wife), but there was almost nothing about his mother, who had of late loomed larger in his imagination. I could conjure up some informed explanations myself, but I didn't want to offer a summarizing perspective on Taita witchcraft beliefs— and even more to the point, I wanted to read what Ngeti had to say.

I was surprised when, instead of a reply, I received an email from Jane, the woman who would later become Ngeti's wife, informing me that Ngeti was now in jail. She was apologetically asking me to bail him out, explaining that although she knew Ngeti's imprisonment was not my responsibility, I was the only one who could help. As Jane explained how Ngeti had been charged and imprisoned for assaulting an mghanga in the port city of Mombasa, I recalled some of his recent emails to me, to which I had failed to respond. I remembered Ngeti describing this old Swahili fellow, for whose authenticity everyone in Ngeti's neighborhood had vouched. Ngeti had hired this mghanga to release a friend's wife from the grasp of a Nigerian witch who had used magic to capture the wife's affections and to keep her from loving her own husband. Ngeti had sent me an email describing the magic pigeon that the old sorcerer had launched to Nigeria to harass the culprit, explaining that "*hii pigeon ni ya kawaida lakini kuruka kwake ni* [this pigeon is ordinary but its flight is] magical. . . . Once he is released into space, time and space become irrelevant." Before Ngeti's very eyes, the old man had set loose the magic pigeon to fly at "light speed" all the way to Nigeria: "The guy just released the dove like they do at the Olympics and voila, it was gone, like stuff gets sucked into a black hole!"

But even after a month of magic pigeon attacks, the Nigerian was still at it and the "lost" wife had still not returned to her husband, Ngeti's friend. This didn't keep the mghanga from demanding more money from Ngeti—after all, this was a very tough case, and clearly this Nigerian was "too powerful." Now I was learning from Jane that Ngeti had grown angry and slapped the old man in the face when he had threatened to curse Ngeti for not adding more money to what had already been paid. That might have been the end of it, but unfortunately this mghanga had a relationship with the police and even performed some jobs for them, helping them to track down criminals and such. Jane's email described how the policemen showed up at their door and how Ngeti had languished for a week in jail waiting for his case to appear in court. At some point the judge had approached Ngeti in private and quoted how much money Ngeti would need to pay to make everything "disappear." The sum was several hundred dollars, which Ngeti didn't have. That's where I came in.

I ended up sending Jane the money via Western Union, and in a couple days I received this message from a freshly freed Ngeti:

Vipi rafiki,

I got the money buddy, on Tuesday. Thanks man. Was with the judge yesterday and we are done now, for good. I made sure he had destroyed my file. He put it in a paper shredder and burnt the results. I am a free man now, and this would not have been possible without your undying commitment. No need to get mushy now, we have been there before. This is another chapter in our lives. All I can say right now is one gargantuan motherfucking "Thank You," and I mean it. I felt like killing the son-of-a-bitch, though, for making so much money out of us while I remain penniless. You know what I could have done with that money, buddy? I could have started a shylocking business and maybe a porno thing on the side. Guys here love porn. Fucking shit. Otherwise I hope you are well my friend . . . . . . Will get back with the story in a day or so. Here are the essays I promised.

Take care, buddy,
Ngeti

Happy about being sprung from jail, Ngeti had delved quickly into writing, producing four essays intended to provide a deeper understanding of witchcraft both in Taita and in his personal life. When I opened and read Ngeti's first attachment at the bottom of his email to me, I found that, in answering my original question about witchcraft, Ngeti had written yet another essay about Taita "nature"—how it was changing, and how people were changed by these changes they had helped produce. This time, the focus was on ants and collective love. There was no overt reference to witchcraft, or *uchawi,* at all in this very ethnographic essay. Rather, Ngeti discussed how Taita's formerly verdant past once produced what Wataita refer to as their collectively "cool" disposition—the habit of generous reciprocity that once bound people across space and time, even after they were dead. When I wrote him back, asking why ants when I had asked him about witchcraft, Ngeti wrote that he wanted readers to "know that things had gone from worse to worst" in general. To understand witchcraft in Taita today, one had first to appreciate that "people's hearts had grown hot" and that everything had degraded—earth, air, water, and above all, soul. Witchcraft itself is not what needs to be explained, for it is only the natural outcome of a bad situation. What needs to be accounted for is how Wataita came to withdraw from each other in the first place—a question that invites a social explanation.

Ngeti's ethnographic vignettes suggest a narrative strategy for dealing with witchcraft, which takes the practice seriously (as being real) while also viewing it as metaphoric of larger social processes. As I mentioned earlier, anthropologists have long tended to think of witchcraft as an epistemological question with a sociological answer. Mainly, why do people believe in something that would seem not to exist? Following from this question, it then becomes the anthropologist's job to identify an alternative rationality in which witchcraft makes sociological and epistemological sense. E. Evans-Pritchard set the tone for this line of thinking in his 1937 work *Oracles, Witchcraft, and Magic among the Azande,* which is framed by the author's equivocation about the reality of witchcraft: at one point, E. P. baldly states that witchcraft cannot exist, but he also describes witnessing the substance of witchcraft flying around at night in the form of a bright light and the fact that, "curiously," the neighbor upon whose house the light came to rest fell ill the next day.[1]

For Evans-Pritchard, the notion that witchcraft was responsible for all misfortunes turned out to be rational because witchcraft explanations could be made to square with Western scientific explanations: a granary could fall on your head because of termites, and yet witches could still have caused it to fall at the exact moment you were sitting underneath it. Epistemologically, witchcraft went beyond scientific explanation, accounting for not only how but also why things happen in the way they do. Witchcraft, Evans-Pritchard famously argued, provides a social explanation for misfortune, as well as a method for dealing with social problems, through divination and the public revelation of buried resentments and conflicts.[2]

More recent analyses of witchcraft in Africa tend to continue the tradition of relating witchcraft ideas to social concerns, while expanding the definition of the social to include capitalism and globalization. And so we learn that Africans accuse those who prosper without work of practicing witchcraft because witchcraft rhetoric is a vernacular commentary on the abuse of power and the invisible sources of visible wealth.[3] In some versions of this argument, witchcraft ideas are, in a way, "rationally" adapted to contemporary conditions, making sense of things like state decline, structural adjustment programs, or casino capitalism in locally idiomatic, or vernacular, terms.[4]

Harry West and others have argued that this idea that witchcraft "beliefs" are mainly metaphors for other, more real, social concerns reduces African knowledges and practices to Western ways of knowing, and so acts to reaffirm and expand Western knowledge and power at the expense of other ways of knowing and being.[5] According to this argument, such radical social constructivism assumes that witches are not real and that what is *really real* is society and social concerns, which are symbolized, in one way or another, by the witch, who represents everything that is wrong with society.

But even if we accept the reality of African ideas about witchcraft and simply allow witches to be actual "forces" in the world, rather than metaphoric beliefs that reveal social truths, it is still the case that witches are *social* beings because they exist in society, and witchcraft beliefs and accusations do refer to social phenomena, including capitalism. Majini do give gifts of money in exchange for the blood of children and sacrificed animals, and it is hard to deny that money has something to do with wages and the market economy, while children and animals are seen as forms of value that are different from, and even morally opposed to, capitalist markets. Similarly, Wataita do admit that witchcraft has become a problem because of land privatization and inequality, and witches do tend to occupy specific positions within society. There are rich witches and poor witches; male witches and female witches; rural witches, urban witches, Muslim witches, and American witches—and the kinds of witchcraft these different kinds of people use reflect these social differences. That means that Taita ideas about of witchcraft are also moral commentaries and modes of cultural critique, in addition to being real experiences. We don't have to ignore the sociological dimensions of witchcraft, or the metaphoric work that witchcraft does, if we want to take other people seriously. And drawing attention to the ambivalent attitudes Africans have toward the reality of witchcraft is probably the truest way to render African experiences of witchcraft, a fact that Evans-Pritchard seems to have implicitly understood and incorporated into his own representations of witchcraft back in 1937.

Ngeti and I have discussed, and tend to accept, the general thrust of the social explanations for witchcraft, even as we leave open the possibility for witchcraft to actually exist. For the most part, the fascination and mystery that Ngeti's stories evoke emerge not from witchcraft itself, which is a fact of life, but from the act of uncovering other people's awesome, buried sentiments and bringing them out into the open. For instance, in the incident narrated above, Ngeti's friend was devastated by the fact that the object of his desire no longer loved him, and he could only make sense of this loss through an explanation involving someone else's supernatural intervention—*not* because he was incapable of reasoning in a different direction, but because his pain prevented him from accepting other possible explanations.[6]

In trying to resolve these emotions by identifying and then eliminating whatever or whoever was blocking the woman's affection for her husband, the friends end up engaging witchcraft sociologically. And out of their efforts, important social facts do emerge. They begin with the sociological fact that witch-finders compete against one another in cities, so it makes sense to look for more virulent forms of counter-magic there. In turn, the Nigerian must have had access to the most virulent forms of witchcraft, since he comes from a more urbanized, "developed" nation, where there is intense market competition. Moreover, it turns out that, in Kenya, witch-finders sometimes assist an inadequate state apparatus, helping police to look for criminals and solve crimes and providing extra revenue in the form of bribes from targets like Ngeti. All of this activity ultimately lures in a judge looking to make a little extra money, and so Ngeti makes a new "friend" who enables him to cut through bureaucracy and burn the past, suggesting that what outsiders call "corruption" is often the very source of justice. Ultimately, all of this sociology emerges from the friends' emotionally motivated efforts to put an end to heartbreak. The affects and moral outrage come first, and invite all of the social structures and circumstances that Ngeti and his friend have to navigate.

The following essays, "A Story about Ants," "Witnessing the Effects of Witchcraft for the First Time," "Family Troubles," and "Do Not Stone a Black Cat, or Anything Else," approach Ngeti's life history from a different angle, uncovering other moments when an invisible reality was revealed to him and shown to interpenetrate visible reality. Taken together, they narrate a shift in Ngeti's understanding of things, as he comes to realize that the Taita ideal of reciprocity was sabotaged by violent private jealousies and desires. With respect to Ngeti's autobiographical narrative, the essays comprise a larger story of lost personal innocence that Ngeti interprets as a loss of innocence for Taita as a whole. In the process, these narratives transport us from the countryside to the city, depicting Ngeti's passage from Taita to Mombasa as an enchanted coming of age.

Vignette #1: A Story about Ants

When I was seven years old or thereabout, I used to see a lot of safari ants around our home and on the many paths that crisscrossed my village. At times we would chance upon them moving in a single file, carrying their eggs and all the unlucky insects that had stupidly crossed their path. Sometimes we would take small sticks and tease them, and we would watch as they ferociously bit down on the sticks and scattered in every direction. At times we would dare each other to stick our fingers right in the middle of the ants and see who could endure the bites without flinching. What we enjoyed most about this game, though, was not seeing who would cry out in pain, but the number of ant heads that would remain clinging to our bloody fingers once we had pulled off the bodies of the biggest ants. The kid with the largest number of bodiless heads clinging to his finger would be the hero.

These insects usually move in a single file, but when they are invading a homestead, they do not adhere to this rule. Thousands of them will come into the compound from all directions with a single mission in their heads, and that is to invade the kitchen and every nook and cranny in the whole house. These ants will invade a home because of the cockroaches, which reside mostly in the kitchen, because of the granary inside this kitchen. The granary looks like a ceiling, but it is made of big logs, which can support the weight of corn and firewood. These granaries are built in the kitchen so that the heat coming from the kitchen fire can dry this corn and firewood. But the heat attracts a lot of cockroaches too, and after a while there is usually a large population of them in the house. Back then, people were not keen on using insecticides to get rid of the roaches, because they said that it would end up poisoning their maize.

Anyway, I remember one time, when I was young, these ants invaded our home. They attacked us in the evening, and since there were way too many roaches in the house, my mother decided to turn this into a blessing and let the ants get rid of the roaches. This meant that we would have to vacate the house and seek shelter somewhere else for at least two days. We quickly grabbed what we could. I remember we had some chickens and a cat. We put them in a box and went to my mother's sister, who was staying not far from us. We had to take the chickens because these ants have been known to kill chickens.

We explained to my aunty what had happened, and she said we were lucky because our house was going to be free of roaches for some time to come. She said she wished they could come to her house after they were done with our home. We stayed with my aunty for two days and went back to our home, which was now free of roaches. And a couple of months later I remember my aunty, together with her kids, coming to stay with us at our place after the ants had invaded her home. In other words, people used to take each other into their homes for days during these invasions. You could not refuse someone who had come to seek shelter at your place. This brought people together in what was considered a trying moment for the invaded family. When these ants attacked, one did not necessarily need to seek shelter at a relative's place—one could even go to a neighbor's home. All the "victims" had to do was carry some food and beddings, and the families would cook and eat together. They would also work in the gardens together and visit the invaded homes to see how the ants' house cleaning was doing.

But nowadays people don't do this kind of thing. Those that are able to get rid of the ants by chemical means do just that, and those that cannot afford the chemicals resort to traditional means of using marigold, stomping around the house, and sprinkling hot ashes on the ants. What is more, these days there aren't so many ants as there used to be. Even the population of roaches has dwindled due to a lack of food in Taita kitchens. People say that the love that was there in those days has waxed cold and that is why there is no rain, and this in turn has affected even the population of the ants, which love humid and wet soil.

A few days after sending me the story about ants, Ngeti sent me another, concerning his first memories of feeling attacked by family and neighbors. This essay, about a poisoned cow and contaminated mangoes, engages the dark underside of reciprocity. What starts as a normative ethnographic description of a cultural practice of gift-giving and debt becomes an anecdote about how actual life was not at all normative and the reality of these practices were not what they seemed. Gifts destroyed relationships rather than generating them. It becomes clear later on that, rightly or wrongly, Ngeti perceived this inversion of the meaning of things to be somehow new, related to growing conflicts over land.

Vignette #2: Witnessing the Effects of Witchcraft for the First Time

I must have been around about six years old when I witnessed the effects of witchcraft in our family. In those days, family members and very close friends engaged in the practice of giving each other domestic animals to rear. This practice helped people who could not afford to buy a cow, a goat, a sheep, or a chicken. This is what happened: let's say John has three cows and Peter has none. These two guys will enter into a deal in which John will give Peter a female cow to take care of. "Legally," this cow still belongs to John, but he has decided to temporarily give up his ownership to Peter with the express purpose of giving Peter the opportunity to own cows of his own in the future. Peter will take care of this cow until it gives birth. When this happens, Peter will sell the milk and spend the money or share the money with John; it all depends on what they had agreed upon when they entered into this deal. They will also share the calves born by the cow that Peter is taking care of. Usually the agreement stipulates that the first calf born to this cow should be given to John; Peter will get to keep the second calf, which will be legally his even if he decides to return the original cow to John. These two guys will continue sharing the calves until Peter decides to return the original cow to its owner. People exchange other animals too, like goats, sheep, even chickens. This practice is called *wuturi* or *kuturuiana*, and it is still alive among the Taita today.

Anyway, back in the 70s my parents were given a cow by my father's maternal uncle. I do not know what the agreement was, but I remember it was a scrawny black cow that looked like it could croak anytime. It had these tiny tits that looked like the tip of a ballpoint pen. I was excited when the cow was brought to our home. I had been watching other kids taking their cows out to graze and couldn't wait to join them, but it turned out that, when our cow grazed, it looked like it felt sorry for the grass that it was feeding on. Its eyes were always teary, and permanent streams of briny fluid ran down to its lips. I wondered why it was so thin and unhappy, and why it was not giving birth so that we could get milk. My parents were also concerned.

Then I heard my mother saying that she sometimes heard footsteps outside the compound and that they usually stopped where the cow used to sleep. She said that every time she heard the footsteps, she would immediately hear the cow pee, which meant that the cow was afraid of whatever was walking in the compound. Things got worse when one day she woke up in the morning and went to check on the cow. She could not believe what she saw: the cow was covered in splotches of blood. The ground nearby was also covered in blood. Mom believed that someone was bewitching the cow. Yes, someone some-where did not want the cow to give birth, and they did not want us to get milk. At this time my mother had not converted to Pentecostalism, but she was a staunch Catholic. I remember her telling us to recite the rosary like a million times in order to ward off whatever evil had been put in the cow. We prayed all right, but things went from worse to worst. One day she woke up and found that someone had actually cut off two of the cow's tits. This gave us goose bumps the size of cherries. I was fucking terrified. Who could do such a thing to a cow that was already dying anyway? My young mind could not comprehend this insanity.

A couple of weeks after the cow had been deprived of its tits, my mother developed a rash on her legs. It got worse by the day, and she was convinced that it had something to do with the blood she found on the cow and the cow itself. She went to the Catholic dispensary, which was run by the nuns at Bura. Most people used to go to this dispensary because they believed that the nuns recited rosaries over all the medicines that they dispensed there. She was given some ointment for her rash, and on top of that she was told not to forget to say the rosary and utter some prayer to some saint of yore for protec-tion and healing. We recited the rosary like crazy until she got well. This was a very scary experience for me. How could God let some people have power over the lives of the people that trusted in Him? Why could He not just wipe the motherfuckers off the surface of the earth and let them burn in hell until they could not burn anymore?

As my mother was nursing her "witchcraft" disease, she heard rumors from some women who lived in the same village as the uncle who had given us the cow. The rumors had it that the uncle had been seen at night at some guy's homestead disturbing the cows. This piece of information freaked out my mother; she did not know what to do. She could not think of a good reason to give the uncle for returning the cow. It was unthinkable and very, very dangerous to confront the uncle with accusations of witchcraft. She just could not take that option, which was no option at all. But she was convinced that this uncle was the one who had done this evil thing to his own cow, which he should have loved. She also believed that this cow gave this "witch" a reason to come to our home and carry out whatever diabolical schemes he had against his nephew's family.

The cow's health continued to deteriorate and all I can remember of its last days is seeing it tethered in the garden, with little to eat, and being left to sleep there. My father's younger brother, who was staying with us at the time, threw clods of earth at the half-dead animal for several afternoons after school, until one day the poor beast, unable to withstand the assault, gave up its ghost. It was buried at the very spot it had died and we planted a mango tree on its grave. One surprising thing about the whole episode is, several decades later, the mango tree has still not been able to produce any mangoes. It has somehow inherited the poor health of the cow it is growing on, and when it flowers, mildew strikes it and all the flowers fall to the ground.

After this my family was given another cow by my father's paternal aunty. This cow was a zebu. Its health was not bad and the family took care of it well. We took it for artificial insemination, and several months down the line it gave birth to a cute little thing. But again there was a problem: the cow had no milk in its udder at all. The udder just hung between its legs like an empty water skin, all shriveled up and useless. I remember we bought a feeding bottle for the calf and milk from a nearby dairy. This was just unbelievable and unheard of. People came to our home to see this freak of nature. Some laughed, while others were shocked just like we were. The aunty who had given us the cow could not believe it either. It was agreed that this must be the work of witchcraft, and the usual suspect was the uncle who had given us the first cow and had played havoc on it. My parents decided to return the cow to the owner, and they closed the door on cows and decided to try their hands rearing sheep and chickens.

In the following passage, a narration of two acts of violence, Ngeti describes the total breakdown of social relationships in his village and in his family: first he describes a fight between his mother and his mother's brother's wife, then the alleged murder of his cousin, by some accounts at the hands of one of his mother's brothers. This essay also concerns the jealousies that accompanied growing inequality, revealing how trust dissolved when people came to see each other as means to an end or as obstacles on the way to the acquisition of wealth. As Wataita struggled over ever smaller pieces of land, and as the well off used their connections with government officials to starve those they pretended to love, the practice of gift exchange was transformed into an act of aggression that could even culminate in murder. The background this essay offers on the conflicts among Ngeti's maternal kin will become important as his overarching narrative of self-discovery unfolds.

Vignette #3: Family Troubles

My mother had six siblings and for as long as I can remember there have been witchcraft accusations between them, and these accusations usually included the in-laws, or my father's family. Almost all of these people have gone to kingdom come now. One of my mother's male siblings was widely thought of as a witch, mostly because he had a retarded daughter, and some said the retardation of his daughter was a sacrifice to majini to strengthen his witchcraft. The youngest sibling, Jack, does not have a kid, and used to get married and divorced like a movie star. He blamed my mother, Monica, for this, that is divorcing his women, by saying that she used witchcraft to chase them away so she could take charge of his shamba, which he had inherited from his father (for he was the last born in the family).

There was a very serious incident in the early 80s, which involved the wife of my mother's brother Valentine, and Jack, the youngest born. Jack alleged that Valentine's wife, Veronica, wanted to poison him so that she and Valentine could inherit Jack's land, as he was the youngest and had inherited most of the land from their father. Their father had a big piece of land of about three acres, and Valentine bought a piece of his own land from their father, but they never got around to demarcating it officially. When their father died, he left the title deed for the property with Valentine. This did not sit well with Jack, but he did not do anything to get the deed from Valentine, for it would have meant going to the Ministry of Lands and getting a guy to come and demarcate the land. This would mean paying those government guys off with money, which Jack could not afford. And Valentine was better off than him and in a better position to defend himself. So

Jack lived his life saying Valentine wanted him dead so he could claim all of Jack's land for himself.

Anyway, one day Jack was taken ill and was bed-ridden, and Valentine's wife Veronica took some milk to this guy. Since he was always suspicious that Valentine and Veronica wanted him dead, Jack did not drink the milk, but rather poured it on some grass. Jack claims that the following day, as he was strolling around his compound, he noticed that the grass where he had poured the milk had completely dried up. The guy informed his sisters, Mary and Monica (my mother). They reasoned that Valentine's wife wanted to use Jack's illness to her advantage, for had the guy taken the milk and died then no one would have suspected Veronica, for the guy was sick and [they would say he'd] most likely had succumbed to this sickness. The trio—my mother, Mary, and Jack—confronted Veronica, and she vehemently denied ever poisoning Jack, "unless they wanted her to start wanting to." The sisters (my mother and Mary) were not satisfied with this, and they informed their brothers, Joseph, Mzungu, and Valentine, who was in Mombasa.

A meeting was called at Jack's place and the story has it that after some time of Jack and his sisters trying to get Veronica to admit that she had actually tried to poison Jack, my mother, Monica, who thought dialogue was not taking them anywhere near their goal, pounced on Veronica and beat the shit out of her. Later Mother was alleged to have said that she wanted to fuck up the woman's liver so she could die a slow and excruciatingly painful death. If that was true, then it meant that my mother was threatening to use witchcraft, which could mean that she was a witch. People said that she literally walked all over Valentine's wife, but I don't know for sure if this is true. Apparently the meeting ended with everyone wanting to rip out each other's body organs and throw them to the dogs, or cook them and eat them with their victims. Anyway, whatever love there once was between these siblings was deep-frozen by this incident and the outcome of this meeting.

There was another major controversy. One of my mother's brothers was called Mzungu, meaning white man. This was actually a nickname, and it's kind of funny how he got it. He was living in Mombasa and the story that we are told is that this guy's wife used to throw away any food that had stayed overnight, but the emphasis has always been put on chapattis because this food is more expensive than other foods. The family saw this wasteful habit as European, hence the nickname Mzungu.

Back in the 60s and early 70s Mzungu used to work with the Kenya police in the traffic department. He made extra money from drivers who had either raped the speed limit or overloaded their vehicles, and as a result he was doing okay by the standard of living in those days. But Mzungu lost his job with the police after publicly beating his mother and sister, and after that he worked with some hotel in Mombasa, but he lost that job too because he found out that the manager was stealing money. Anyway, the guy returned to Taita with his family in the late 1980s. In Taita this guy had no source of income and had several mouths to feed, so he resorted to going from house to house asking for small stuff like sugar, tea leaves, salt, and matchsticks. Other stuff he just stole from people's shambas, like maize, bananas, beans, vegetables, and sugarcane. This peripatetic begging and the stealing was done not by him, but by his children. The kids would be divided up to visit different houses for different stuff. One kid would go to house A and ask for sugar, another kid would go to house B and ask for tea leaves, another kid would go to house C and ask for milk, and so on. The family came to be nicknamed the *wenim-viringo*, or circles, because of their habit of going around to homesteads asking for small stuff.

A couple of years after Mzungu lost his job, his nephew Thomas was killed. Thomas was my mother's sister's son. Thomas was a secondary school teacher, and his body was found one morning half submerged in the water under some bridge close to where he taught. The postmortem revealed that the guy had not drowned, as those who killed him wanted it to appear, but had been killed somewhere else and his body later dumped in the stream. Some folks who lived a couple of kilometers from where the body was found claimed that, the previous night, they had heard someone pleading with people who were beating him up. They added that they heard the person say, "Uncle, why are you killing me, please do not kill me!" Further investigations by the family showed that, the previous day, Tom had been seen in the company of his maternal uncle, Mzungu, and some second cousins drinking at some bar in Wundanyi. These guys are known by society to be not so nice. Later on, some people would interpret this as a ritual killing committed by the family to improve its magic and get itself out of poverty. All I know is that Mzungu was a powerful, violent man, and his hanging out in the community indirectly begging for things made a lot of people nervous.

Around this time my mother was already a Pentecostal and she woke up one morning and went to her only sister, whose son had been violently murdered, and she told her that her dead son Thomas had appeared to her in a dream. Thomas had told my mother that he had been killed by his uncle Mzungu, her brother, who had beaten her sister some years back, together with her sister's daughter. Given my mother's influence in the family and her sister's desperation to figure out who had murdered her son Thomas, the sister believed that her dead son had actually been killed by her brother Mzungu. She confronted her brother with this news. She did this coz Taitas believe that the dead do not die but they are out there watching over them. When the brother asked where she had gotten such preposterous information, she said she had gotten it from my mother. Now, given my mother's history as a fearless woman, Mzungu did not dare to face my mother with this information, but rather chose to go around the village telling people that my mother had accused him of killing his nephew Thomas. But whoever heard this story thought that maybe Mzungu was capable of doing such a thing coz his life had taken a very drastic change for the worse.

So the killing of the nephew, Thomas, was not necessarily about Thomas but about Mzungu's sisters, one of whom was my mother. They each had given birth to now-adult male children who were expected to help their parents in their old age. The sister had a son who was remitting money back home, while Mzungu's male kids were not employed. There were times when Mzungu would go to his sister with the intention of borrowing sugar or salt and the sister would tell him that he should not depend on her since Mzungu had male children who were capable of working and taking care of him. This did not sit well with Mzungu, so he thought by killing the nephew he would be making sure that his sister did not benefit from the fruits of her womb. If Mzungu could kill his sister's son, Thomas, it also meant that, as far as my mother was concerned, he could kill me, and now would want to more than ever.

Mzungu and Monica transcended Taita social boundaries, as well as others likewise taken for granted. Mzungu was almost, but not quite, white, and some felt that Monica's actions made her manlike. Many saw them as capable of violence, and some thought they were witches. According to Ngeti, witchcraft may have been Mzungu's only way of acting on his situation. Monica, however, had other options. Seeking to escape the conflicts back home in order to protect her family, Monica sent Ngeti to live with his father in Mombasa, and for a time she joined him there. But when they arrived in the city, they found that its cosmopolitanism was no guarantee against witch-craft. Rather, the city offered new dangers and temptations, as well as new forms of witchcraft, ones explicitly associated with the lure of money and sex. Ngeti captures the mystique of Mombasa and the invisible dangers that threatened people, in what his family at first took to be a safe haven from Taita's witches. In moving us from the country to the city, this passage also shifts focus from Ngeti's childhood to his adolescence, setting the stage for future chapters.

Vignette #4: Do Not Stone a Cat, or Anything Else

We eventually left for Mombasa, hoping to leave witchcraft behind us. This house that my parents and I eventually moved to in Mombasa was owned by a Taita couple from Bura, which is a boulder's throw from my home area. It was believed back then that the Taita did not have the heart or courage to own jinnis because they were Christians. Also by nature they are said to be quiet and do not like bringing suffering to anyone in order to get rich quick. We heard numerous stories about these jinnis. According to the stories related to us by the grown-ups, these creatures were invisible as well as invincible. They could do things that were impossible, like walk into a closed room through the walls, make your hair stand on end, and leave through the roof. Or cause two or more cars to crash into each other, sucking all the blood from the accident victims before it hit the ground. There would be all of these disjointed body parts strewn all over the place but you would not see a single drop of blood.

These stories were both fascinating and terrifying. We were told how they could shape-shift into anything that they wanted, from the most beautiful to the most hideous creatures imaginable. We were told that there were female and male jinnis and they pullulated like flies. They could be bought and they could be sold. They were cheap to obtain but very expensive to maintain. There were people who specialized in keeping these jinnis and they were called *wafugaji wa majini* (herders of majini). Most of these breeders were bush doctors. The stories we heard were that most of the people who bought these jinnis were the Swahili folks who would keep several jinnis that would bring them money, but all this at the expense of one of the family members' sanity, good health, and general well-being.

One could buy a jinni for, say, a hundred shillings (a little over a dollar), but that person would have to sacrifice the life of the beloved of the family, usually the first-born child or one of the children who was loved so much by the parents. The jinnis knew who was loved in the family, so there was no way of pulling a fast one on them, or so we were told. The sacrifice required that whoever was given up as the sacrifice would end up being mentally retarded. We were told such a person would spend the rest of his life in a world of incoherence, full of babbling bullshit, eyes crazy and popping out of his sockets, and always drooling at the mouth—in short, totally loco. We were told that, whenever we saw a boy or a girl who was retarded and whose family had all the good things in life, that was a sign that they were in possession of jinnis that brought them money. By "good things" they meant stuff like a television, a car, a good attractive house with electricity and tap water and well dressed members of the family. We were told that these jinnis would sometimes walk around the neighborhood pilfering people's money and taking it back to their masters. They mostly stole from people who were not Muslims. Sometimes these jinnis would go to the bank and spirit away a lot of money for their owners. In return for this service, they sucked the blood of the unfortunate member of that family and deprived them of their mental faculties. When they were done siphoning the blood of their sacrifice then they sometimes killed them.

As we grew older we were told that these jinnis sometimes would stray from their homes at night in search of prurient fun and more blood. If you dreamed that you were balling a beautiful slender woman with long sleek black hair, then chances were it was a jinni. These jinnis would screw the females in the neighborhood, or if they had predilections for pederasty and homosexuality, they would hump the men and boys too. Apart from the jinnis that lived in people's houses, there were those that were said to be homeless. These were said to have the tendency of morphing into women clad in *buibui,* the traditional black robe worn by Muslim women at the coast. They also liked to take on feline features at night. We were warned against stoning and kicking cats during the day or at night. We were told not to talk to any strange beautiful women.

This warning was driven home with a story of a guy who had viciously kicked a black cat on his way home from a bar. This guy lived in a house that had single rooms for several tenants. When he got into his single room he pulled out a matchbox and struck a match to light a kerosene lamp that he had left at the usual place, and this was on a nail in the wall, but the match went out before he could light the lamp. Several matches went out, and the guy started cursing and was ready to give up on the lamp when he heard a voice bark, "Light that lamp quickly!" The guy was drunk and did not think much about the voice. He struck another match so he could see his bed, for he had decided he was not going to light the fucking lamp anyway. He heard the voice again and this time he felt a slap on his face. The guy screamed, dropped the box of matches, and groped in the darkness for the door, but he ran into a wall. He screamed some more with all his might and he heard the voice bark at him again, "I have told you to light that lamp. Stop screaming!!" The guy was shocked beyond words and continued groping for the door, all the while calling out to the neighbors to come to his rescue.

Then, suddenly, the room was filled with light and he almost had a fit when he saw his own shadow on the wall in front of him. He frantically turned around to see where the door was, but what he saw made him pee in his pants. He saw his dear lamp suspended in the middle of the room, gently swaying from side to side like a hammock in a gentle breeze. Then it glided toward another wall and hung itself on the nail he had hammered into that wall. By now he had emptied his bladder on himself and whatever alcohol he had had in his head was gone. Then the lamp glided across the room again and planted itself on the table, and he heard the voice say, "Sit down quickly!" He inched his way toward the table and pulled out a chair and glanced around the room furtively to see where the door was, but to his surprise the door had miraculously merged with the walls and it was nowhere to be seen. He was in a mud box with no doors or windows. Nothing happened for a couple minutes. It was deadly quiet. He wondered why the neighbors were not coming to save him from this hell he felt trapped in. He looked at the flame of the lamp and it looked like a serpentine tongue throbbing rhythmically like a cardiovascular organ. He swallowed hard, but his mouth was as dry as limestone. He silently prayed to God to get him out of this nightmare.

Then he saw a cat's paw and a human arm lying side by side on the table. The paw was the size of a human hand. The paw and the arm were cut off at their elbows, and there was no torso attached to them. The poor guy wished for death and felt the blood drain from his head. The paw started clawing at the table, leaving deep, ugly grooves in it, and the fingers of the hand started rapping on the table. The guy closed his eyes and opened his mouth to scream, but no sound came out. It was a typical silent scream. "There is no one who is going to help you today. It is only you and I," he heard the voice say to him. He slowly closed his mouth and stared at the two limbs. The paw continued clawing and the fingers continued to rap the table. Then, suddenly, the limbs were gone as fast as they had appeared. "Why did you kick me on your way home?" the voice enquired. "I did not kick you," the terrified guy whispered. As he said this, a black cat materialized on the table. They stared at each other like long-lost pals and the guy saw a vision of himself in the streets kicking a cat. The cat on the table turned into his leg dressed in trousers from the hip down. He saw his shoe on the leg, and the tip of it was covered in what looked like black fur covered in blood. He violently pushed back his chair and blindly ran into the wall, screaming his head off. He felt a kick on his ass, then another one, and another. He turned around and saw the leg swinging to and fro from the knee down, preparing to deliver another blow. Then he felt the kick in his balls and whatever beer and food was in his stomach came rushing out of his mouth like crude oil. Then he passed out. The guy was woken up the following morning by neighbors who found him sprawled on the floor just outside his room. He narrated his ordeal to his neighbors, who said they had heard nothing; if anything, they had had the most relaxing sleep in months. We were told the guy packed his stuff and went back to his rural home.

I heard stories of men who found themselves naked on baobab trees in the morning after a long scabrous night with some cutie. These escapades would start with a guy getting stopped by a woman who pretended to have lost her way to some place. The guy would offer to take her there, but on the way the lady would suddenly seem to realize that she was already at the place she was looking for. She would invite the guy inside for a drink and a chat. Once inside, one thing would lead to another. Guys who had such experiences would say how the woman lived in a posh house with all the things that a man could dream of. It was always stuff like TVs, big music systems, fridges, sofa sets, and self-contained houses (meaning, houses with toilets).

There was a way to guard oneself against these nefarious beings, we were told. One of the most effective ways to make sure that one's house was a no-go area for these jinnis was to eat pork once in a while. One could also anoint oneself with the oil rendered from boiling the pork. Another defense was a talisman made of any pig bone. This bone was hung with a string inside the room and it was believed it could ward off legions of jinnis. Another defense was marijuana, which was placed somewhere in the house. I remember seeing my parents hanging pig bones on the door and windows of the house that they had moved to. They said this kept out the jinnis from a neighbor's house that they believed had jinnis.

I would like to draw attention to what I take to be the main themes of these essays and their overarching narrative arc. As a child in Mgange, Ngeti witnessed people coming together to help one another and found this generative reciprocity mirrored in nature. Later he saw people fighting over nature-as-property and living things (ants, cows, grass, people) dying as a result. The severing of social relationships brought about a world of witchcraft, and the severed relationships were in turn brought about by new fears about witchcraft—all of which was underpinned by a new regime of private property embodied in registered title deeds and a realm of law that was all too easy for some people to manipulate.

Ngeti sees this personal shift in his own understanding of things to also represent a historical transformation in the way the world works: people used to selflessly come together in times of need, and "nature" reflected this good-heartedness; now, they do not. People have been violently disentangled from each other and from nature, and this has happened alongside a new favoring of property and individualism, as people have come to possess nature, and their own individualized selves, as property. There is irony in Ngeti's description of the past, especially in his essay on ants, because, although he describes a Paradise Lost, he has always wanted to break from the past and live in a world unencumbered by other people's sentiments, emotions, and histories, so to become a free and autonomous subject himself.

By the time we get to the city of Mombasa in the final vignette, we find a world of anonymous "hook-ups" in which people relate to each other solely as things. Ngeti again interweaves the lost innocence of his own adolescence with the lost innocence of Taita people, corrupted as they have been by wage labor migration to the city and the qualitatively different forms of witchcraft that are to be found there. In the city, we find a new kind of enchantment, in which unfettered desire has the capacity to transform the physical properties of things and turn the world completely upside down, as if one were to find oneself hanging from a baobab tree in the early morning hours. Forced to leave Taita as "modern" refugees, in Mombasa Taita people were at the mercy of capricious spirits who dangled false wealth in front of them and fed on their accumulated social histories, embodied in livestock and children. When they brought majini back to Taita, they married the dangerous consequences of infinite desire with the historical resentments and duplicity of rural life—a deadly combination indeed.

Witches and majini were the real, terrible reality underlying fake visible reality. Ngeti wanted to both see this reality and free himself from it. He wanted a future world in which people said what they thought and did what they said, and he wanted his own intentions to be realized as actions that also bore fruit. Doing this often seemed to mean freeing himself from the past's hold on him, but in his efforts to break from the past he was to enter a world where nothing meant what it seemed to mean and where every single moment held forth simultaneous promises of salvation and damnation. And so we follow Ngeti on his sojourn into the world of the Pentecostals, as he recalls his memories of a young adulthood in which he tried to grasp a transparent future that was forever just out of reach.

FIVE

The Power of Prayer

I was a new creation, and the old nature had passed away.

NGETI, *on becoming "saved"*
in Pentecostalism

A FEW YEARS AGO, NGETI and I were in central Kenya conducting field-work on Mungiki, a neotraditionalist Kikuyu religious movement and occasional transport mafia composed mostly of unemployed male youth, who often receive support from powerful politicians. There we met Grace, a very well educated Kikuyu religious leader in her fifties. Grace, who had long struggled with diabetes and kidney troubles, told us that she had cured these ailments herself by visiting a Chinese herbal clinic in Murang'a, where she bought "Magic Chinese Detoxipads." These are soft, herb-filled cotton pads that you place in your shoes, under your feet, to suck the toxins out of your body. The idea is that, as you walk around during the day, the herbs in the pads are doing their work and after a few days of this internal cleansing you'll be nearly impervious to disease, which results from the weakening of the body due to the progressive build-up of toxins. By the end of the day, the pads turn black with gunk. The fetid material that was hidden in your body is now revealed on the pad, which can be easily discarded and forgotten as you continue to do whatever it was that you were doing to make yourself so filthy in the first place. Grace urged me to buy the pads, if only for prevention of future disease, and being inclined to experiment, I decided to try them out.

Chinese herbal medicine clinics are sprouting up all over the region—part of a larger phenomenon of Chinese investment and involvement in the continent, as well as of African interest in Chinese things. Grace's enthusiastic endorsement of the pads also signaled her openness to Chinese culture, which she felt was circulating around Africa in and through these pads, which in turn represented China. But Ngeti felt skeptical about the Chinese, and also of the pads. He suspected that Chinese investment in African roads and infrastructure was superficial and self-interested. Like the Chinese-manufactured umbrellas that he often complains about ("This is a fake umbrella, bwana!"), he believes the roads will not last and that, anyway, they were built for the purpose of extracting minerals and other goods and resources from Africa. Similar to Grace, Ngeti often implies that objects embody the moral qualities of the people who made them. Or as Ngeti would put it, usually in reference to a particularly impressive piece of camping gear from REI, "People say that whites are bad guys, but how can you be bad when you have created this amazing thing?" And so, according to him, the virtues of the West are fused in, and emerge from, its material products, whereas the fact that Chinese goods quickly fall apart signifies that the sweet promises that accompany Chinese investment and development support will likewise collapse, revealing a reality of naked greed.

As a salesman in Mombasa in his twenties, Ngeti depended for his livelihood on cheap Chinese imports like umbrellas, backpacks, abdominal exercise devices, radios, and clocks, which he carried around with him in a ridiculous mass on foot. These often spurious and dilapidated things, unloaded at the port in huge quantities, forced him to learn how to spin stories with alacrity. Once, a customer to whom he had sold a cheap backpack confronted him on the street: after the stranger had washed the pack for the first time, the color had vanished and the pack had fallen apart. The man threatened to have Ngeti arrested, but Ngeti, thinking fast, convinced his former customer that the small preservation packets that had been inside the backpack, which everyone of course throws away, had contained a special solvent. Ngeti's assailant was supposed to have mixed the contents of the packet with the water in which the knapsack was washed so as to preserve the color and integrity of the fabric. But he had failed to do so, and so naturally the backpack had dissolved. Would he like to buy another backpack? Ngeti's charisma had won the day, and the customer turned accuser became customer once again, ultimately buying some more questionable things from Ngeti.

During the Magic Chinese Detoxipad episode, Ngeti and I were staying in cheap lodgings in the Kikuyu district of Murang'a, from which many anticolonial Mau Mau insurgents once hailed. One evening, after a long day of walking around and interviewing people about Mungiki, I peeled off the formerly white pads from my feet and showed them to Ngeti, in all of their ugliness: the cotton was black with goo. Ngeti, ironically ever the skeptic, immediately protested: "If there was really that much dirt in your body, you'd be dead, bwana! Why don't we open up one of those new pads?" So we cut open a clean pad with a knife, and out came a caked, greenish powder. "Hmm. . . Smells like soy sauce and ginger," Ngeti muttered, sniffing. Ngeti knows about soy sauce because I used to bring bottles of it up to the hills from the lowland Taita town of Voi to spice up the daily fare of boiled beans and maize. "Let me see what happens when I get it wet," he offered. Jumping to the sink, Ngeti turned on the faucet to moisten the powder, and before our eyes appeared the same sticky black gunk that had been on the bottom of my pad. Ngeti had made his point: it was the sweat from my foot that was turning the pad moist and the powder viscous, not "dirt" from inside my body.

In exposing the pad in this way, Ngeti felt he was also exposing the character of the Chinese: "These people want to take over the world with trickery!" he warned in Swahili, all the while shaking his head. The pads were a fake miracle, a dissimulation designed to cheat Africans of their money while potentially endangering their well-being. There were serious moral risks associated with living in a world where things and institutions did not do what they were intended to do, but often did something opposite—a world where signs were permanently and dangerously unleashed from referents. Tawdry products, like fake herbal medicines, ephemeral backpacks, and the "crazy" Kamba antiwitchcraft rituals described in the previous chapter, create dishonesty on a public scale, as people are forced to dissimulate to survive, just as Ngeti had while working as a salesman in Mombasa.[1]

Pentecostal practice is a technique that promises to usher in a world of unadulterated truth, in which God reveals the invisible reality underlying appearances to those who have freed themselves from satanic social entanglements and desires. As the fastest-growing religion in Africa, Pentecostalism is also one of the many "things" that circulates around Kenya and Africa, and Kenyans see it as a religion that is at once global and local. This is not because Pentecostalism originally came from somewhere else—so did Catholicism and Anglicanism, after all. Pentecostalism is perceived as global because it is widespread beyond Kenya's national boundaries, and it became popular during a period when Kenya was suddenly awash in powerful foreign things and institutions, like NGOs.[2] At the same time, it has become localized because churches break off and proliferate quickly in Kenya, operating independently without much intervention from "outside." Also, Pentecostal beliefs and practices have intertwined with historically enduring ones—including practices of mediumship, testimony, and ritualized cleansing—while also altering them. So Pentecostalism is a domesticated global "thing" through which Kenyans also act on globalization. Pentecostals are explicit about this, "using"

Pentecostalism to mitigate the dangers of globalization, from cheap imported clothing to technology to structural adjustment programs to foreign films—all of which are interpreted and cleansed through Pentecostal ritual.[3] Pentecostalism also allows people to reinterpret and make sense of the meanings of local, historically enduring practices and relationships, such as a "traditional" ritual, or a curse, or a family relationship gone bad.

In Kenya as elsewhere in Africa, Pentecostalism is quickly eclipsing historically entrenched Christian religions that came with colonialism. In Kenya and the Taita Hills, the Catholic and Anglican churches are recognized as "mainline churches": in Taita, these churches once effectively divided the hills into two mutually opposed cultural spheres whose denizens were discouraged from intermarrying, and who each viewed the other as different kinds of people. These divided regions also received differential support from government in the struggle for "development," the "Anglican side" tending to benefit from their ties to political leaders like Jomo Kenyatta, while the "Catholic side" was sidelined. In creating a new religious dispensation, Pentecostalism works to transcend these divisions and to transform the residues of the colonial past and its continued influence on contemporary Kenyan life. After all, the mainstream Christian churches are still widely seen as the backbone of Kenyan modernity, because mainline Christianity and education went hand in hand and the early generation of mission-educated children went on to become the postcolonial nation's business and political leaders. Politicians have long boasted of their "mainline" religious faith and have frequently made the point that they represent modernity and Christianity through their actions and policies. In the postcolonial period, this mainline Christian elite went on to create a political culture in which so called "big men" helped each other to "eat" resources from the state and the international community, while often demonstrating a callous disregard for the "backward" rural *wananchi* (citizens), enmired in witchcraft and savagery. The popular critique of this elite has long been couched in a religious idiom: "Guess what?! The sanctimonious Christian president is actually a devil worshiper in league with a global conspiracy of satanists that wants to literally eat the poor!"

In dissolving old hierarchies and entanglements, Pentecostalism creates direct communication between a saved individual (or a community of saved people) and the Divine. All of this "breaking with the past," as Birgit Meyer calls it, is beyond rhetoric: it is produced in powerful rituals that leave their mark on converts, and it is perpetuated in the daily, ritualized task of "testifying" about one's sins and the positive consequences of one's new communicative relationship with God.[4] It is in and through these rituals, followed up by immersion in the Bible and constant interactions with other saved people, that one is able to change the course of one's life—producing positive outcomes for oneself, which depend on God's sustained interest and involvement. One of the most powerful and commonly discussed of these rituals is that of "speaking in tongues," in which adherents speak God's language and are transformed, through communications that the converts don't actually remember or understand.[5] Ngeti describes his receipt of this gift from a Nigerian Pentecostal below.

Some scholars have recently pointed to the politically revolutionary aspects of Pentecostalism in Africa.[6] In the political theory that undergirds Pentecostalism in Kenya, the entire society can be changed forever through the individuals that constitute it—in other words, if every person's "desire nature" could only be changed, then society would also be forever transformed. The individuated subject that is produced through Pentecostal ritual is able to see things as they actually are because of his or her new, unmediated relationship to God: Is this a good person or a bad person? Is this cell phone of God or of Satan? Is this politician concerned with things of this world or things of God? In this way, Pentecostalism theoretically allows people to cut through the chaotic jumble of worldly appearances, just as Ngeti cut through my Chinese Magic Detoxipad, and to replace dissimulation and trickery with frank confession and testimony.[7] All individuals, male or female, young or old, are in a position to accomplish this personal transformation so long as they are "right with" God. Thus it is that Pentecostal ritual is largely concerned with the production of a bounded, protected self—an autonomous individual impervious to curses as well as temptations. Pentecostals "use" ritual to create a new community of interconnected subjects who share in the same soul and desire nature, who speak God's language (the gift of speaking in tongues), and whose desires are regulated, such that they can participate in society without being corrupted by it.

However, as Ruth Marshall has pointed out in her book on the "Pentecostal revolution" in Nigeria, this individual is not the same as the individual of Western political thought, and African Pentecostalism is not trying to produce a modernity that resembles an idealized Western modernity, based on secular reason. As she puts it, "This individualism is by no means that of the secular subject. . . . In the place of a politics of reasoned deliberation [Pentecostalism offers] a politics of affect, motivated by the desire or passion for God; in the place of an agency born from the exercise of human reason ... [it offers] the performative power of prayer and the agency of supernatural forces; in the place of a teleology of progress [it offers] the urgency of the messianic instant."[8]

Ngeti does not dwell on any of this in his own memories of early encounters with Pentecostalism. Instead he writes of the excitement of his newfound intimacy with a group of people with whom he now shared a common spirit and purpose, one that transcended kinship, ethnicity, history, and locality. Ngeti also focuses on the guilt that he felt for the lack of direction in his life, which he seemed to think was his fault. Pentecostalism made him feel loved and lovable again, and his new friendship with the preacher-prophet Patroba endowed him with a new family in the city. Moreover, Pentecostalism offered Ngeti an opportunity to disconnect from his past and rendered his break with the Catholic church, and his leaving the seminary, sensible as part of a larger life history that was singularly his. Suddenly, his repetitive lack of direction would give way to a life in which miracles could happen at any time. The redundant rhythm without meaning would be replaced by an experience of time in which every instant mattered and every experience was filled with meaning.

I begin this chapter with an email that Ngeti wrote me in March 2004, describing his adolescence in Mombasa and focusing on his visits to sex workers there. "The Five Shillings Herpes," Ngeti's title, is not about Pentecostalism at all, but the juxtaposition of imagery in this essay and later ones conveys a great deal about why Ngeti was attracted to this religion in the first place. Ngeti entered into these urban misadventures with a spirit of discovery, all the while hoping to establish a connection with another person. The women workers he encounters in these surrogate homes are mostly annoyed by his drawn-out intimacy and seem not to like his efforts at transparency, aided by matches and, later, a cheap flashlight. In these places, darkness and dissimulation were absolutely essential for business, and despite Ngeti's best efforts to create transparency through "inspection," things were never as they appeared: the woman who finally convinces him of her cleanness, and whom Ngeti makes his girlfriend, is the one who leaves him with a painful reminder that he carries to this day.

THE FIVE SHILLINGS HERPES

Hi buddy,
Hope all is well over there. Things are not so cool here; I have this outbreak of herpes that is giving me hell. Tell me, does herpes kill a guy and does it transmogrify into something life threatening later in

life? It's crazy how people get these venereal diseases. Let me tell you how I got this shit. This is gonna make part of our narrative, OK?

Back in the 80s, when I was still in secondary school, myself and a friend of mine whose family house we had rented experimented with prostitutes. They were cheap by today's standards, but back then they were damn expensive for teenage boys like us. One shot used to cost five shillings [about a U.S. quarter], and I would save my lunch money so I could get a fuck in the evening. Back then there was no fear of catching AIDS, and the other venereal diseases were curable by swallowing a couple tablets of ampicillin or tetracycline, which almost all sexually active teenagers had in their pockets, so we never bothered about using condoms. Condoms were scarce those days anyway, and I hated the idea of cumming into a fuckin' rubber.

Anyway, come evening, my friend and I would disappear for a couple of hours to visit the prostitutes. Most of the prostitutes were from neighboring Tanzania and Uganda, and we had heard stories that women from these countries were great fucks. They had rented houses around the neighborhood, and these houses had no electricity, so the fear of being seen by prying eyes was minimal or not there at all. We would appear out of the darkness in front of these women and inspect them by the light of a match that each one of us carried. We would strike the match and lean forward and inspect their faces and thighs, which were always seductively exposed so that one wanted to see the entire package. It was fun, inspecting these beautiful and not-so-beautiful women by the light of a match. But at first it was scary, so I would grab the first woman who happened to be close, not bother with her physical appearance, and proceed into a room that had one bed and a lantern light sitting in a corner, its tongue of flame flickering eerily, inviting me into this den of carnal debauchery.

Most of the rooms I got serviced in permanently smelled of fresh cum and kerosene smoke. The woman would throw herself on the bed, legs wide open and ready to fuck. There was no foreplay, no kissing, no nothing. I had read novels where a guy would drive a woman nuts with desire just by playing with her erogenous zones. But this was like jerking off inside a goddamn closet. The only difference was that this "closet" was always drippy with cum from the previous customers and it could talk back to me. After I was done with the woman, she would yank out a dank, moldy rag from under the mattress and wipe my tool. I cannot tell you the multiplicity of fungal infections I picked up from these rags. Some were smooth, and some were as rough as the boots of a hillbilly. I remember one time I started kissing one of these women, trying to impress her with my fucking skills, but she would have none of it. She pushed me away and told me that if I wanted to kiss and caress, then I had better find myself a girlfriend and do the shit I wanted to do to *her*. But as far as she was concerned, she was there for business and not love, so I better get my act together, get it over with, and let her screw the next guy in the line. I was pissed. I was paying a load of money here, and I deserved to feel some woman flesh in my teenage hands. Damn, what the hell was wrong with this woman?

This went on for some time, and I moved from using match light to inspect my prey to using a flashlight, which I had bought after not getting laid for a couple weeks. I hated the matches because they always went out before I had had a good look at the women, and sometimes the women would blow out the damn matches. After I had screwed like a hundred of these women, I decided to settle on one of them, and that was the one who gave me herpes. She was young, probably in her early twenties; she had the fairest, smoothest, most silky thighs I had ever seen. She was the only one who would remove her clothes for me, let me touch her, kiss her entire body, and actually have an orgasm while I spliced her in half. We got close to a point where she would let me fuck her on credit, and when I had an extra shilling I would let her have it. Strangely enough, I did not get clap from these escapades. The only thing I got was the five shillings herpes.

These trips to women did have their heart-stopping moments, though. I remember one day cops raiding this whorehouse while I was inside. I had picked up a woman as usual, and while I was doing my thing, the door flew open and in walked three cops. They had AK47s hanging from their shoulders. I froze on the woman and my dick went flaccid in an instant. Before I knew what was happening, one of them yanked me from off the woman and wondered out loud, "And you, young boy, what are you doing in here, you should be at home doing your homework!" He glared at me, all the while shaking his head in disbelief. I had not paid the five shillings yet, so I zipped up my shorts, stuck my shaking hand in my pockets, and fished out the money and extended it to the cop. To my utter disbelief, he took it and pushed me toward the door, and I fled without looking back. I could not believe my luck on that day. I stayed away from the brothel for two months, but I still went back anyway, to see my whore girlfriend.

So buddy, this is how I got my herpes. For less than a quarter, I got them herpes.

Later next time,
buddy.

Ngeti's writing links bodily illness with social corruption, depicting an urban society in total decay, and comes to a brief, dramatic head in his encounter with a policeman, who seems to be transformed into a surrogate prostitute himself. I have another interpretation of this exchange with the policeman, which is that, in accepting Ngeti's offer, the policeman was acknowledging Ngeti's manhood and agreeing to participate with him in an exchange relationship that was greater than, and in a sense more moral than, law. But this was an exchange that took place on the backs of, and because of the labor of, socially stigmatized and mostly foreign women. One thing is clear: from Ngeti's perspective, things definitely weren't what they seemed in Mombasa, just as the majini spirits that hailed from there concealed their true, demonic nature under false beauty and wealth. The look of innocence concealed unseemly truths, and those who would protect were not above corrupting the innocent, even if they sometimes found themselves shaking their heads in dismay.

Pentecostalism, Ngeti suggests in the essay that follows (written before "The Five Shillings Herpes," in December 2003), was like a new day dawning on this darkness, and it appealed to him as he grew increasingly bored and frustrated with his daily life. Later, the intimacy, openness, and manifest equality of Pentecostal ritual extirpated Ngeti's guilt and made him want to cry. It also introduced him to a newfound desire for God's love, as well as a whole new level of eroticism.

ENTER THE PENTECOSTALS

They were like a heavy cloud that threatened to darken the earth, yet promised rain. Their coming was like dawn in a land that had been in darkness for eons. Their voice opened prisons and dungeons, and their words loosed chains and shackles, and the fetters on the prisoners' feet were broken, and they came out singing and rejoicing. Then the sun rose over the horizon of ignorance, and its beams of wisdom, knowledge, and understanding illuminated the earth below. As the sun rose higher, those that had dwelt in the land of gloom began to see. They heard and understood that which had been hidden from before the beginning of the earth. But as the sun rose higher and higher, its heat scorched the seed and the tender shoots and they began to shrivel and droop. Some died and some were on the verge of dying.

, After the events at Lunga-Lunga, I went to live in Nakuru [in the Rift Valley] with my paternal uncle with the intention of getting a job so I could start fending for myself. I had tried getting a job in Mombasa but to no avail. I recall this time of my life as a period of searching for myself and carving out an identity all my own, moving away from what had been inculcated into me as a boy. Things like going to church were matters for those who did not appreciate the hallucinatory effects of bhang and qat. Church was for those who pretended not to appreciate the joys of screwing and all the other forbidden fruits. I had stopped going to church altogether coz deep down I had decided that no one who fucked like me and used highs like me was gonna tell me anything about the God above. I read the Bible only when I was high and listened to reggae music coz I considered its philosophical message about emancipation from mental slavery very appropriate during this particular time, when I wanted to free myself from the shackles of religion and tradition. Anything that did not go down well with me or crossed my path was outright Babylonian.

I managed to get a job as a booking clerk in Kisumu [a city on the shore of Lake Victoria, in Luoland]. It was when I was working in this town that I received a letter from Taita (from my mother) telling me that they, that is my mother and my three sisters, had found a new religion—that is, they had become "born-again" Christians. They told me how the Catholic Church was not ready to mingle with those that had been caught in this wave of Protestantism and that they had been ostracized. This took place after the parish priest had written my father (who was in Mombasa) a letter informing him that his wife and three daughters were at risk of being excommunicated on account of what the Catholic Church deemed an outright act of repudiation. Several other women were kicked out of the church for questioning, not vociferously of course, some of the Catholic activities, like the relevance of the rosary, the litany, the idols in the church, etc. Personally, I had no confidence in the church, so this news made no difference to me.

This change of faith in our family was largely influenced by a born-again man named Patroba, from a rural town called Werugha. The family came to know of him through a friend of my mother's, Mama Esther, who fed her stories about how this guy prayed for people and in the end they received their miracles. Mama Esther told Mom how this guy had prayed for her son and he finally got married. Earlier, this guy had failed to marry because of witchcraft in the neighborhood, and this is how the witchcraft worked: On the day of the wedding, the bride did not show up at the church. According to the man of God Patroba, witchcraft had been used to confuse the bride, to make her loathe the whole idea of getting married to this guy. Patroba was held to be a prophet, a man who was able to see into the future and the past simultaneously, delivering messages *ex cathedra* from God. This guy claimed to be a spiritual healer, too, and this was attested to by many who had no end of rhapsodies about the various diseases and afflictions that had vanished after they had been prayed for by this guy.

In our family, the lead singer of Patroba's wonder-working spiritual gift was my mother, who had by now been recruited into this guy's group of what I call "prayer warriors." These are born-again Christians who dedicate themselves to continuous prayers. She told us of his miraculous healing of her hypertension, migraines, and other afflictions. We had known her as a perpetual pill-popper for any ailment that chanced upon her, so this was a new thing. Of particular interest was Patroba's healing of my sister's case of epilepsy, and this had the effect of convincing Mother and my sisters that this guy was sent to help the family in its search for a God who was near. According to them, my sister had started suffering epileptic fits just like that. This was before Patroba walked into the religious picture of the family. Sister was taken to old man Mwarashu (the traditional Taita healer we went to, Jimmy, who gave you that soporific stuff back in '99 for your bowels) and was diagnosed with an affliction whose root cause was said to be demonic. No exorcism was performed, but a regimen of herbal medicines was prescribed and, on top of that, she was told not to eat any food that had been covered with a lid, or any kind of meat, or bananas upon which a bird had built its nest.

See, when Taitas are cooking, they usually cover the pots to keep the steam inside or, when they have eaten and some of the food remains, they cover it to keep the roaches off. Birds like making their nests in the space between the bunches of bananas, and Sister was not supposed to eat these bananas, because they are open to dangers from outside, through the birds who are actually witches. I was told there was a time she suffered a fit immediately after eating a banana on which a bird had built a nest. The demons did not go away, but there was relief as a result of following Doc Mwarashu's orders. This happened in the late 80s, early 90s.

Anyway, when this guy got into the family picture, I was told that he prayed for my sister and her epilepsy just left her. No bullshit with bananas. Her affliction was attributed to some ancestral sin on either the father's side or mother's side of the family. Other miracles happened in the family that had the effect of making Patroba take root.

More next time, buddy.

Ngeti

As is often the case, Pentecostalism entered Ngeti's household through the women in the family while the men were away. For a while, Ngeti's mother and sisters saw a protector in Patroba, whose direct and, in a way, "modern" relationship with God would enable him to become a kind of father figure at home while Ngeti and his father were in Mombasa. Ngeti's father, Charles, was the last holdout, and would never completely trust Patroba or approve of his involvement in the family, although he did allow Patroba to enter into the home and pray for him. Patroba claimed that this act of prayer was successful, because Charles acquired a better position at work soon after. But Charles never paid Patroba the tithe he had promised, and for years Patroba asserted that God was angry at his refusal to make good on his debts.

At first, Ngeti was not particularly interested in his mother's and sisters' conversion, but he was positively struck by his first visit, with his mother, to a Pentecostal church in Mombasa. In the essay below, "Response to an Outer Call," it is clear that Ngeti wanted to please his mother, and perhaps he worried that he no longer deserved his mother's love.

When I first came to know Ngeti in the late 1990s, he was already a committed Pentecostal, and everywhere we went other Taita Pentecostals would ask us if I was also saved. "Not yet" was always his ready reply. "I'm working on him, little by little," he would sometimes add. One Sunday I decided to walk with him up a hill to his church. I heard the singing and the divine language of speaking in tongues long before I saw the church, and so I was well braced for the loudness of the scene when I entered. Pentecostal churches overflow their material limits, constituting a loud, undulating movement of people, colors, and noise—a fusion of sounds and scents designed to create a new kind of experience and a new kind of person. Everything that takes place in the church is oriented toward putting people in contact with a divine power that has the capacity to obliterate the past and transform reality forever—in particular, people's subjective states and, through them, politics and society.

The ceremony lasted for hours, and everyone in the church was very aware, and approving, of my presence. Their smiling eyes and nods greeted me with an enthusiasm that I found more than a little annoying. What struck me most about the ceremony was that, although there was a preacher orchestrating what was happening, the "ordinary" people in the church were at the center of what was going on, and a spirit of vocal testimony had gripped almost everyone. One old man loudly confessed to poisoning his neighbors. A woman admitted to sleeping with married men. Another man declared that he had stolen maize from his neighbor's plot. I was impressed by the openness of the scene: *How can this guy who just confessed to murder go and walk around the village after this?*, I wondered to myself. In this atmosphere, everything was sayable and also no longer mattered, because all of these past acts belonged to people who no longer existed and who therefore could never be legitimately punished. The "saved" remembered their reckless former selves, exploding with desire, as if these were the inhabitants of a dream from which they had thankfully awoken. The preacher coupled this spirit of transparent testimony with his own revelations about the secret things that were happening in this community, which involved lurid descriptions of obscene acts. Among the many things he said in his angry voice that challenged Satan himself, the following is forever etched in my memory:

> There are those here who fornicate with other people's spouses!
> There are those here who fornicate with goats!
> There are those who fornicate with chickens!
> There are even those who fornicate with water!

For years I wondered how people fornicate with water. I was also very intrigued by how, rather than repressing sexuality, these people were enumerating nearly every possible sexual act, laying out the realm of human possibility for all to see, only to destroy it, at least in theory, and move on.

But I grew nervous when the preacher turned to me and bellowed, "We have a guest with us today! We welcome him to our home and ask him to introduce himself to us."

I silently cursed Ngeti for making me do this, but stood up warily and addressed the crowd, in Swahili: "Greetings. My name is Jimmy. Thank you for welcoming me here today. I am a student from America doing research on the lives of Taita people, on the issues that affect your lives. Along the way, I have heard that Taita has many saved people, and I did not know what this being saved was. So that is why I am here, to find out what being saved is all about. Thank you for allowing me to observe."

In Kenya, Americans are known to be the most notorious devil worshipers in the world, many having sold their moral selves for monetary wealth. The preacher, seeing an opportunity to win a very strategic soul for God, continued: "Have you been saved?"

"Ah, no, not yet," I said, growing alarmed.

"Will you come and be saved right now?"

"No, thank you, but I can't right now," I managed.

"Why not?" he continued, as silence gripped the long hall.

"I really don't know enough about it, and don't feel ready," I said, hoping for salvation that I never received.

"There is nothing you need to know. There is only the Lord, my friend."

"I will think about it, and then perhaps I will, but I cannot quickly come to such an important decision without putting a lot of thought into it."

"But there is no time like the present, and later, once you've left us, it will be even harder for you to make such a decision, seeing as you have never made it before."

And so on. The eyes of every single person in that church were now on me, but there was no way I was going to be saved. I suppose I didn't want to declare something that I didn't feel committed to, but there was more to it than that. These people were inviting me to open up to them and leave something of myself behind, to let go of my inhibitions and enter this effervescent community that could make miracles happen. I simply didn't want to join in, and wasn't interested in sharing myself with them. Unfortunately, by not letting my guard down before them to release the secret guilt that everyone knew I shared, I was rejecting their love and giving Satan a foothold in their community, thereby placing them all in a kind of jeopardy. As we left the church, everyone backed away from me, and some shot angry looks in my direction. "Now you did it," Ngeti gently chided me. "Now they know for certain you're a devil worshiper."

When Ngeti visited a Pentecostal church for the first time, he did not share my hesitation. Unlike me, Ngeti genuinely wanted to be cleansed and to become the upright, moral man that others wanted him to be. The noisy, high-tech communitarian enthusiasm that galvanized and changed Ngeti during his early visits to churches and crusades was viscerally exciting and even transgressive. Ngeti discerns sex in all of this excitement and imagines that he smells menstrual blood. Here, for the first time in these writings, he is more concerned about the devil than about nearby relatives, living or dead. He wrote this essay in January 2004, recounting his conversion in April 1995.

RESPONSE TO AN OUTER CALL

I cannot remember the last time I had been to church before this day. I had given up the whole idea of going to church for reasons that, to be sincere, I cannot begin to explain. But I think, subconsciously, the idea of worshiping someone or something that I had no direct perception of was not up my street. I was a young man then, barely in my twenties; I was beginning to enjoy life in the youthful sense of the word. I was taking notice of girls and appreciating the things that made them interesting. Pure animal instinct. There were little vices to be experimented with, things like alcohol, cigarettes, and even drugs, mainly Mary Jane. I was not ready to listen to anyone who was against these things, God or human. Yet life is one big road with lots of signs.

I was in Mombasa at this time, trying to make things work out for myself. I had been out for ten years since my final exam. I was bored, depressed, and seething inside with inscrutable rage at the way things were in my life—no job, no money. It simply sucked. My mother was already a converted Pentecostal, and she was into praying for people with Patroba, who preached to her and prayed over her myriad health problems, from migraine to high blood pressure. My three other siblings, the sisters, had also been converted, though their conversion was a result of the fact that they were staying with Mother. The old man was the type you can safely describe as having one foot in church and the other in the secular world. He had his weaknesses and he made no apologies for them. Anyway, on this particular day my mother had come to Mombasa from Taita, and she was miffed when she asked me whether I went to church and I said I did not. She went to a Pentecostal church, of course. Not wanting to be rude and put her off and make her think I was an asshole, I said it was okay for us to visit her church. And off we went. Boy, was she happy!

From half a mile away, I could hear the church choir singing their hearts out to God. Every now and then you could hear ululations of victory, interspersed with shouted "hallelujahs" and "glories" and thousands of "Thank you, Jesus!"es. As we moved closer to the church, the music got louder as it streamed out of the state-of-the-art public address system. The speakers spewed thousands of watts of music. The church was one motherfucking tent spread on hundreds of iron bars and wood beams. The whole area was filled with hundreds of wooden benches. I imagined the conflagration that could happen here were this place to go up in flames. Hellish thoughts.

The church was packed to the maximum; the fans above were doing a shoddy job of keeping the frenzied, probably sexually excited crowd below cool. The music blared from the thousand-plus-watts speakers. The hallelujahs rent the air, and this had the effect of making the congregation more hysterical. The lips of those who believed themselves prophets and prophetesses prophesied, and those that could speak in tongues gave full rein to this spiritual gift. The air was charged with the presence of the invisible God, moving upon the work of His hands setting them free. I stood there, drinking in the scenery like it was some forbidden brew. People sang themselves hoarse in the name of their Creator. You could see the veins sticking out of their necks and foreheads as they tried to bring the Most High to this sanctuary. Others were seated on the benches with their heads bowed, heavy with metallic issues they could not comprehend, as they offered their supplications to God. There were free-flowing tears and emotions. Some spoke in tongues and prophesied. The whole scene was chaotic yet very touching. There was a myriad of smells from this crowd. Sweat mixed with cheap perfume, bad breath, and the smell of dirty socks in well-polished shoes, all swirled around the church like jinnis streaming out of bottles. And I can swear I smelled menstrual blood from a lady standing in front of me.

I sang along with the congregants, making every effort to look like one of them, though deep down I knew I wasn't like them. I looked at them as those whose sins had been washed away by their God. Feelings of guilt washed over me like a wave of halitosis.

"Oh, hallelujah!! Oh, Jesus!!" the pastor roared. "This is the day of salvation and when you hear the Lord's voice do not harden your hearts, brethren, do not let yourselves perish in the rebellion of Korah!" I was like, "Who the fuck is Korah and what did he do?" But whatever he did, it sure was black enough to have found its way into the Bible. It was like standing on the shores of a sea and watching people board a ship that promised to deliver them safely to whatever port they were sailing to without taking into account the many dangers that could befall the vessel while still at sea. The captain kept beckoning, the songs raged on, emotions flowed freely. People were possessed by what they believed was the power of the Holy Ghost.

Coincidently, on this day the church was celebrating, or rather commemorating, the Last Supper, as this was Easter month. The pastor was like, "No one should approach the table of the Lord if he knows he is not right with his maker." To these people and their pastor, being "right" with God meant only one thing, and that is being saved. Before the Last Supper, the pastor preached something to this effect, how the Son of God went to the cross for the sins of the nations, and how He was making ready to come and reward those that had heeded His voice through his servants, and consign to eternal damnation those that had ignored His gracious voice. Visions of fiery hell with roasted guys screaming at the top of their voices asking to be given a second chance invaded my mind's eye. I imagined myself among these unfortunate beings, probably in a worse part of hell because I had been given a chance, not at some open-air evangelical crusade, but in the very house of this terrible God.

Intelligent voices reasoned with me. The devil tugged my left ear, filling it with stuff like, "Well, Ngeti, this ain't the time for this shit. There is that brown lady who should be screwed by you and no other. You do love blowjobs and giving head—or is it muff diving? There is this ganja that has to be smoked by you and your friends, man, there's nothing for you here now. Do not listen to this crap; this is a bunch of confused guys, get out and run for your life. The world still needs you, and I need you to go places with." The angel on the other ear pleaded just as fervently: "Hell was never meant for you. Only Lucifer and his rebels were meant to go there. Do not listen to him; there is nothing that he can give you. He was, he is, he will always be a liar. All these people can't possibly be crazy to believe in Jesus as their personal savior. Join them and be a part of the family. Heaven is real, just as hell is equally real."

I wrestled with these voices, the proverbial saying that the spirit is willing but the flesh is weak manifesting itself. The pastor finished preaching and, as is usual at such meetings, he asked if there was anyone who wanted to cross over to heaven and abandon Satan. Several hands shot up, some timidly, some with resolve. Cacophonous clapping by those who had already given their lives to the Lord followed. More tongues rent the air and suffused it with the "presence" of the Lord. "When one soul is won over into the Kingdom of the Most High, the whole heaven rejoices!" the pastor roared into the microphone. "Oh, I can see the devil and his army trembling before the King of Kings!" he continued.

I shot up from the seat and lumbered to the altar to join my new-found brethren, and together we let our tears stream from our eyes, and there were enough tears from among us to sink the fucking Titanic. Tears of guilt for what we had done against the Most High. I cannot tell what it is that brings those tears, but I think these are tears of anger, desperation, and a desire to belong, which the world does not readily offer but religion offers on a fucking silver platter.

"Lift up your hands to the Lord and repeat this prayer after me," the pastor instructed the flock gathered in front of him. We all lifted our hands toward heaven and waited to be led through the prayer of penance. This is the prayer said by the pastor, and which the neophytes repeat after him: "Lord Jesus, I'm a sinner and I come before you for forgiveness. I believe you are the Son of God and you died on the cross because of my sins. Wash away my sins with your precious blood and come into my heart. I leave the devil and all his lies and I promise to follow you and do your will. Guide me to the church where your holy spirit will teach me and lead me in your paths of life. Delete my name from the Book of Death and write it in the Lamb's Book of Life. I ask this in the name of Jesus Christ, our Lord and Savior."

More clapping and ululation and "Thank You, Lord"s followed. Then followed the commemoration of the Last Supper. We ate pieces of bread and some red soda, which was followed by more outpouring of spiritual emotions. And so began a long arduous journey, fraught with trials and tribulations, to the kingdom of God.

Ngeti is very clear about the fact that, at the time, he felt remorse for what he had failed to accomplish, especially given all of the money and work that his family had put into protecting their only son from witches. At this time, Ngeti was seen by many as a lost cause disappearing behind a thick blanket of marijuana smoke, in a region where smoking bhang is highly stigmatized. His conversion to Pentecostalism assuaged these feelings, but Ngeti's memories suggest that he also felt, or perhaps only now feels, that there was something sinister beneath the signs of moral rectitude and salvation from desire that Pentecostalism offered on a "fucking silver platter." The well-polished shoes concealed sweaty socks, and the sickeningly sweet smell of jinnis filled the air. At the same time, the moment he entered the church and felt the vibrant community as a sensual, aromatic, and sexual presence around him, Ngeti's imagination also conjured up Satan as a threat. Ngeti envisions Satan trying to burn the parishioners in a conflagration, imagines himself having a conversation with Satan, and later theorizes that his conversion has made Satan angry. Suddenly, after being lost for years, Ngeti had become important, if only for Satan. These crusade rituals made the devil palpably present, and for Ngeti, this was a change. Unlike the witch, the devil was not a family member or neighbor, but a universal figure who was everywhere on the globe—an enemy that Kenyans and Americans have in common and that links them in a global ecumene. But the devil works through family and kin and so barrels through global and local constellations of power and belonging, corrupting them all.

Probably even more important than these public rituals was Ngeti's mother's new friend, Patroba, who would now become Ngeti's closest companion and, later, the person who would convince him of the satanic essence of the non-Christian ritual cleansings in which he had participated at his parents' behest. Patroba's prophetic work, which Ngeti says resembled that of a traditional healer with Christian paraphernalia, placed Ngeti at the center of a cosmic battle in which God was personally vested. Suddenly, as the following email essays (written in December 2003) describe, key figures in Ngeti's life were transformed into characters in an unfolding moral drama in which Ngeti's very survival was at stake.

MEETING WITH PATROBA

My first meeting with Patroba was in 1992, several months after returning to Mombasa from Kisumu after losing my job. This was after gulping stories about the miracles that this guy, who had been born into the poorest of families and was said to have been ostracized as a child by his own father, performed in the name of God. I went there with Mother, who was now spending a lot of time with this guy praying for people. I had lost my job, was penniless, and was looking for a miracle. At this time of my life I wouldn't say I was such a staunch Christian. Four years had elapsed since I was last inside a church, and I was full of questions about the Catholic doctrines. It was more out of curiosity than religious piety that I went to see this guy who was said to be performing signs and wonders. I went there expecting to see a man with a white beard in a camel skin that clung to a lean body acquainted with long days of fasting, maybe a water skin hanging carelessly on his left shoulder. But I met a medium-built black guy sans beard, but with a ready word exalting the goodness of the Most High, holding a Bible in his hand as if it were the Mosaic tablets of stone from Mount Sinai.

We went through the motions of introduction—like, "This is the man of God, and the Lord is using him mightily"; "This is my son whom I told you about, the Lord has brought him back home like He said He would." These guys informed me that my staying in Kisumu and Nakuru was influenced by the devil, who wanted me to waste myself out there and never think of going back to Taita. They had prayed fervently to God so that He could bring me back and be close to home, and there were still some people out there with diabolical schemes against my life, but God was going to fight for me. This was all music to my ears. I thought, well, things are gonna be fine, let's wait and see.

Patroba opened his Bible and read a psalm about the goodness of the Lord in my life and told me to lay my hands on the pages that he had read, palms down. He told me that I was actually laying hold of the feet of Jesus, and he thanked God for bringing me back to Mombasa, and he said other things in xenoglossia (tongues), opened this good and bound that evil out of my life, cast out this demon and rebuked the other, undid shackles and chains in several spheres of my life. And there followed plenty of "Thank you Lord"s for the whole world.

After this encounter, I continued to smoke various smokable things, but followed by countless sessions of prayers with this man of God. There was no end to the litany of good things that were going to happen in my life, uttered in the languages of men and of angels. I kept looking for a job, did odd jobs here and there, and life went on always looking forward to fulfillment of the promises of God. This guy kept coming to our place in Taita with more promises of good from God. Patroba would pick up mother, together with her friend, Mama Esther, who had introduced her to this guy, and they would take off to Mombasa or Taveta for prayers, coz according to the man of God these prayers were more effective than those that were said in the house. Every time that mother came home from these trips there were some messages from God—stuff like "The Lord told us in Taveta that there was somebody planning to harm us with witchcraft, but the Lord has averted the crisis," and many more stories about how they were praying for people with demons and how these demons left their host screaming, "These are servants of God! We are leaving!" How they were praying for people with various maladies, how financial and marital problems were solved through their prayers.

I watched as this guy initiated a smooth religious transition in the family. Mother threw away her rosary, saying it was blatant idol worship. She gave away her Catholic prayer books, saying people were not supposed to recite prayers like they were nursery rhymes. She would give us stories about how this Patroba guy was so close to God that he literally saw Jesus every fifteen minutes of his waking hours. She told us a story about how one day this guy had gone to pray for somebody in Kishushe [in the Taita lowlands] and was benighted on the way. God literally struck a true rock and this guy Patroba stepped inside this rock and found himself in a spacious room furnished with a bed and a table, on which was a Bible. The guy spent the whole night in this rock talking to God. She also told us that, when somebody gave this guy cheap food like *ugali* [maize meal] and *sukuma wiki* [bitter greens], this food would turn into, say, *nyama* [beef] and chapatti or a McDonald's burger.[9] Sad to say, our God-hungry minds soaked up these incredible stories like puppies lapping milk, and for some inexplicable reason we thought ourselves to be damn lucky to have found such a guy, and consequently became putty in his hands.

At the time, my life had fallen into a crazy routine that was driving me crazy—it was like, I would stay in Taita for a couple of months then go to Mombasa to try and get work, fail to secure any, then go back to Taita and try my hands at farming. That would go on for a while and go up in smoke. I recall one time applying for a job in a company that my father had worked for and in which he had influence. We went for the interview, passed the interview, and were waiting to be taken for a medical check-up, when suddenly the company said it was not employing anyone in our group. It is interesting to note that every time I raised issues pertaining to progress in my life, Patroba always attributed my problems to what he called a "secret hatred" that my father felt toward me. The argument was based on a veritable truth, that Taita fathers have this congenital dislike for their sons, especially if they are first born. This has to do with the fact that, when they want to get married, there's dowry [bridewealth] to pay and this is not economically healthy for the family. I have inquired about this from old men, and they have said that it is true, that Taita men prefer the first three or four children in the family to be girls, so that when it is the turn for the boys to get married he has something to give. Anyway, my woes were attributed to this, and the solution from God for this problem was that the old man should buy me a shirt and this Taita curse would be lifted up from me. The old man was of course never confronted with this reality, coz God was going to deal with him in his own sweet time.

Around this time, there was this girl, and we'd been friends for close to eight years and planned to get married sometime in the future. Everyone in my family knew about her. One day Mother comes from one of her trips and confronts me with this story that the Lord told them that this girl was not fit to be my wife, coz she comes from a family of witches, that her parents are not "clean people." She said there was no way the "profane" was going to be joined to the "holy," our family, which had chosen to seek and follow God. I was not to tell this girl that we were not going to get married after all, and these guys told me that they had prayed to God so that this girl could jilt me. They also reasoned that if I left this girl, her family would bewitch me. It was the hardest time in my life. I was in Taita, and the girl was in Mombasa, and believe it or not, less than six months after the witch-craft news I heard that this girl was getting married to a guy she had apparently jilted before we met. It was fucking crazy.

The family continued to rely on Patroba for advice, listening to stories about how the Lord was preparing me for great wealth and prosperity. I swallowed this, just like I swallowed the bush doctors' stories. References were made to my earlier contact with the bush doctors—especially the trip to Lunga-Lunga—and some of my woes were attributed to it. The idea was that what was done to me back there was nothing but the opposite of what we thought was done. There was always someone out there trying to kill me or just fuck me over. One day Mother comes from those trips and gives me two *madafu* (this is a coconut that is not mature but is edible and has a lot of water) and tells me that they were instructed by God to give these to me to eat and drink so that they can rid me of the Lunga-Lunga rituals and some unspecified witchcraft. Nothing much changed in the family. I was still jobless, saw the old folks fight over money, the old man saying he has no money and the wife saying the guy is just mean and that he is being used by the devil so he can distract her from following and serving God.

I recall there was a ritual that was performed on the old man by this Patroba guy. The purpose of this ritual was to get the old man promoted at his place of work. He had stayed for a long time without getting promoted, and according to Patroba, this was coz most of the guys at his place of work were using witchcraft to get themselves promoted and at the same time hinder others from getting promoted. The ritual involved the slaughter of a sheep at home, and when we had gutted the animal, Patroba took some of the animal's shit and made the sign of the cross on the old man's forehead. He said that those who had used witchcraft to hinder the old man from progressing were in for a shock. A couple of months after this ritual, Dad got promoted.

In short, there was this perpetual fight of good over evil and the promises that one day God was gonna be the victor, for God's time is not man's time. I became close to Patroba, thought of him as my spiritual guide, and had confidence that God was actually using him to guide the lost souls into the path of life. I was a very patient guy when it came to listening to this guy as he explained biblical truths in a way that left no doubt in me that this guy was really some super-duper man of God.

I'M A PENTECOSTAL TOO

The first thing that a born-again Christian is supposed to do is to give witness to people about his newfound faith in Jesus, the son of God, who said that whoever would be ashamed of the Son of Man, the Son of Man would also be ashamed of him on that great and terrible day. These are the words that kept ringing in my ears and head. At first I thought it was gonna be hard to walk around telling my neighbors and friends that I had been saved. This was something that the other saved people before me had experienced, and they encouraged me to shame the devil.

I started the witnessing work that night at the house where I was staying. At first it was hard for those who had known me as a Rastafarian to believe that I had been converted to Protestantism. Not that I was a staunch Rasta, but I had carved myself an image of a cool rebel. I never went to church, listened only to reggae music, and the whole of society looked at me as one who could not be saved. Now I was saved, and there were skeptics who thought this was just a passing thing. But there were others who wanted to buy Jesus a beer for work well done. My family was so happy, especially my mother, who had spent a lot of time with Patroba praying to this God to save me. To her, her prayers had been answered. Nothing was impossible with this God of the Israelites.

And so started the long journey to heaven, a journey that I had been warned would not be easy because I had just pissed off the devil and his buddies. Now he was going to come at me with all the weapons in his arsenal and bomb my ass back to antediluvian times. He was going to try every trick in his black book that has made him notorious since time immemorial. My only weapon was to call upon the name of Jesus in prayer, read the Bible, and buffet my flesh with fast like the prophets of old. I attended church every Sunday, fasted, read the Bible, and watched my tongue and my flesh. I was "dead to the world," or was supposed to be. I was a new creation, and the old nature had passed away. The medusa in me had been slain, and out of her dead body sprang Pegasus, who would be used by this Jesus to conquer and vanquish his foes, both real and most probably imagined. I learned to pray aloud and sing Pentecostal songs; I greeted the brethren, "Praise the Lord, Brother or Sister!" I learned to detect the devil and his agents by listening to people talk, and every time I saw something that suggested the presence of the devil, I would loudly say, "In the Name of Jesus, devil, you have no authority, you are a liar!" I had to be careful about what I listened to and watched on the radio and TV. I was not supposed to associate myself with stuff that would open "doorways" for the devil, as this would surely bring about my downfall.

I recall giving away my collection of reggae music, because this kind of music was another one of those doorways that the devil used to mess people's lives. We were told during those home Bible study sessions that the devil was the most cunning of all creatures that God had created, and that since he had been in charge of every orchestral composition in heaven prior to his ignominious fall from grace, he had resorted to using this talent to entertain humans in the form of rock music, reggae, blues, and all earthly beats that did not offer glory to God. I had close to sixty audiotapes, which I had bought when I was working in Kisumu. One time, some of my closest buddies asked me whether I was serious about this salvation thing, wondering how it was going to be possible for me to go without smoking pot. People were like, well, if Ngeti can be saved, then everybody is going to be.

Being saved was not easy. One false move on the part of the believer and he or she was dead meat. One's spiritual growth was measured by the number of days that one fasted in a week and the time spent during any one given prayer session. The demons were all over the place: in the water, in the food, in the clothes that people wore, in the money, in the TV, in the cars, in the technology. We were told that technology had its provenance in the deep blue seas, like majini. Every nook and cranny was crammed full of grinning, fiendish demons, with bloody hands and gnarled fingers gripping pieces of human flesh. These demons were responsible for a lot of misfortunes. There were demons of poverty, demons of joblessness, demons of high blood pressure, demons of diabetes, demons of cancer, demons of infertility, demons of fornication, garrisons of silicon-clad demons to ensure that the Internet was one hundred percent pornographic, demons and more demons *ad infinitum*.

The first few months of my salvation were spent entirely on fasting and attending home Bible studies. At these meetings, new converts were asked to give witness and say what the Lord had done for them since they turned a new page in their lives. The witnessing was mostly confined to banal things like, "I used to smoke bhang and drink alcohol, but the Lord has removed these things from my life. I feel fresh and invigorated; I do not suffer from shortage of breath like I used to." And the gathering would go, "Hallelujah, glory to Jesus!" and shit like that. Another guy would go, "I was a very bad person. I used to invade other people's houses and sleep with their wives. I was a thief; I used to sneak into other people's gardens and steal maize, bananas, and beans. But these days I do not steal. If I want something, I ask the owner for it." Hallelujah!

We were made to believe that salvation is the key to the eternal life that other religions were preaching about. There was acrimonious reference to the Muslims as being the children of Lucifer, and they were doomed to burn in eternal fire. Catholics were looked at as idol worshipers of the deepest dye. We were told our archenemy was the devil, who was capable of manipulating the physical world to unbelievable proportions. He influenced the finance minister to hike the prices of essential commodities like meat, cooking fat, and medicine, and influenced the World Bank and the IMF to stop giving aid to third world countries, especially Kenya. He manipulated the media like TV, to get the people in charge to start showing programs and adverts that promoted promiscuity. AIDS was the rod of God to humans because they had stopped thinking with their heads and were now thinking with their genitals.

It is interesting that, for Kenyan Pentecostals, all the institutions and forces that the West has recently equated with transparency and openness—technology, media, and the removal of barriers to "free trade"—were actually blocking openness and transparency by preventing "open access" to a more real and true divine power. Not only did this suggest that Pentecostals discerned sinister intentions in these interventions; it also meant that an alternative to the "new world order" was being manufactured through Pentecostal practice. For Ngeti, all of this introduced drama and risk into his life—which, at the very least, helped him to experience the passage of time in a different, more dynamic way.

Fasting made his mystical states and cosmic journeys all the more real for Ngeti. In the remainder of his essay, he describes the time he misconstrued the remnants of a Swahili lunch for human sacrifice:

I recall how, one day, after I had come out of a three-day fast, I decided to walk down to the beach, as I was wont, to commune with the Most High. This is what Jesus used to do, and I was a disciple of this guy.

During the walk, I inadvertently chanced upon a shrine that was used either for devil-worshiping rituals or traditional healing rituals—for me, these were the same. This shrine was at the edge of the beach under a huge tree. There was this big area full of strange-looking stuff. On the ground there was a black pot sitting on three stones, and under the pot was burnt wood. It looked liked someone had cooked something. There were plates on the ground, too, and several pieces of variously colored cloth. I saw a bowl filled with a red pigment, which at first glance looked like blood. Several bottles hung from pieces of red, blue, green, and black cloth from the low-hanging branches of this huge tree. I took in my surroundings in thirty frightfully suffocating seconds. I felt that I was in the presence of very real evil.

I weighed my odds quickly, and my newly saved psyche told me that He who was in me was stronger than whoever ruled this shrine. I was a soldier in God's army and I was armed to the teeth with devastating, spiritual weapons of mass destruction. My hair stood on end, my whole flesh goosed up, my tongue swelled exponentially in my mouth, and I thought I was going to pass out. But I launched into a Swahili hymn, which we were told would send the demons scurrying for cover. "There is power, power, wonder-working power, in the precious blood of the lamb," I chanted at the top of my voice several times, before I switched to the English version of the same song. I labored on, eyes darting from side to side, ready to run for my dear life if anything untoward happened. But nothing happened. Only the sound of the waves rushing in from the sea.

There is a common belief among the coastal people that all jinnis came from the sea and lived in the sea, and I felt there were many jinnis where I was standing at that moment. I bent down and grabbed a couple of bottles filled with some red stuff, which I later discovered was a food-coloring pigment very popular with Swahili people when they are cooking a spiced rice dish called *biriyani*. I also grabbed several pieces of white kerchief and walked with these to the edge of the water, then threw them into the swelling waves. What happened next convinced me that there truly were demons at this place: the pieces of white kerchief disappeared immediately as they touched the water. They did not fucking float, as would have been the case normally. This left me momentarily dazed, staring at the waves lapping around my feet in disbelief. I whirled around and ran the whole length of the beach, imagining long watery hands sticking out of the sea and pulling me into the underworld. I was fucking spooked.

Ngeti's relationship with God was still tenuous: he could now see things he couldn't before, and also not see things that he probably could see before (like the food coloring used to make biriyani), but he could still be frightened by Islamic spirits. He was beginning to feel strong enough in his new relationship with God that he could at least think about standing up to forces that had frightened him and held him back his entire life. But he would become spiritually stronger only after receiving the gift of speaking in tongues.

The language of the divine is quite literally a gift, conferred on already saved parishioners by master virtuosos in a public ceremony. Typically, this spiritual patron hails from another, faraway country (in Ngeti's case, Nigeria), and his or her upwardly mobile foreignness is the social foundation upon which his or her knowledge depends. The purpose of this language is to transform the state of the soul by strengthening one's relationship to God, expurgating sin, and deflecting demonic influences both from the spirit world and from the immediate social environment. Ngeti continues in this email to tell the story of the time he received this gift:

I continued praying and fasting, and four months after giving my life to Jesus we were baptized at the sea. On this day, there had come some renowned preacher from Nigeria. He was at our church to preside over what was called a Revival Crusade. We were baptized in the morning, hundreds of us, and in the evening there was this revival crusade at the church. On this day this Nigerian informed us that God had told him that we were going to be filled with the Holy Spirit and we were going to speak in tongues. We were all excited because being filled with the Holy Spirit was what every believer longed for, for this was an unequivocal indication that the Almighty God had put his seal upon the believer. Being filled with the Holy Spirit meant that one could see into the invisible world of the spirit, either in the waking hours or in sleep. Dreams played a very important role in the life of a believer, for in dreams God communicated with his child. Every dream was to be taken seriously, for in them were esoteric messages that could not be conveyed verbally. In dreams the believer could see God or his angels. All this was possible if you were filled with the Holy Spirit. Anyway, the church was packed to its fullest on this day of "Pentecost."
After the Nigerian had finished preaching, he told us to start praying or say anything to God, pour out our hearts and souls to our Father in heaven. And pour out our heart to the Father of all flesh we did, the whole bunch of us. Several minutes into praying, something took over my vocal cords and I started uttering stuff in a language that did not make sense to me at all. It sounded like any language in the world only I did not know which, and I did not care. I enthusiastically walked this xenoglossic path like a maniac for almost three hours nonstop. It was crazy, only back then it did not sound crazy. Funny what people can do with religion. I spoke in tongues from that day on for over seven years, and not once did I know what the fuck I was saying in this crazy language. One thing I recall, though, is, every time I spoke in this strange language I would get slight headaches, and back then I thought it must be the devil trying to stop me from speaking in these tongues. There was a belief that when one spoke in tongues he was actually speaking the language of God and angels, and the devil could never decipher

this language. This was an advantage to the believer because if you prayed in human language the chances of the devil listening in on your prayers were very high and he could hijack those prayers and throw them to hell, and when that happened then you would not receive what you had prayed for. It was a life of constantly looking over one's shoulder.

The thing is that with the new religion everything that happened had meaning. For example, I remember there reached a time that I decided to have what I call a dreams and visions book, and I remember this one dream that I recorded in this book. I had this dream in the year 2000, sometime in January. This is how I recorded it:

I'm at home (Taita) walking about the compound, when suddenly I look on the ground and a plague of locusts and an assortment of other creepy-crawlies greet my eyes. I ask myself what could be causing this agitation among these guys. Is it ants? But no, there are no ants anywhere. Then, just as suddenly, the grass on which these locusts are disappears and these monsters start marching toward the avocado tree that grew in our garden. I follow these little fellows toward this tree, stepping on several along the way, and they go, pop, pop, pop under my feet. I wondered what was attracting them to the tree in the thousands. Suddenly an idea comes to my mind. "There must be a python under the avocado tree," I concluded, and immediately got scared. I broke into a run toward the tree, and as I neared it I cast my eyes frantically around watching out for a python. Then I saw it, or so I thought. It was coiled into a black thing that could as well have been anything from a cat to a molehill or an old piece of rug.

Providence came to my aid, for I miraculously found myself clutching a good-sized raw avocado, which in the hands of a person under the influence of several liters of adrenalin could cause irreversible damage to whatever was on the ground. I let go the fruit and didn't wait to see the results because I was reminded by my scared mind that pythons do fly when threatened with danger, so I endeavored to create a gap big enough to fit a planet in, between it and me. No whooshing sound over my head, no slippery muscles crushing my body. Nothing. Only silence. Did I kill the fucking python or was it after all an old piece of rug?

End of dream, but it is immediately followed by another dream. I'm with another guy at home doing something. Then I hear a *thud thud* sound under the avocado tree. Same tree. I suggest to this guy to go check it out. There are a lot of raw avocados on the ground, and more are falling. We look up in the tree, lots of fruits waiting to fall down. Then I see a guy, head sticking out between the foliage, grinning like a psycho. I order him to climb down and give me enough

making party, for each of these siblings had a grievance against another. My mother had not been on good terms with her brother Mzungu since she accused him of murdering his nephew. And there was no love lost between her and Valentine's family for her kicking the shit out of Valentine's wife a couple of years earlier. She told them that the Lord had shown her that their wrangling was chasing away their blessings and that, had it not been for this conflict, most of them would be driving cars and owning big-time businesses. She told them to think about the wealth that their father had: the guy, we are told, had a flock of sheep, a herd of cows, and about fifty donkeys. She said none of the wealth of their father had rubbed off on any of them, but the Lord was about to do something wonderful in each of their families. So there was a fund-raising, which realized enough money to buy a couple kilos of rice and a sheep.

The day was Saturday and most of the grandchildren were there, those who were in Taita anyway. Some of the adults boycotted the party, saying it was a waste of time. My mother was in charge of the ceremony, and she led the gathering in prayers and songs, quoting stuff from the Bible about forgiving those that had wronged others and God Almighty. Those that were there, like Valentine's wife, said she did not have anything against my mother. But the husband, my mother's brother Valentine, who did not attend the party, had made his stand very clear on the day they had had a meeting to try and resolve the acrimony between their younger brother and his wife, and which had ended with my mother beating the living daylight out of his wife. He said he would never forgive my mother for beating his wife. Another conspicuous absentee was Mzungu, who said he would rather take a walk with Lucifer in hell than be seen eating together with my mother.

Take care buddy,
Ngeti

Many things are important about Pentecostalism in Kenya and Africa. More than an abstract "belief system," this is a mode of social action whose practitioners hope to radically reconstruct themselves and society in a way that really is revolutionary. We can see from Ngeti's story that this mode of action did have real, powerful consequences. Part of what is striking in Ngeti's story is how this religion thrust marginalized, even scorned, people into positions of authority, often with the potential for wealth acquisition. At the same time, it cast aspersions on people who had acquired wealth and respectability through conventional means, including schooling, politics, and participation in the mainline churches. Patroba was a nobody from a poor family, and Monica was a woman widely held to be dangerously powerful by the society, and by her own family, but the Pentecostal spirit turned them into people at once powerful and virtuous. This capacity to innovate and transform was symbolized in the very rituals that produced transformation for individuals and the larger society. A central underlying feature of all of this is the rupturing and redirection of ordinary, incremental time.

Much has been made, of late, of African Pentecostalism's orientation to time and temporality, in part because time seems to be central to the changes that Pentecostals try to produce.[10] Birgit Meyer has discussed how Ghanaian Pentecostals try to create a complete break with the past, severing the hold of tradition and past events upon their lives, which enables them to proceed unmolested into the future.[11] Charles Piot has argued of Togo that disenchantment with the senior male guardians of tradition and the past has fueled this interest in creating a clean slate on which to write a new future.[12] Ruth Marshall, in her writings on Nigerian Pentecostalism, takes this idea further, arguing that Pentecostalism pulverizes the "historical time" (what Walter Benjamin referred to as "empty, homogenous time") through which, to paraphrase Marx, the past is made to weigh like a nightmare on the brains of the living.[13] She shows how ritualized miracles and the act of salvation impregnates every moment with possibility, theorizing that "in the messianic conception of time, the arrival of the messiah may be accomplished 'at any instant,' in the very heart of history, pulverizing the coherence and continuity of historical time into innumerable messianic instants in which the radically new becomes possible."[14]

In an article that is as much about economics as it is about religion, Jane Guyer has argued that evangelical Christianity's orientation toward a miraculous, or "prophetic," time is born of lived experience in post-Fordist times.[15] She uses Pierre Bourdieu's concept of a "generative schema" to discuss the relationship between structural changes taking place globally and perceptions of, and orientations to, time.[16] Simply put, the institutional structures through which people once built incremental futures no longer exist, or they appear to be broken, and instead people find themselves subject to sudden, momentous shocks that rupture their experience of time. So there is an elective affinity (not a causal connection) between these popular new religions and neoliberal, post-Fordist capitalism.

The relationship that Ngeti fostered through Patroba suggests an interesting strategy, as well as a changing dispensation toward success and development. Two men with no obvious historical connection to one another (they were not kin or neighbors, nor did they attend the same school) decide to enter into a kind of work with each other. The work is not "economic" in the sense that we give to that term in the West, but the outcome of this work is intended to benefit each of them materially as much as spiritually. The general attitude reflects the dismantling of coherent structures that characterized structural adjustment: these people are looking for miraculous opportunities that will come suddenly, independent of any mediating structures or historical relationships. Patroba and Ngeti feel the need to be flexible, moving from place to place as God wishes, always ready for something good to happen. What stance could be better suited to what David Harvey refers to as the regime of "flexible accumulation," in which established geographic boundaries and sedimented relationships give way to a mobility that sets itself down for a moment only to pick itself back up again and start anew?[17] Moreover, Ngeti and Patroba hoped that by structurally readjusting their desire natures and suffering through extreme austerity measures, they would suddenly burst ahead into a bountiful future—an idea that also fit quite well with the neoliberal economic thought that undergirded the withdrawal of the World Bank and IMF from loan programs during this period.

The problem was that Pentecostal temporality was paradoxical—it cultivated the anticipation of miraculous transformation while also insisting on the need for patience in the face of "God's time," which is not "man's" (to paraphrase Ngeti in a later passage). The tension between these infinite hopes and the boring routine in which Ngeti found himself was starting to wear on him, and in his frustration he took to marking time so that he could look back and know what exactly he had been doing with his days. Which brings us to Ngeti's diary.

SIX

Works and Days

Hope kept me going. Every day was a miracle day for me.

NGETI, *on his hopes for wealth while serving as
a disciple for his Pentecostal guru, Patroba*

The Lord told him he should buy Alcatel.

NGETI, *on God's advice, spoken through Patroba, concerning what
brand of cell phone his prospective business partner, William,
should purchase*

NGETI HAS BEEN COMING UP with new business ideas nonstop for as
long as we've known each other, always hoping that one day I'd be sold and
want to join in with him on something particularly credible. He continued
to try to persuade me to enter into business with him, via email, long after I
left Taita and returned home. Some of Ngeti's ideas have included loan shark-
ing, "matching" African wives with Chinese bachelors, using the Internet to
make divination and witchcraft accessible to foreign consumers via a website,
selling pirated pornographic DVDs on the street, and establishing a church
in which the tithes would be returned to congregants as low-interest-bearing
"believers' loans." Eventually, gemstone mining in the Taita Hills captured
Ngeti's imagination: right there in his neighborhood there was more wealth
than he could ever expend, if only it could be accessed! All that was needed
was the right set of connections—the right government geologist, the right
foreign investor with money for machines, the right buyers. Why look somewhere else when salvation was so close, and the means for achieving it so
direct? But after spending months in the wilderness using money that I had
given him to blow up holes in the ground with dynamite, Ngeti began to
realize what a bad bet this was. But no matter. He had become habituated to
waiting for a miraculous rebound after a long period of austerity.

Ngeti used to have different ideas about how he could become successful,
in the total sense of the term. He held other assumptions about what kinds

of dispositions and orientations to people, geographical location, and time were likely to be fruitful for him, based mostly on the experiences of others and the stories he was told. Recall that Ngeti had spent many years searching for formal employment in cities, at first following in his maternal grandfather's footsteps by demonstrating an interest in the Catholic priesthood, and later looking into transportation, like his father. But he had difficulty finding employment in these areas, took to selling cheap imported products, and dreamed of obtaining the start-up capital necessary to launch a small business, usually one geared to an investor or customer base outside of Kenya. Ngeti became interested in business as he grew exhausted from what he called the "crazy routine" of migrating back and forth between Taita and Mombasa, first trying to find a job, then "trying his luck" at farming.

It was in this time of mind-numbing repetition that he also started to listen to the Pentecostals, and I don't think this was coincidental. There was something homologous about entrepreneurship and Pentecostalism—these activities, and the ideas that undergirded them, seemed to nourish each other, though in a way that Ngeti did not fully understand or perhaps even think much about. Call it an elective affinity. Both paths encouraged practitioners to look beyond established authorities, to set off on their own, and to develop disciplined personal accounting skills as they patiently waited for their miracles. Of all the businesses available to young men of Ngeti's age, starting a new church was one of the most appealing. Not only did it make financial sense (a church can be started cheaply and pays for itself), but in this arena material success and transcendent meaning are conjoined. The church fuses the ideal of small business enterprise with the religious practice of steadfast preparedness, of readying oneself for a miracle. Pentecostalism, in particular, is a model spiritual and economic concern for a new generation seeking independence from the old state-centered ways of getting ahead. It also speaks to long- established African understandings of the relationships among morality, testimony, and success.

Like many young men of his generation, Ngeti saw his shift to thinking about business as a break with Taita tradition. He was going to be innovative, to try and come up with something new—even if it was the case that he didn't have much of a choice at all. Anyway, he tended to see business not as something that was forced on him by a lack of opportunities, but as an idea that he had come up with on his own. To be successful in business, it was best not to be submissive in the face of authority, but to be ready at any time with a new concept, however iconoclastic. For example, you didn't want to blindly accept such Taita customs as naming your kids after your parents—what if they became like them and spent all their time waiting to inherit land!?—or having your wife move into your parents' house to help your mother with the cooking (what anthropologists call virilocality). Pentecostalism encouraged people to break from the past, often in very transgressive ways—such as repudiating your senior relatives and rejecting the visible and invisible powers they wield over you through cursing, inheritance, and naming practices. Pentecostalism's emphasis on direct communication also made sense to Taita entrepreneurs, as did the sudden "miraculous time" of Pentecostalism, through which a period of waiting might give way to a sudden resurgence in prosperity as the result of a good deal. History—relying on that which came before—did not seem like a particularly good foundation anymore. Indeed, history seemed to be a big part of the problem.

Ngeti was trying to find a foundation for his own free will through Pentecostalism, but he ended up feeling enslaved to an increasingly erratic spiritual patron who had achieved near total power over his life and whom he genuinely feared. By the onset of the new millennium, Ngeti had been working with Patroba for over five years. For the most part they prayed together, but, like all of Patroba's disciples, Ngeti also did odd jobs for Patroba. At some point, Ngeti became aware of how much work and time he was putting into trying to produce miracles that went unrealized, and he started to feel increasingly alone and abandoned. Like a shipwrecked Crusoe, he began to obsessively keep track of all his days, focusing especially on the moments of hope that went into the work of miracle making, when he and Patroba laid the foundations for the expected unexpected.

This chapter comprises excerpts from Ngeti's diary, written over a one-year period during which he was starting to question some of the rituals in which he engaged with Patroba. To write these sections for me, Ngeti went back to his physical diary, from the year 2000, and typed up what he found, often including his own interpretations and observations from the "present," about three or four years after he wrote the diary. During the year that he kept this diary, Ngeti hoped to enter into a business venture involving Patroba and another young convert with entrepreneurial ambitions named William. Both William and Ngeti hoped that their spiritual salvation would manifest financially and viewed successful business as proof of the reality of what they were doing spiritually. Over time they began to doubt the power of both this patron, Patroba, and even God himself, who definitely seemed to be losing the war against his exiled former servant, Satan. When the diary begins, William, Patroba, and Ngeti (whom Ngeti often refers to collectively as "the trio") had just returned to Mombasa from Nairobi on an airplane, after looking into buying a *matatu* (passenger minivan) there. Ngeti was inspired by this trip, believing that it augured well for his continued business success under Patroba.

By this time, Patroba had broken off his relationship with Ngeti's parents. Ngeti's mother and father had grown to feel that nothing good had come from their dealings with the prophet, and they began to take account of how much they had given him, in terms of money and assistance, over the years. For his part, Patroba felt that Ngeti's father still owed him the tithe he had promised years before. At one point, Ngeti's father, who had always resented the influence Patroba had over the family, ordered Ngeti to stop seeing his spiritual patron and, when Ngeti refused, warned that Ngeti would die when he died. This apparently meant that Ngeti would not inherit land from his father, but Ngeti interpreted this as a curse and as possible proof that his parents were in fact witches. Ngeti defied his parents, and in his guilt became all the more worried that they wanted to sacrifice him to demonic agents.

Ngeti's diary from this one-year period with Patroba is long. I have not included everything, but have left enough of the original to convey a sense of what Ngeti did on a daily basis, and what "working" with Patroba entailed. I believe it presents a rare illustration of one particular version of everyday Pentecostal life, as well as an insight into the kind of world these male actors were trying to produce through ritual. Some important themes emerge from these diaries as well that may not be immediately evident, and certain details may seem obscure or puzzling; I have put my interpretations at the end of the chapter for the sake of readability.

Monday, June 20th

I'm in Mombasa. Patroba and I go to Likoni for prayers, and while praying he tells me that he had seen the Lord with hot coals in his hands and he was using these to burn off all the ropes that were binding me in my life. He tells me I must resist the advances of my white lady friends.

Sunday, June 25th

Patroba, William, and I go to Kwale for prayers, and the Lord tells me that he was going to cleanse me of all the filthiness that came upon me when I consulted mediums before He called me into His kingdom.

Friday, June 30th

I prayed with Patroba, and the Lord told me to be *huru*, free, that he has food on the table for me and I shouldn't feel like a stranger in Patroba's house. Patroba tells me that the Lord is about to do something for me. We pray to the Lord to bring the dollars from America and for me to get the opportunity to study computers, marketing, and advertising.

Monday, July 10th

While praying at night, the Lord speaks through Patroba and says that my help will come from Jimmy and that I should pray for him always. He says that the hands of Mother are calling me back to Taita. Patroba says I have had enough problems and he does not want me to go home. But He, the Lord, has good things in store for me. He also urges me to refuse the carnal desires of my white lady friends.

Earlier on in the day, the trio, that is Patroba, William, and I, had gone to a town called Mariakani, about 60 kilometers from Mombasa town. The purpose was to go and pray so that the Lord could give us the gift of rearing domestic animals, especially cattle. We felt that we deserved to have these animals just like the biblical patriots Abraham, Isaac, and Jacob. To make our prayers be heard, Patroba told us that the Lord had told him that we should eat *ugali* and *nyama choma* [maize meal and roast meat] in this town, something we did in obedience to the Lord's voice.

Tuesday, July 11th

In the evening, while praying at Patroba's place, the Lord says that my sister should leave her job or else she is going to die from fornicating too much. He said he had brought me to Mombasa to help her. The Lord warns us against playing around with his servant Patroba, saying that He had killed women like Mama Esther and Mrs. Mwabili because they had not believed in his servant Patroba.

Mama Esther is the woman who introduced my mother to this guy Patroba. One day, Mama Esther fell sick at our home. They had just come back from Patroba, where they had spent like four days at Kishushe, in the Taita lowlands, praying for various people. This woman managed to go back home, but her condition got worse and she was taken to Wesu hospital, where she died after about one week. Mrs. Mwabili was one of the people that Patroba had prayed for. She was a widow. This woman died in her sleep, and Patroba told me that she had been given poisoned tea by my mother because she, Mrs. Mwabili, had refused to lend Mother some money.

Later I would wonder: did Patroba kill these women because they stopped praying with him or perhaps as a sacrifice to increase his power?

Thursday, July 13th

The Lord says that we should not be afraid of thugs. He says the toilet where my folks had hidden their jinnis was not working because of the prayers that we were saying to oust the jinnis.

Saturday, July 15th

The Lord tells me through Patroba that I will grow fat, for he is the one who watches over my health. He also says that Jimmy is planning to do big things. I should "be free" with William and Patroba because they love me. He asks me, Where is it written that a man should work so that he can eat? He has made me eat like Saul in the Bible. I have no fucking idea how this Saul guy ate or what the fuck he ate. I understand there were lots of figs then and they were used, I think, as money. You could buy a guy as a slave for a couple of figs, I think.

Later on I think that this is a lie from God Himself, because I know it's written in the Bible that you must work if you expect to eat. God cannot contradict Himself, so this guy must have been uttering stuff from his spirit-drunk head.

Sunday, July 16th

Spent the whole day in Patroba's house watching TV. In the evening while praying, the Lord says, "Peace William, peace Ngeti, you love Patroba, you did not complain about spending the whole day in the house. That is very good." He also tells me that I will get a certificate for all the hardships that I have gone through in my life.

Sunday, July 30th

During evening prayers the Lord tells me that he has a case to sort out with me, so I should be at Patroba's place early in the morning. Earlier in the day, William had asked the Lord, through Patroba, what kind of a mobile phone he should buy. The Lord told him he should buy Alcatel. The guy wanted to buy a car and he asked the Lord where he should buy it, and the Lord told him to buy it from some Asians in town. But instead William bought it from some other guy and not the Asians. But the Lord was not pissed, because He never asked why he had not bought it from the Asians as He had commanded him.

Monday, July 31st

Went to Kwale with Patroba for prayers and he tells me that I am victorious and that he has seen the Lord removing my parents far from me. This God tells me that this guy I am staying with, William, is about to give me monetary help. He tells me I should leave everything about my life to Him, the Lord. He says he knows the wickedness of my parents and their cruelty toward me.

Sunday, August 6th

The trio plus Patroba's wife and their two kids leave for Voi. Patroba's wife's father, Mtongolo, stays in Voi. He is a staunch Catholic and does not believe in people changing their religion, as we had done. He frowns upon Pentecostalism, saying it is a foreign religion. The only true religion is Catholicism. Patroba tells me that I should consider the trips that we were making as a way of serving the Lord. The Lord tells me that He knows about the old folks and that He is going to deal with them. By this He means he will make them disown and confess their witchcraft. Later at night, God speaks through Patroba, telling him, "The tradition of Mtongolo I do not want," meaning God repudiated Patroba's father-in-law's Catholicism right there in front of us.

Monday, August 7th

While praying in the morning at this hotel the Lord tells me that I should go to Taita, then I was going to fall sick. On this day I watch as this guy Patroba spends money buying household furniture worth thousands of shillings. He buys a wall unit, a dining table, and sofa sets. The guy spends like over sixty thousand [about $800] on this stuff. All this time I am like, well, the Lord is really performing miracles for this guy, I think some of these miracles will rub off on me sometime soon. But now I think somehow he was able to prosper by "tying" me. But at the time, this is what kept me going, hoping that maybe today was gonna be my lucky day too, today the Lord was gonna pull out my file from his cabinet and say, "The time is now ripe to visit this son of mine," and prove to him that all his toil has not been for naught. Hope kept me going, every day was a miracle day to me. If nothing happened, then I would wonder if it was something that I had done or not done. I was panting for these blessings like a desert traveler pants for the sight of an oasis.

While at Voi, we are informed that this guy's mother had been diagnosed with diabetes. We go up to Saghasa to take the stuff that this guy had bought at Voi and see his mother. Later I watch this guy who seemed to be invincible reduced to tears by the sight of his sick mother.

Friday, August 18th

This William guy had bought a car about two months ago, so traveling had become easier for us. Went with Patroba to Shela beach for prayers. The Lord tells me to forget about my father. In the evening he tells the trio to go back to Taita and see Mercy. Mercy is Patroba's last-born daughter. She is about six months old. The Lord says that the kid is an mzungu [white person/European], meaning she is smart. This kid Mercy had been born with plastic teeth and, according to popular belief, that was not a good sign. People believed that when such a kid is born, it meant that the parents were not clean people, that they could be witches. When we prayed, sometimes the Lord would comment on this and say that He was the one who had created the kid with the plastic teeth and this was His miracle and He had a reason for it.

Later William confides in me that he does not think the Lord is ordering some of these trips that we are making. He thinks Patroba is taking advantage of the availability of his car.

Saturday, August 26th

The trio leaves for Voi. Patroba is on his way to Taita. We go to William's shamba [plot] near Voi, to see his cattle and worker. While praying, Patroba tells us that he can see Jimmy coming. He also tells us that the Lord had changed his plans for going to Taita. We end up cruising around town like rednecks. Later, much later, around seven o'clock, Patroba tells us that the Lord has told him that all of us will go to Taita instead of going back to Mombasa. We go to Saghasa, his place, at the whims of this guy. On this day while sitting at Mwasela's filling station, Patroba tells us that the Lord had forgiven Mwasela for not tithing to Patroba. Mwasela is a Taita tycoon who owns a matatu business by the name of Frontline Safaris. Patroba claimed that if it were not for his prayers then this guy's business would have gone down.

Sunday, August 27th

We leave Saghasa for Mombasa. In the evening, William and I wonder if all that Patroba says is really from the Lord or just from his own fucking head. Since William bought the car there have been too many trips, which we begin to doubt were actually ordered by the Lord. We do not say anything to Patroba, though, and we do nothing to make him see our displeasure with his Lord.

Friday, September 8th

God tells me, through Patroba, that ten years ago my paternal uncle had tried to poison me when I was staying with him in Nakuru because I was eating his food. He tells me to go to the house where my father used to stay and pray, that our house in Taita has demons but that He had removed them. He also asks me why I do not believe that He can do things for me.

I thought it was funny that God asked that, because at this time I was beginning to question this guy and his "God says" messages. I had a feeling that Patroba wanted to control every aspect of my life. He wanted to know when I crapped and when I pissed. Yet somehow I did not have the courage to just quit this bullshit, because there was this promise of taking care of William's business. I did not want to piss off these guys. At times when questions came to my mind I would dismiss them as being stuff from the devil who has for all these years given me hell on earth. I was not going to let him have the last laugh, no fucking way. I wanted to weather out whatever storms he threw at me in the name of Jesus. And that was that.

Friday, September 15th

I prayed and the Lord tells me that getting married is not a sin for me. He said he was going to deal with my mother. He tells me there is some hidden treasure for me. He commands me to go home to Taita and pray at home because my father had said that he would not let me inherit anything from him.

Monday, September 18th

Patroba reads me a letter from the old folks and he tells me that the Lord had removed the rod from them. I had given him the letter because I thought maybe there were some jinnis in the letter from the old folks.

Tuesday, September 19th

We pray and the Lord tells me that the old folks at home have blessed me. He tells me that he stopped me from marrying Loice because her family was not "clean." Loice was some lady I wanted to marry back in 1997, but things did not turn out well. I was seeing Patroba then, but I was not told that her family was not clean until today. The Lord instructs me to go to Likoni and wash my feet with seawater after praying. This prayer washing was meant to cleanse me of some witchcraft that was placed in me by Loice's family.

Monday, September 25th

We pray and the Lord tells me to go get the money that William had promised to give me so I could register with some NGO that was giving people loans to start small-scale businesses. The Lord says he wants me to start doing something. I go to Willy and he gives me a cheque for three thousand [about $40,] but things do not turn out okay. This leaves God with egg streaming down His fucking glorious face. Shame on Him!

Wednesday, September 27th

Patroba is not in, so his wife takes the mantle of prophesying on his behalf. The Lord tells me through her that He is about to answer my prayers. He says that I loathe myself because of how things are in my life. He also says that a rival Pentecostal preacher named Cyrus is in trouble because he did not do the work of "burning" the majini at home properly. He was afraid of them. He also adds that I am too brainy and that is how I was created.

I wonder why the Lord is turning this prophesying thing into a family business. Why can't he use me or William to do the prophesying, or any other person for that matter? Something was definitely not right here, and for some crazy reason we did not do anything about it. Or was it because Patroba had very powerful demons, which just rooted us to one place and made us immobile? Why did we not have the guts to face this guy and tell him to his fucking face that we thought he was just full of shit and he should get someone else to pray for him?

Sunday, October 8th

There was a time when my dog Misty disappeared from home for some days, and when it reappeared, its two balls had been ripped off. Today the Lord spoke through this guy and he said that when this dog had disappeared, my mother knew where it was. According to this Lord, the dog had been used in a satanic ritual that was meant to prevent me from getting married. Its balls had been used in this particular witchcraft ritual. Now, to deliver me from this "curse," I was to buy a bun and a chapatti, hold this stuff in my hands behind my back, and utter some short prayer to God while facing toward the wilderness. This ritual was supposedly meant to open my marriage plans.

Wednesday, October 11th

We pray in the evening and the Lord tells me to go and rub myself down with salt, then wash myself. This ritual was meant to cleanse me of some evil that was either committed by my grandparents or by my parents, I do not remember which was which. I was also told to start preaching to William's brother, who is a drunkard and who keeps coming to the house with a new fuck every night. He tells me that he did not bring me to Mombasa to watch television. He threatens to frustrate my plans if I do not do what He tells me to do. He tells me I am walking on a sharp sword. He says He wants my mother to come to Mombasa and talk to Patroba. This same night I wash myself with salt, and boy, do I smell bad.

Hey man [Ngeti is now addressing me in a side note], have you ever rubbed yourself down with salt? Fuck, for some crazy reasons, the body smells more than shit when you do this. That day [returning to his story] I was in the bathroom and took like half a kilogram of this mineral and started doing the rubbing. First, the salt stings you like a swarm of psychopathic bees, then slowly the stench begins to rise from within the *corpus* and hits your olfactory organs with the force of an exploding TNT bomb. Your whole surrounding is soon saturated with this fetid stench that would make a morgue smell like a perfume shop. All this time I was like, well, what the hell is going on here, I mean this God that was into all sorts of rituals and nothing coming out of them. Yes, I used to ask myself questions, man, as to how I was almost always subjected to some crazy shit like this.

Tuesday, October 17th

The Lord says that the trio should go into serious praying because there was witchcraft in my mother's heart, which she was planning to use to destroy the three of us. We are to start praying for the plans that we have with Jimmy. (What plans did we have my brother, I do not recall?) The Lord says something about Jimmy coming with a Land Cruiser. Very funny. I think my mind had been fried to senselessness by all these messages of fear and animosity from God. But I kept lapping up these stories like chocolate syrup.

Tuesday, October 24th

While praying the Lord tells me that he had taken hold of me so he could execute his judgment upon my old man for saying that I was not going to inherit anything from him. He also tells me that Betty, the girl I was seeing, is saying in her heart that if I'm serious about our relationship, then I should give her some money as a token of my commitment to her.

Friday, November 3rd

I leave Saghasa for Mombasa. When I arrive, I am told by Patroba's wife that my mother is in the house with Patroba and they are praying. It does not go well with my mother. There is too much anger in me. I just do not want to see her. I feel she has come to do more witchcraft, so my plans do not go well and I have to go back to Taita. We do not talk much. Later we see her off and we leave her at the bus stage. Later at night while praying, the Lord says, "Ngeti, today I have drunk water from you . . . you did not show your mother any disrespect . . . you greeted her."

Sunday, November 5th

Patroba comes to William's to pick us up so we can go to Kwale for prayers. He tells me that the Lord has removed all the curses that my father had placed on me. He says I will get married to Betty.

Later at night the Lord speaks to me through Patroba's wife, Olympia, saying that He was going to fight for me to the end. He tells me to be free. He says that the people at Voi, that is Mtongolo and his wife, are saying that Patroba is misleading William, and the Lord asks William if it was true that Patroba was misleading him. William says, "No, it is not true." The Lord says He is going to bless William with a wife from America. He should only believe.

Monday, November 6th

We went to Jane, Patroba's wife's elder sister, to deliver some message from the Lord. This lady had found her own place and was staying alone. She is almost 50 and she is not married. I recall there was a ritual, which Patroba said the Lord had ordered him to perform so this lady could get married. It was revealed by the Lord through Patroba that when this lady was young her mother had gone to a witchdoctor to have this lady "tied" so she could not have sex with any man until she was married. All her sexual desires had been "stored" somewhere for safekeeping until the day she would need them. But something went wrong at the witchdoctor's and the lady was made repulsive to men. The ritual involved the slaughtering of a male sheep and roasting the balls of this animal, and Patroba would pray over them and give them to this lady to eat. Usually, according to Taita customs, women are not allowed to eat animals' balls. I was at this ceremony, but so far nothing has happened to this lady. She is still "repulsive" to men.

Monday, November 13th

We pray and the Lord tells Patroba to tell me to wait for the Lord. He is going to help me get married. He tells me that my father keeps saying that he wasted his money by sending me to school and his hatred has contributed to my being jobless.

Wednesday, November 15th

I am with Patroba and we pray and the Lord says that, when I was young, my mother used to touch my private parts a lot, so I should go to a place called Timbila and pray and I would be cleansed of this filthiness.

Thursday, November 16th

During the day, Patroba tells me that the Lord wants the three of us to go to Taveta/Timbila over the weekend and there is no more wasting time. The Lord wants my plans of marrying to succeed immediately. In the evening, while praying, the Lord says that he had wanted us to go to Taveta earlier and he blames Patroba for not listening to His voice properly. Patroba claims he can hear the bell for the trip to Taveta ringing. Later William asks me how on earth we were supposed to know when to go to Taveta if Patroba didn't tell us, and if this was really coming from the Lord?

Saturday, November 18th

The trio goes to Taveta. On the way, we pick up a group of people who had been stranded due to lack of transport. At Timbila I washed my hands in some murky stream. I was supposed to wash my whole body, but when the Lord saw how dirty it was He stopped me and told me to just wash my hands. At this stream we also found some kids fetching water, and the Lord later says they were angels. At the stream the Lord says, "It is finished," meaning the curses placed on me. Later we go to some restaurant to eat, and Patroba says that the Lord had given him an envelope for the prayers that he had said for me at the stream. Patroba says that some years ago they had come here with mother and Mama Esther for prayer and that it was at this place that my mother had commented that Taita men do no like it when their wives give birth to male first-borns. He said this trip here was somehow delivering me from this traditional curse from my father.

Sunday, November 19th

The trio leaves for Mombasa, and the Lord tells me that I should not think that he does not care about me. He hurts when I hurt. On this day William and I take my sister to Magongo, where she was staying. I got the chance to pray at the place where my father used to stay. I had been commanded by God to do this.

Tuesday, November 21st

We pray, and God gets very angry with Jane, Patroba's sister-in-law, for refusing to stay with Patroba's dogs. This guy had bought two puppies and had decided to keep them at this lady's place while he waited to take them to Taita. This lady was not fond of dogs. They would go scrapping all over her compound, and she had asked Patroba to make plans to take them away. This did not sit well with this guy. So on this day while praying, God is like, in Swahili, "Jane, you are refusing to stay with the dogs of the servant of God. You have forgotten all that the servant has done for you. Now you have a good job because of the prayers of the servant. If you do not want to stay with those dogs then I will deal with you. Patroba, take those dogs to my son William."

When the lady heard this she literally threw herself at the feet of this guy and begged God to forgive her. She said she would stay with the dogs. It is funny now, but back then it was serious shit. We were all frozen in our seats waiting for thunder, brimstone, and fire. We were all asking God to forgive Jane for being so stupid as to piss God off.

Friday, November 24th

While praying at Patroba's place at night, the Lord says there is a maternal grandfather's tree that was blocking a lot of people's blessings and holding them in the roots so they do not make any progress in life. This tree, the Lord claims that it killed King David. He tells me that the knife that I used to carry when I was a young man took away my blessings. Yes, it is true. When I quit school back in the 80s, long before I was saved, I used to carry a dagger to the discos and I would pull it out and stick it to whatever unfortunate girl had agreed to dance with me. I would take them out in the middle of the night and just rub the cold razor-sharp blade up and down their quivering thighs in some dark corner as they begged me not to hurt them. I feel bad, and I don't know what I was thinking back then.

Tuesday, November 28th

On this day Patroba, myself, and another guy go to Malindi for prayers as commanded by the Lord the previous night. This other guy, called Amos, is a "born-again" guy and he was making plans to get married, and the Lord instructed him to go to Malindi with us. We did not go with Williams's car but with the car of another lady whom Patroba prays for. This woman's husband is in the States for studies, and he has been gone for like three months now. She has been letting Patroba use their cars to go on these trips, because she thought it was a way of helping the Ministry of God through Patroba. Anyway, the trip to Malindi is fine, we get there and say the prayers. And as usual the Lord has something to say to me regarding my parents. On this day I had pains in my chest and I asked this guy what could be the matter, and he had a ready answer. The pain was in fact a result of my mother's witchcraft. The guy laid his hand on me and went haywire with the xenoglossia.

But on our way to Mombasa we got into an accident. The car we were in rammed into another car and our car got badly damaged: a burst radiator and other shit in the bonnet [hood]. Patroba was pretty shaken by this. We all were. The guy whose car we rammed wanted his car repaired by us and there was some agreement on that.

Patroba looks lost, because he knows we are asking ourselves why the Lord did not show him this accident was about to happen. During the usual evening prayers, the Lord gives us the reason for the accident. The Lord says that this woman who was letting Patroba use her cars is not doing it wholeheartedly because her husband is not a "born-again" guy. Another person blamed for this accident was the driver, who happened to be Patroba's first cousin. According to the Lord, this guy had received curses from his father because he was not getting along with his parents. They had some unmentioned bitterness against their son. Others blamed for the accident were Patroba's spiritual rivals. The Lord said that they were envious of Patroba's spiritual gift. It was claimed by the Lord that they were praying against Patroba's gift and they wanted him dead. Later Patroba told us that before someone acquired wealth they had to make some sacrifices. This was in reference to this woman who had given out the car. He said that this was a minor hitch on our part.

These were the most absurd statements to have come out of this guy's mouth, but for some reason we did not question his "wisdom." Several days earlier, Olympia, Patroba's wife, told me that she had complained about her husband using this woman's cars to go on these frequent trips. When these cars were not available, the guy would just sit around the house saying the Lord wanted him to relax, but as soon as this woman availed her cars to this guy, he was always on the move. She told me that when she suggested that her husband stop using these cars, Patroba started speaking to her in tongues and told her that the Lord wanted her to tell him when Patroba was going to start having fun.

Tuesday, December 5th

While praying, the Lord mentions a sheep that I had taken to Patroba some five years ago. This was a gift from my mother to Patroba, but now I was being told that this sheep was for "blinding" Patroba to the real nature of my mother. She did not want the guy to see her witchcraft, thus the sheep was meant to make him feel that she was a nice person. The food that this guy ate in our home was to make him "blind" to the true nature of mother. He says that my mother poisoned this woman, Mrs. Mwabili. He tells me to continue praying, since I had washed my hands at Timbila. He also warned me against Jane, Patroba's sister-in-law, saying that she was a person who liked to inspect people, a nosey person in short. He also said my life was not always going to be the way it was, you know, no money, no job and shit like that. He said he was going to give me a job when the time was right for Him to do so. He insisted that I should not mention what he has told me about my parents to them at all. Never.

Friday, December 8th

While praying, the Lord tells me through his usual mouthpiece Patroba that I should start witnessing to people. Just wake up one morning and stop everyone I met on the road and tell them something like, "I am called Ngeti and Jesus is Lord and Savior of my life. I am going to heaven, I have been forgiven my sins and am a man of God. I have been washed in the blood of the lamb. I love Jesus very much. I am passing though many things, but I don't look astray. I am fixed on the cross of Jesus. Satan has no power over my life." People give witness, according to Pentecostal teachers, the first few months after they are saved. This is to saturate their subconscious minds with this newfound situation in their lives. I believed I was past this stage. Why was God telling me to do it?

Wednesday, December 13th

The Lord tells me that my folks have left their witchcraft and it is in the shamba [fields], in the *nyika* [plains]. He says that this witchcraft is no longer effective because its "chair, its stool and support," that is me, have been liberated from its suffocating and oppressive power by the blood of Jesus fucking Christ. The Lord tells me to forgive them and go see them.

I went, as the Lord requested, to buy cow intestines and bananas for the old folks. This ritual was to bring me blessings from these guys, because they had refused to bless me. The Lord was going to take their blessings and give them to me. I did buy these intestines and bananas. The strangest thing, though, is, the more I performed these rituals, the more things got bad for me, while Patroba was progressing. It was like he was magically stealing something from me!

Monday, December 18th

It is almost X-mass and I'm feeling like shit. I feel very low. Am depressed, badly depressed. Am full of questions about this God who seems to be doing fucking nothing for me. I decide to tell Patroba that I am not going to Taita for X-mass. I can feel the guy is not happy with this report because, for like two weeks he had been telling us that the Lord wanted all of us to go to Taita for X-mass. I did not give a fuck. I had made up my mind I was not going and that was it. We prayed and, surprisingly, the Lord said nothing. Later William tried talking me into going, but I remained adamant. To me there was nothing to celebrate. Patroba's wife was also not for the idea of going, and her reason was she did not want her husband taking the cars again. William had bought a car at this time, but his car was so small it could not carry all the guys and the entire luggage, so the Lord said that they should take that lady's pick-up truck, which they did. When Patroba's wife expressed her concern, God talked her down and she fell sick overnight. Later she told me that, when they prayed, the Lord asked her why she was resisting His will. Nothing happened to me, though, but I became increasingly depressed.

The guys leave for Taita without me on the 23rd and they come back on the 26th.

Friday, December 29th

We pray and the Lord says nothing. Of late He had been saying nothing at all and I concluded that Patroba was still angry that I had refused to go to Taita. I started wondering why it would have been so important for me to go when I was not in the mood. I know the guy felt bad that I had defied him and his messages. I think he could feel I was beginning to question this God that spoke through him.

Tuesday, January 2nd

My sister comes in from Taita. I decide to violate Patroba's will and tell her all what the Lord has been saying concerning the old folks. She is shocked. I told her I did not want anything to do with my parents—they had screwed up my life so bad I did not think I was gonna forgive them. I still believed that these people were witches. As long as I was still jobless and not married I believed they were the reason for this and they were directly responsible.

On this day Sis had brought us some corn from home. When she was gone we prayed, and the Lord said that we should throw away the corn because it was full of demons. The corn was thrown away.

Wednesday, January 3rd

I informed Patroba about my decision to tell my sister what the Lord had been telling about my folks. The guy looks disturbed. He tells me I should not have done that. He said he had plans to woo Mother down to Mombasa so he could take her to Kwale for prayers, where she would confess her witchcraft. The guy is not happy. He goes into his bedroom and stays there for like one hour. I wonder what he was doing?

Saturday, January 6th

I am so depressed. The world feels so small, as if I could straddle it and shit down its windpipe. At night, while praying, I launch into unexpected xenoglossia. Then suddenly the Lord speaks through Patroba's wife and addresses me, in Swahili: "Ngeti, I do not want your noise!"

Wednesday, January 17th

My father comes to Mombasa to make peace with Patroba. While praying the Lord tells the old man, in Swahili, "All right, all right, there is no curse on you, Charles, the business is not dead . . . Monica (my mother) should stop being the chairlady of Mchana village. She should remove that picture of Yusufu (this was some Swahili guy in Mombasa who was a bush doctor whom my father used to consult and they became good friends and he would bail out my father with money). Charles, welcome Patroba to your home. Ngeti will marry when you are still alive. Do not be afraid to go say hallo to the in-laws. Patroba, give the old man some little food . . . (meaning some money)."

The following day Patroba gives the old man eight thousand shillings [roughly $100], but I can tell he's not happy about it. Also, he tells me that William had a lot of money in the bank, but he did not understand why the guy was not doing anything. Patroba tells me he is not happy with the way William is handling the situation.

Saturday, January 27th

Went for prayers and the Lord tells me, "You should involve your parents in your marriage plans and I will do a miracle. I have cleaned your homestead, it is a new homestead now. They have left their things (meaning their witchcraft). Believe it or not it is I the Lord." I do not say anything, but I feel like shit, I have a feeling this guy does not like me anymore and he wants to kick me out and send me back to Taita. The messages are coming from his head. But I am confused, I do not know what to believe. I think I am too depressed to be rational. The world is full of enemies and I am still seething inside with anger toward my parents for wrecking my life, and I am pissed at God for being such a slow actor. Yet I keep on hoping that maybe someday things will turn out fine.

Friday, February 16th

I chatted with Patroba's wife, Olympia, and she suggests that I tell William that I want to go back to Taita, since whatever plans I had come for to Mombasa were not materializing. She is quick to tell me that I should not feel like she was forcing me into this idea. I had a feeling she had discussed this with her husband but the guy did not have the guts to tell me this. I had seen this day coming, of these guys getting rid of me. Personally I doubted if there was any matatu business plan from the beginning.

Sunday, February 18th

The Lord said that my old man fooled Patroba when he came to Mombasa and that he did not come with good intentions. He said that the family is saying in their hearts that Patroba spent a lot of their money and it was time that Patroba started repaying them. The Lord says that the money that Patroba gave the old man when he came to Mombasa was payment for the timber and other building material that my family had given this guy when he was building his house. I remember my mother had given this guy a lot of timber for the roofing of his house, and I also recall spending like the whole day painting this timber with some chemical to keep it from getting eaten by termites. This was close to ten years earlier. In short, our family had done a lot for this guy, and to see how things were in the family after all of this work was devastating. When I think of it now, I think we were taken advantage of because of our own greed.

Monday, March 12th

We pray and I try to explain to Patroba why I had not felt like going to Taita at Christmas. But the guy just sits there flipping through the Bible like I was not addressing him. I knew he was trying to make me feel guilty for defying him by not going to Taita with them at Christmas. I tell the guy I feel bad about eating in his house day in and day out, that I have a gut feeling that they do not like it. Patroba says he had no idea that the Lord would turn around and make an issue out of my not going to Taita for X-mass. The guy tells me that his wife keeps nagging him about me and that his mother asked him to tell me to leave so that I could create room for his brothers to come and stay with him. These were blatant lies but there was nothing I could do. I did not want to go to Taita because of my parents' witchcraft. There was nothing for me in Taita. I was in a fix. I was between a rock and a fucking hard place.

The Lord tells me, through Patroba, when praying, in Swahili, "Your father is the biggest witch of your plans and life. Do not forget what I told you. He must die first before you succeed. But I will look into this thing. My hand will guide you. When you were young you went and acted the way you liked, but now, listen to me, listen to my servant. His spiritual gift is very fierce. Mama Esther died because she used to say that Patroba is a liar. Eat the food, you walked on rocks with my servant. Look for a job. Go to your sisters and they will help you."

Tuesday, March 13th

In the evening while praying, the Lord tells Patroba to give me fare for my Taita trip. He said that I was blocking Patroba's blessings by continuing to stay in Mombasa.

Wednesday, March 15th

In the evening, while praying, the Lord tells me, "Ngeti, make haste and go to Taita so I can finish with your father [meaning kill him]. You have your things to do and I have mine."

So here God is saying he wants to kill my dad, and this promise is what God and Patroba are using to get me to go home. He was also saying that he murdered people who didn't listen to Patroba, which could have been a threat on my life.

Earlier in the day Patroba had given me a thousand shillings [roughly $13] in front of his wife, something I took to mean that he was showing his wife that he was finally getting rid of me and they do not need me anymore.

Thursday, March 16th

On this day I leave Mombasa for Taita. Little did I know that this was the last day that I would ever see Patroba alive. The next time that I saw him, he was in a coffin. I still believed that he was the servant of God. But after reading this diary years after his death, I have come to conclude that the guy was just full of shit and that I was stupid to have believed everything that he said in the name of God.

Over the years I have thought maybe the guy had jinnis, just like the other men of God who we heard were going to the devil to get powers to perform miracles and oppress people and close their minds to reason. They used these powers to have people follow them without question. They had a reason for every hard time that a guy went through. And it was always about witchcraft in the family, or some curse from the ancestors, some sin that was committed by grandparents, and God was revisiting this sin. There was always an envious neighbor trying to retard your "*maendeleo*" (development) and blocking your blessing. The men of God of the late 80s and early 90s were just like the witchdoctors of the 70s and before, when our parents would spend sleepless nights listening for footsteps outside their homes. Our parents had gone to healers who were dressed like they were going to a Halloween costume party, and now they and their kids were going to healers who wore designer clothes and held shiny Bibles in the place of sooty pots, calabashes, and skulls and crossbones. It is a vicious circle.

Many a time I have said if he were alive today, I would have ripped off Patroba's fucking balls and fed them to the dogs. Am I angry? Yes, I am angry. I have lost faith in God and I think that is good, for I feel more liberated by this newfound freedom of the spirit. Anyway, shit happens, but one thing I know is this: I have no time for any kind of God. If there is hell, then I have made up my mind to go there. No apologies.

A few years before writing this diary, Ngeti had felt the presence of God in church, and it had moved him to the point of tears. God had seized Ngeti and spoken through him in an alien language that shook and changed him, so he knew what it was like to experience God as an entity that was not only real, but actually inside of him, and yet also distinct from him. He understood what it was like to feel himself as an alien person whose voice and body belonged to Someone Else, and to wonder what this power was and from where it came. Later, reflecting on this experience, he thought maybe it was guilt for all the things he had done, coupled with the desire to belong, "which religion offers up on a silver fucking platter." It is clear from his recollections that this powerful feeling had something to do with the experience of being surrounded by the emotional outpourings of others and the empathy this engendered. He had to watch others experience God and speak in tongues before he could do so.

In *When God Talks Back,* a book about how American evangelicals learn to recognize and experience the presence of God in their lives, Tanya Luhrmann recounts the various everyday rituals that evangelicals perform in order to ready themselves for God's presence.[1] The evangelicals at the Chicago church where Luhrmann conducted her research understood God's presence as friendly and supportive, and they actively prepared themselves, and their minds, for God's communications, learning to discern the voice of God from the nearly endless stream of thoughts and impressions that came to them on a daily basis. Much as Ngeti established a relationship with the world beyond

Kenya by "pretending" to know English as a small boy, and thereby developing a "soft spot" for this remote and powerful language, so too did these Chicago evangelicals ready themselves for "pretend" dates with God by performing such mundane acts as, for example, making sandwiches. Like the child Ngeti, they readied their minds and bodies for a particular kind of experience, which Luhrmann understands as being more real than "real," rather than an illusion or mistake. The kind of relationship that Luhrmann's evangelicals want to develop with God is similar to the kind of relationship Ngeti wanted to develop, first with the faraway world of the Wazungu, and later with God.

Like the God described by Luhrmann, the God that spoke to Ngeti was interested in his daily affairs, in his life, and in him. It is easy to understand why Ngeti would be interested in a God like this, after having experienced Him through the Catholic priests who acted as intermediaries during his youth. As he once put it to me, why should he care about the God of priests who had a habit of getting drunk in the bars and running after young local girls, only to finally leave town on the backs of the very motorcycles that the community had bought for them? So, Ngeti wanted an intimate God that he could connect to, like his evangelical counterparts in Chicago.

Unlike the God experienced by the Chicago evangelicals, however, Ngeti's God was never exactly a supportive friend. Rather, He was a powerful and demanding taskmaster who wanted to separate Ngeti from his destructive practices and from the hold of the past. This God was jealous and seemed to want proof that Ngeti was loyal to Him above all else. Perhaps this is because a friendly, convivial God was less promising than a God capable of ordering another reality into existence, who could vanquish the false idols of a generation past and bring forth a new era in which one's work actually paid off as wealth and respectability. What was needed was a power that could transform reality, in the way that most understood Christianity to have done in the past, when it turned people away from darkness and toward light, before it was sullied by Kenya's kleptocratic elite and by Kenyans themselves.

Even if the Pentecostals Ngeti knew were looking for a more heavy-handed and forceful God, capable of moving ancient mountains, there was a big difference between the way Ngeti experienced God when he was in church and the way he experienced Him under Patroba. In church, there was inspirational movement and the sharing of painful but liberating emotions, as well as undertones of mystery and sexuality. But under Patroba, Ngeti was asked to remain in a state of perpetual apprenticeship; his job there was not to talk and share, but to listen, obey, and wait. In fact, when he tried to connect with God directly by allowing His voice to speak through him in xenoglossia, God spoke through Patroba's wife, in Patroba's absence, and told Ngeti to shut up, referring to his words as "noise" rather than divine language. Here we have a divine tug of war between two manifestations of God sitting together at cross-purposes at the same table, one inside of Ngeti, and one outside of him. In short, there is a direct conflict between the idea of God that Ngeti was attracted to and the one that Patroba and those around him promoted: Ngeti was open to a God who was available to anyone who could hear Him, but Patroba, and those who extolled him, suggested that God played favorites. Not only did He pursue relationships with particular individuals, but He tended to cultivate relationships within particular families. And so God seemed to submit to human social conventions—passing from a man to his wife, for example—rather than making His own rules.

For a while, Patroba did a decent job of managing Ngeti's experience of time while they all waited for William to cough up the money for the matatu business. He engineered miracles and messages from God in such a way as to nurture hope in Ngeti while minimizing disappointment in the face of tedium. But eventually Ngeti had had enough. Somewhere along the line God had changed. No longer a transcendent divine, confident and patient, He had become shrill, venal, and boastful, a narcissistic spiritual bully preoccupied with very particular memories and resentments. For Ngeti, this God was, like a Taita ancestral spirit, interested in Ngeti's personal life for reasons that seemed to have less to do with him than with God's own self-aggrandizement. No longer a living presence inside him, God had become the very kind of spiritual power from which Ngeti had been working to escape. As Ngeti came to doubt Patroba's messages, his quixotic rituals, and his peripatetic journeys, he eventually found himself staring into the face of a vulnerable, perhaps even pathological, man. God in turn lashed out with angry and opaque exhortations that began to make Him look sillier still.

When Patroba presented himself as the mouthpiece of God or even as God walking on earth, he was taking on a hefty risk, because it meant that all of Patroba's actions, especially his mistakes and slip-ups, would be critically read and evaluated as evidence that God did not actually speak through him. Interestingly, this is exactly the kind of danger that African politicians expose themselves to when they claim that they embody the state or when they take on powers that verge on the celestial. In this way, such "big men" have accrued all of the blame for happenings that were not always their fault—from declining world prices for particular commodities to the traumatic impacts of structural adjustment programs. The comparison is not arbitrary: in a sense, Patroba was channeling the authority of an earlier generation of political big men who had lost respect and value in a time when they had very little to offer. Political life, and with it the ideal of the strong masculine political leader, had been irreparably damaged, but religion provide a space for this model of masculine moral authority to flourish once more.

Patroba's assumption of such awesome power leads to similar kinds of quandaries, as when Ngeti asks why car accidents are happening when Patroba should be able to see them beforehand. As Ngeti got to know Patroba better, he inevitably came to see him as human: Patroba cried when his mother was sick, liked availing himself of a free car, and became petulant when his sister-in-law wouldn't take car of his dogs. This doubt was engendered by Ngeti's new relationship to God under Patroba, in which God was synonymous with a person who was not Ngeti (i.e., Patroba), rather than being a force that could be inside Ngeti. Interestingly, as Ngeti grew more dubious, Patroba tried to recreate the original experiences that brought Ngeti to Pentecostalism in the first place, by instructing him to go out and testify to people on the street, for example, so that he might feel God inside himself again. Even Patroba knew that, for God to be compelling to the practitioner, she or he needed to feel Him on the inside, at least from time to time.

Patroba's alleged powers would not have been believable if they were not naturalized through daily tasks and work. Much of the work that Ngeti and Patroba engaged in was aimed at severing attachments to the past and conjuring up a new set of attachments that were ordained by God (the words Ngeti uses for this are "tying" and "untying"). So Ngeti is asked to cut himself off from his mother and father and from other people back home who carry past resentments in their hearts, at the same time as prayer forges relationships and networks with new people, often from faraway places. God does not want the tradition of Mtongolo, Patroba's father-in-law—that is, the practice of Catholicism, which Ngeti and Patroba now see as a retrograde tradition of old men. Prayer is intended to generate fruitful relationships with William, with me, with NGOs, and with computer education schools, and these new, generative relationships are somehow conditional upon the destruction of the old, deleterious relationships or networks. Through prayer, Ngeti can disconnect himself from his parents' curses, even if some of the prayers he performs seem to conjure up the ghost of non-Christian Taita ritual, and so the Taita past. This concern over network creation and destruction carries over into things like everyday commodity purchases, as when God helps Ngeti and William to discern which commodities are associated with evil social networks, and which are not. The Indian car dealer and Alcatel are good, but other constellations of things and people might not be—and when you're trying to remake yourself by connecting with a globalized world that is outside of you, making the right consumer choices is of paramount importance.

Birthing these networks through prayer and social collaboration, even if only by eating roast meat together in the railway town of Voi, is seen as crucially important, even more important than "work" in the conventional sense of the word. Thus it is that God/Patroba advises Ngeti to wait for me to come back from the States with a good opportunity, and asks him where it is written that people should work to eat. Ngeti later reads this question as evidence that Patroba was confused, since the God of the Bible clearly says that you must work to eat, but Patroba was probably also reflecting on the consequences of diminished opportunities in jobs that were once coveted by men like Ngeti. Wage labor has dried up, and so "work" in the way that Ngeti's parents knew it was not sufficient to fill one's stomach, and it was also not required. After all, some were making fortunes by establishing CBOs (community-based organizations) and NGOs, and using their positions to write funding proposals to agencies in the United States and elsewhere. Patroba was conditioning Ngeti to a new kind of economy and encouraging him to go into business with his newfound Pentecostal social network.

The acquisition of the car seemed to aid in their work of network creation—allowing them to travel to sever old ties through prayer and to meet with others more quickly. But all of this world creation and destruction didn't seem to be as earth-shatteringly transformative as Ngeti had hoped. In fact, the car made Ngeti doubt Patroba ever more, as the accelerated space-time of their actions—doing more spiritual things at a faster rate over larger distances—came to be at increasingly absurd odds with the product of their work. Which seemed, at the end of the day, to be nothing at all. It is not hard to make a parallel between, on the one hand, the post-Fordist efforts of Patroba to create a successful future in lieu of older methods like Catholicism and wage labor and, on the other, the rhetoric of neoliberal economists at the World Bank, who hoped that by destroying the public sector they would magically open up opportunities in the private sector. Instead, the civil service bureaucracies they helped to downsize left people broke and unemployed, with no discernible options. In the same way, God/Patroba's work of disconnecting Ngeti from historic connections to people and places seemed as radical as the short, sharp shock of structural adjustment, but they left Ngeti with more pain than promise. And, like those civil servants who found themselves unemployed, Ngeti found himself waiting for a rebound far longer than he had expected.

This interest in creating and severing ties comes to light in concerns over birth and birthing as well as death: some things from the past have to die in order to give birth to a new future. Many of the daily rituals force Ngeti to divest himself of attachments and emotions from the past, such as the knife that he used to rub against girls' thighs at the disco. He also has to go to places where "sins" were committed in the past, even when these sins were not committed by him, so that these actions will not continue to influence his present and future. They go to where his father lived in Mombasa and pray over the fact that his mother touched his private parts and his uncle wanted to poison him. And of course they pray over the poisoned ground of Ngeti's home back in Taita, over the old tree with deep historic roots that go back to the time of King David, and over the gifts that may still bear the trace of past sins and conflicts—like corn from his sister. And they work to give birth to new businesses, new marriages, new educational opportunities, new relationships, and new selves. Sometimes all of this birth and death work can become explicitly violent, as when it is revealed that certain people—like Mrs. Mwabili, Mama Esther, and Ngeti's father, Charles—might have to die if Patroba and Ngeti are to finally give birth to a new world.

The emphasis on birth and death takes many forms. For example, Patroba suggests that in his daughter's teeth one can find evidence for his ability to birth a new world, and so avoid a death that would be certain if one adhered to the practices of the past. Patroba's daughter had what is described as plastic teeth (*meno ya plastic* in Swahili) and should have died, but instead she lived. Though extremely brief, this is one of the most ethnographically interesting episodes in the diary, and it needs a little background. Plastic teeth disease is a relatively recent regional affliction that affects infants and young children. Paralleling the spread of AIDS, it demonstrates symptoms, such as diarrhea and wasting, that are similar. The child who suffers from the disease is born with fully formed "plastic" teeth, which, if extracted, appear to move as if they were alive. The disease renders eating almost impossible and is fatal if not treated by a specialist. In a sense, the child has been taken over by plastic, a substance that epitomizes, for many people in the region, the dislocating, dangerous, and dehumanizing potentials of contemporary life. The parents of a child born with this disease are often accused of having lost their moorings in local values and morality, having become seduced by foreign values, particularly money. They are often said to be "dirty people" who would gladly sacrifice their loved ones and neighbors for money or luxury commodities.

In a brilliant essay on plastic teeth affliction among the Haya, a Tanzanian ethnic group that is culturally, historically, and geographically very close to Wataita, Brad Weiss argues that this disease relates to Haya perceptions of the disruption of normative temporal processes resulting from rapid social change. Haya hold that teeth are supposed to develop at a predictable rate, and the emergence of teeth is linked to the process through which an infant becomes a social being, as teeth mediate between the person and the social world—most iconically, in the act of eating. But plastic teeth simply emerge ready-made before the child has gone through teething, and so the plastic teeth result in, and are symbolically equated with, abrogated socialization and related bodily wasting. As Weiss puts it, "In a time of increasing land fragmentation, a collapsing coffee market, incomprehensible currency devaluations, and growing rates of HIV seropositivity, the Haya experience an increasingly eclipsed capacity to control the forces that give their lives meaning."[2] For Weiss, plastic teeth symbolize these social and temporal processes, thus serving as indexes of larger social crises. For his part, Ngeti does not delve into these issues in his explanation of plastic teeth, observing simply that people who give birth to children with plastic teeth are said to be "bad" or "dirty" people. They are, in short, witches, or at least witchlike.

Patroba's life was radically different from that of most Taita males. Again, he had rejected patriarchal Taita custom to the extent of repudiating his own father, something that is supposed to bring untold misfortune. After all, his actions implied rejection of his entire patrilineage and his male ancestors. Patroba had also rejected the tradition of Catholicism, a fact that clearly upset Mtongolo, his wife's father, to whom he was supposed to be paying bridewealth. But strangely, not only did Patroba survive his revolutionary acts, but he visibly prospered. It is tempting to argue that the rumors that circulated about Patroba's daughter's plastic teeth reflected local attitudes about Patroba—that his rejection of Taita tradition had now revealed itself in this "modern" disease that also symbolized the negative dimensions of modern life. The fact that he calls his child an mzungu, or European, lends itself to this interpretation. But significantly, this was not simply a malicious rumor that circulated about Patroba; it was in fact a disease that Patroba took for granted as being real. Patroba knew that his daughter had plastic teeth and never once questioned the diagnosis.

What was important, for Patroba, was that his daughter did not die, even though he never went to a specialist. More than this, Patroba reinterpreted the very meaning of plastic teeth, while accepting that the disease was in fact a deadly epidemic. Patroba suggested that, rather than meaning he was "dirty" or a witch, these plastic teeth meant that he and his child were somehow special, for they had been granted a sacred task. God knew the reason for giving Patroba a child with plastic teeth, and He had allowed that child to live, thus showcasing to the world that it is possible to live with plastic teeth. Moreover, Patroba's manifest mobility and financial success did not diminish his morality. In other words, he could be a fast-paced modern subject who moved from place to place, had lots of money, rejected tradition, and had a child with plastic teeth, and he could still be okay—more than okay. God would allow Patroba, and all Wataita who followed in his path, to be outwardly modern, to reject aspects of Taita history, and to continue to be healthy, both physically and financially. They need not be afraid, so long as they were saved.

I think part of what Patroba was doing was seizing hold of the capacity to create the future by taking direct control over social production at a time when masculine virtue and value seemed threatened by larger structural transformations, including the decline of the state, the absence of sustainable employment, and the inability of men's wages to make ends meet. Patroba revitalized an older model of masculinity by developing male partnerships that resembled the blood brotherhood pacts of an earlier generation, when men became kin and business partners with one another through ritual. For Patroba, mastering the future meant intervening directly in gendered relations and the management of sexual activity. On the most prosaic level, Patroba tried to use ritual to turn Ngeti into a respectable adult male, by helping him to marry and get a job or an education. He did this in opposition to the alleged plans of Ngeti's mother, a woman who, according to Patroba, was working to steal the future from her son and make it her own. Building up Ngeti's masculine power meant minimizing the power of women (and older men) over Ngeti's life, and so Patroba instructed Ngeti not to spend too much time with women or allow them to control his life. And Patroba often demonized women and their power as being morally questionable, particularly in his discussions of Ngeti's mother, certain white women, and Mrs. Mwabili and Mama Esther.

But the story isn't so simple. At times, Patroba comes across as almost feminist, praying alongside women, sharing the voice of God with his wife, and seemingly admonishing Ngeti for his violent threats against girls in his teenage past. He instructs his own sister-in-law to transgress against gerontocratic male authority and to eat the testicles of a goat in order to escape a curse that her mother had inadvertently placed on her when she tried to control her sexuality prior to marriage. The injunction that the "repulsive" sister-in-law eat testicles violates long-held Taita understandings about who should eat what kinds of meat, but Patroba's practice implied that a direct line of communication with God meant the old rules and taboos need no longer apply. In fact, Patroba's enthusiasm for breaking gender norms seems to go too far for Ngeti, whose doubt is flamed by Patroba's wife taking on the role of God in prayer. Patroba didn't mainly want to control the power of women; rather, he wanted to assume power over how men and women related to one another, so that gendered relationships would no longer be the same. This usually meant channeling gendered relations into morally respectable structures, like marriage and childbirth, but it also could mean using divine power to rebirth the world at a quotidian level, beginning with gender and sexuality.

But despite all these rituals and rhetorics of death and rebirth, Ngeti was at an impasse and felt that the promise of radical change was again slipping through his fingers. Now, expelled from Mombasa, he was going to carry the logic of destruction and rebirth back to Taita to wage war on his own home.

SEVEN

A Confrontation

So we'd pray and Patroba would be like, "Well, Ngeti,
you're doubting God." Well fuck you, God! Why is it
taking you so long to do stuff?

NGETI

AND NOW WE ARRIVE, FINALLY, at the unfortunate climax to Ngeti's story, an event that allowed him to partially realize his dreams of independence while leaving him really alone for the first time in his life. Ngeti, fed up with empty promises from Patroba and goaded by his mentor's warning that confronting his parents meant death, decided to bring everything out in the open in the spirit of transparency. In defying God and social mores in this direct way, he put the transgressive spirit of Pentecostalism, democratic political reform, and his entire generation into action. If Ngeti was not cursed before, as he believed, it is quite possible that the goings-on described in this chapter accomplished the job, in that he has been left with a profound sense of guilt ever since.

In 2003, I received an email from Ngeti's sister informing me that Patroba had died and that Ngeti was in a tailspin. As far as Ngeti was concerned, this meant that all of his plans and his time spent working for Patroba and helping him to pray for people, had amounted to nothing. At this point, I knew that Ngeti had grown disillusioned with prayer, with Pentecostalism, and with Patroba. I also knew that Ngeti had come to believe that his mother might be a witch. But I didn't yet know that the preacher Patroba, Monica's one-time friend and spiritual colleague, had been directly involved in creating and fueling this belief, probably out of spite for Monica, who no longer prayed with him and who claimed that Patroba owed them money. Later, I received this email from Ngeti:

Hallo Rafiki! So on December 31st, 2002, I decided to be a very
Catholic guy and went and bought myself a bottle of wine ... or devil's

piss as we were told to call it at the church. What is to be will be so let it be, I told myself as I made the decision to leave behind this life that was a fucking lie through and through. I have decided to let go this illusion of heaven and liberate the noosphere from the biosphere. I am human and if God had meant me to be anything else, that is what I would have been. Anyway, if the first white missionaries who came to Africa had been believers of some interplanetary monster god, other than the god they came with, then we would have toed the line and believed in this god.

Anyway, I started to wonder why this god who we read in the Bible is the creator of all, who is not partial and who loves all people equally, would choose to tell some people, like Patroba, shit about other people, like me. I have watched myself and others go to church from January to January expecting to grow "spiritually," as it is written in the Bible, but nothing ever happened. Every Sunday we would be told that God was going to do some wonderful things in our lives beyond our wildest dreams, that whatever tribulation we were going thru, it was for our own sake, for we were getting refined by God. We had a great reward in heaven, our tears were gonna be turned into Pepsi Cola or some other nice thing that we could not afford on earth . . .

I was very determined to bring sense into my life, so I visited this Lunga-Lunga town where I had been taken to "be tied" by the bush doctors so that I could not be bewitched. The purpose of this trip, which I made with my brother-in-law and his praying cousin, a prophet-ess of some renown, was catharsis. I wanted to see the place that had brought me so much suffering. I wanted to confront the demons and tell them to go fuck themselves. I was a child of God and they had no frigging right to mess around with my life.

Anyways, now I have decided in my heart that this salvation thing is all bullshit. I am more influenced by you now. I recall those times that you would sit with these people up in Taita and sip *bangara* [home-made sugarcane beer] with them, not giving a hoot whether the God in the clouds cared or not. You had your things that you had to do, things that you did not have time to explain to God because He wouldn't care anyway. Anyways, these days I'm thinking about becoming a devil worshipper. Who knows, Jimmy. When you come back here again, I think you'll find me a very rich man. *Rafiki yako*, Ngeti

I went back to Kenya in the summer of 2003, eager to see Ngeti and his family. Ngeti and I met in Nairobi and, before going to Taita, did some research together in rural western Kenya, among Luo people in a remote village named Wasare that was facing extinction due to a hydroelectric dam project bringing electricity to the nearby city of Kisumu. The people of

Wasare had recently been visited by a nineteenth-century ancestress named Omieri, who appeared to them in the form of a twenty-foot python. The appearance of Omieri had divided the entire region, and even the nation, on spiritual and ideological grounds. What exactly was this python? Was it truly a returned ancestress (as many people believed)? Was it perhaps the physical incarnation of the devil? Or was it simply a python? A local NGO composed of Luo academics and unemployed former civil servants tried to get the most of all worlds: they wanted to use what they called the "Omieri python," which they held to be an ancestor and a python, to obtain money from the government and foreign donors. Their plan was to build a snake park to protect Omieri and other wildlife, while bringing in tourist revenue instead of rain. The revenue stream would be proof that Omieri was really a local totemic resource and a source of collective pride and prosperity.

But a Luo Anglican archbishop had read in the newspaper about this community that "worshiped" a snake, Satan's well-known emissary, and threatened to go to the town, pour gasoline on Omieri, and set her on fire. When local male youths learned of his intention, they formed an impromptu militia and declared that they would fight to the death to protect their rains. Meanwhile, a local Luo herpetologist tried to convince everyone that the snake was just a snake—to no avail. (In all honesty, his arguments didn't even win *me* over.) But even those who believed the python was their ancestress disagreed as to how it should be dealt with: some wanted to use Omieri to generate commerce, while others thought placing Omieri in a park would be like imprisoning her and could lead to bad fortune. They felt that it was not good to make a profit from Omieri. Some felt that Omieri was supposed to help women, while others, especially men, disagreed and saw Omieri as a symbol of masculine authority, arguing that a senior man had turned this woman into a python as a curse for her incestuous relationship with her husband's brother. Eventually, Omieri left of her own accord, but only after another dam broke and drowned out the town, leaving people to wonder why this sequence of events had occurred and what it all meant.

The conflict surrounding Omieri, and all of the work that went into lifting her up and bringing her down, both augmented her importance and made her a cipher for the Luo community in general and for all of its concerns (which is not to say that Omieri was not also an ancestor). It reminded me of how the ritual work that went into healing Ngeti helped to convince him that he was bewitched, thus conferring substance to Ngeti's concerns and a kind of sacrality to his life. Ngeti, a "foreigner" in Luoland, thought the inflated sense of hope and danger surrounding Omieri was absurd, even when he took into account the new hydroelectric dam that threatened to wipe out the community and its wildlife, "Omieris" included. But I sometimes found it equally absurd that he had no problem believing that every event in his life was exploding with cosmological significance. It sometimes seemed to me that Pentecostalism had goaded his sense of self-importance, making Ngeti's biography seem more cosmically significant than it actually was.

When we were done researching the Omieri situation, Ngeti and I took a bus to the Taita Hills. It was the first time he had been home in over a year. As far as I had known, Ngeti had always gotten on extremely well with his parents and really looked up to his mother, and so Ngeti's recent reversal in thought was still difficult for me to comprehend. When we finally arrived in Mgange, Ngeti's mother, Monica, was uncharacteristically cool. She looked sad and hurt, and she greeted us without much warmth. Ngeti quickly went into the sitting room to talk with his parents, while I made a fast retreat to Ngeti's room, on what had become his side of the house. I could hear them from across the compound, Monica angrily wondering how Ngeti could have believed the things he'd said. She just couldn't understand what she could ever have done to Ngeti to deserve the treatment he had meted out on her.

Ngeti was mostly quiet. I heard Charles, his father, saying that all of this was Patroba's fault, adding that this false preacher, this man of the devil, wanted to sow discord in the family so that he might profit from it, like a parasitic bird. I remember thinking that Patroba was an unfairly easy target, seeing as he was dead. After some time, Monica burst into the room where I was waiting. Clearly upset, she put her hands on my head and intoned, "Jimmy, your paths are clear!," a phrase meant to imply that there was nothing in Monica's heart that was binding me or holding me back from anything I wanted in life. I thanked her dumbly, but, despite all my warm feelings for Monica, one worrisome thought did enter my head: "If she is opening my ways now, were they closed before, and if so, who closed them?" Was it that Ngeti's paranoia was becoming contagious, or was there something in the small ritual performance itself, and perhaps in all ritual performances, that produced ambivalence, a sense that something powerful was being concealed and revealed all at once?

Monica left the room, and after a time Ngeti's father, Charles, came in along with Ngeti, and the three of us chatted for a while over sweetened tea about life in the U.S. and in Nairobi. Charles asked about my own parents, who were beginning to struggle with old age, and he urged me to bring them to Taita, which, unfortunately, I never did. It was clear to me that Charles wanted things in the family to get better and for Ngeti's relationship with his mother to improve. The two of them were being especially congenial and respectful toward each other. But Ngeti and I didn't stay the night. Instead, we made our way on foot down the hill to the larger town of Wundanyi, and when we arrived I bought us Tusker beers and roast goat meat with plenty of hot chilis on the side. I urged Ngeti to fill in the blanks that were left open in this narrative. How had he arrived at this point with his parents? Ngeti set about telling me his story, and I pulled out my tape recorder; as we talked we moved back and forth between Kiswahili, Kidawida (or Kitaita), and English—all of which I have rendered here in English.

Ngeti narrated his recent falling-out with his parents. He told me about the diviners, and about Lunga-Lunga, in painstaking detail, then moved on to Patroba's warnings about his parents and the ensuing conflict between Patroba and his parents. Along the way, he threw up a host of other conflicts and issues—this mother's brother's or that father's brother's concern about his mother, various speculations about the occult underpinning of his sisters' poor romantic choices, and so on.

I interjected. "But Patroba was the first person to bring all this up about your mother, right? What made you listen to him?"

"Well, I believed in him and he was my friend. But in the beginning I did find it hard to believe." Ngeti responded between bites of roast goat. "But then one day my mother scared me when I went home from Mombasa. The old man, my father, was there, and Mother was there. They had called this meeting to discuss things. The family was going down, you know. There was no money. It was just the three of us, we're sitting there, and they start telling me, 'Okay, you've been going to this guy Patroba, and he's not a good guy. He's been praying for the family, and it has become poor.' You see? They thought Patroba was bewitching us. There were some rituals we used to perform in the family with Patroba. He'd come around and say, 'Okay, the Lord says you should kill a goat to cleanse the homestead,' and there was that particular time when you were here and we did it back in '98. Remember?"

"Yeah, I remember," I said. "We ate blood sausage. It was delicious."

"Anyway, my mother says, 'Don't go to this guy anymore. He is a devil worshiper.' She started doubting him because we weren't getting good things from the Lord. Because Patroba kept telling us that the Lord said we were going to be okay, and we weren't okay. And Mother also said that she talked to God in her dreams, and God told her that this was not a good guy."

"So how did you take this?" I asked.

"So, I was like, 'Okay, you guys have your own problems with this guy, but they're not my problems. I'm not going to involve myself with your problems.' So at this particular moment, Mother leaves the kitchen, I don't know where she went, and later on she comes back, and there is this feeling of a presence or force, and I realized that something is not right here. I felt this wave of cold, there were goose pimples all over me. This goes on for a long minute, everything is disoriented in the room. And I said, 'Okay, there's no way you're going to tell me that just because the family is broke, Patroba is responsible.' And you know, how do I know Mother is clean? Mother has also been recruited, like me, into these groups that call themselves Prayer Warriors. They go and pray in Mombasa. She used to go with Patroba and this other woman, Mrs. Mwabili, who died mysteriously, and back then there was talk that either Patroba or my mother might have killed this woman. You know, with these Pentecostal prayer groups, it's hard to tell what they are doing. And you know, how they were converted. All the miracles they used to receive, the healings in their body. No one really knows what that is. And in the back of my head, I have these stories, like, 'Oh, I've also been told that you guys are not good. Okay, I'll move along with these guys, but someday I'll know the truth of what's happening.'"

"So, can you explain the cold you were feeling? What did you think that was? Were you just nervous because you were defying your parents?"

"I thought maybe these were majini," Ngeti responded. "And from then on in they were upset with me because I keep going to this guy they've lost faith in, and they attribute their bankruptcy to his promises. They believed that this guy was doing the opposite of what he said he was doing. They can't understand why I don't come around, so they think that by threatening me with curses, I'll come around."

So Ngeti rebelled against his parents and went to Mombasa to be with Patroba, at the very same time that William was seeking spiritual help for his new business venture: the matatu business. Ngeti filled me in on this business, and how frustrating it was that things never came to fruition. Patroba blamed the delays on Ngeti's parents, but Ngeti grew tired of all the mixed messages from God, to say nothing of the waiting. In particular, he never understood why he had to go to specific places to pray, if in fact God was everywhere. The idea of going to particular locations struck Ngeti as somehow demonic, partly because Pentecostals equate an overt concern with locality and history with "traditional" culture and, by extension, devil worship. The universal God is supposed to transcend specific histories—this was one of the reasons why the Luo Anglicans had wanted to kill Omieri.

"I think these may be specific places for demons," Ngeti said. "You see, the city of Malindi has a long history of rituals—rituals of people being killed or disappearing. And it's actually always by the edge of the sea that we'd go to pray [majini are believed to come from the sea]. We don't go to someone's house, we just go to the sea, we pray for five minutes, and then we go back. Very short trips, actually. God was always like, 'I remove this curse because you went to Kilifi,' or 'I remove this curse because you went to Kwale.'"

"And you started wondering, why the fuck does God care if you're in Kilifi?" I added.

"Yeah! I mean, God is supposed to be everywhere, but now he wants me to be in Kilifi to get rid of some imaginary curse! But, you know, I'm not telling anyone. I'm stringing them along, but I have my doubts, and I want to see where it goes. Okay, he would pray, and I'm really pissed, and inside I'm saying, 'Fuck God and his promises!' It's taking too long for God to come through with his promises, you know? So we'd pray and this guy would be like, 'Well, Ngeti, you're doubting God.' And I'm like, 'Whew! Ai! How does this guy know?' You know, he says, 'you're doubting God, you think God is taking too long to answer you,' you know. [Laughs]. It knocks me off, you know? I think, 'Mmm . . . so God actually knows what I'm thinking about, huh? Well, fuck you, God! Why is it taking you so long to do stuff?! I'm rebellious! I don't give a shit if You do Your worst to me or not. I'm a man of few days, God, and I'm not going to live forever!'"

"So you confronted your parents?" I asked.

"Yes, because I wanted to find out if I'd die or not. Patroba had said that if I confront my parents with these stories, we'd both die. So I decided to tell them. I was taking my life in my own hands for once. My life was making no sense to me at all, yet here I was praying more than John the Baptist himself, and nothing meaningful happening. All I ever heard from this God was shit like, 'In my own sweet time I will do this and that for you, Ngeti.' I had been listening to this bullshit for the last ten years or so. Ten years, more than ten, believing and worshiping a God who is not clearly perceived, but seen through a fucking frosted glass of doctrines and dogmas! I had concluded that I was the living dead, in that I was not making any progress, not being married and having no money. In very simple language, I was as good as dead already. So I decided to talk to my paternal uncle, my father's brother, about what Patroba had told me. Even though I was starting to doubt Patroba, I somehow believed in his messages about my parents."

Ngeti pushed his plate away, pulled a lone Sportsman cigarette from his shirt pocket, struggled for a while with some damp matches, and began to smoke. "When I got back to Taita, I told this uncle how God had spoken to me concerning my mother's witchcraft, which she had inherited from her father, and that she had decided to use me as a 'chair' to strengthen this witchcraft. I told him the Lord had told me that, when they took me to Lunga-Lunga back in the 80s, they took me there so they could mess up my life, and not to help me as they had made me believe. You know what he told me, Jimmy? That they had known all along that my mother was a witch, but they had not told me because they were not sure how I would have reacted! He also told me that a couple of days earlier my father had gone to him and told him that I was not helping them with any work, like cutting grass for the cow, which was a disappointment when it came to giving milk. The cow gave so little milk, it was not enough to rinse one's mouth with. I had decided that I would help with household chores only when I felt like it and not when my parents told me to. I kept telling myself, if they thought they had 'tied' me to stay in Taita so I could help them with their shamba work, they were in for a rude awakening. But now that I knew my parents were circulating grievances, I thought this would be a good pretext for having a meeting where I could turn the tables on them . . ."

"Okay, so wait a second, Ngeti," I interjected. "So you go to Mombasa and the business with William and Patroba doesn't pan out, and you're fed up, and now you go back to Taita and you find yourself stuck, farming and helping out your parents around the home. Did it ever occur to you that you were just upset and frustrated, and you blamed the people closest to you, partly because they had had an influence on your life course that you didn't want or choose?"

"Yes, but wait," Ngeti insisted. "There was more than that! There was a confession! Okay, so my father's brother told me that the old man had already told him that I was not getting along with mother. I told him I wanted to hold my own meeting with them and confront them with the truth about their witchcraft against me. I told my uncle that I would call my three maternal uncles to be witnesses as I exposed these guys and their black art to the whole fucking world! I then visited each of my maternal uncles and told them what I had told my other uncle, and they too were all like, 'We know that your mother is not a good person, but everything has its own time and this is the time for the world to know that she is not a good person.'

"And I was like, what the fucking fuck?! All this time these guys knew this woman was not a good person and they didn't say fuck?! Fuck the whole lot of them! I was both angry and encouraged, for now I knew that I was not going to be making any false allegations."

"Really?!" I asked, self-consciously mocking Ngeti's confident empiricism. "You know that those guys never liked your mother."

"Hold on, bwana," Ngeti urged, confident that I would at least come to understand, if not share, his point of view. "My paternal uncle talked with my father and he agreed to arrange a meeting, which would be attended by all my uncles. Neither my father nor my mother knew that this meeting was going to be about me accusing them of witchcraft. They thought they were going to be discussing my uncooperative attitude toward them. My paternal uncle, Venny, chaired the meeting, and three of my maternal uncles were present, plus one of my cousins. The atmosphere was super charged with a multiplicity of emotions. I knew both my maternal and paternal uncles were with me because I had briefed them on the agenda of the meeting. Valentine was there, and I knew he was seething with subdued rage at his sister for beating the shit out of his wife some years back. Mzungu was spoiling for a fight with my mother for accusing him of killing his nephew back in the 80s. And my mother's family's last born had his own bones to pick with his sister for messing up his marriages. There were a lot more unvoiced grievances, and everyone was playing their cards below the table.

"My father began by complaining that I was not helping them with any work and was not being the child they thought I should be. I was waking up late, while they woke up at six to work in the shamba. He touched on how they had sent me to Lunga-Lunga thinking that they were helping me, and they did it in good faith. He also said they believed that whatever was done to me back there was not good and that was why I was not making any progress. He said bush doctors had cheated people out of their money, and many families were suffering as a result, not just ours. He talked about the charms that they were given by the bush doctor to come and plant in the compound to ward off the evil men in the neighborhood, and said these had been removed by Mother and Patroba when she got saved. Mother echoed the old man's story, and she kept blaming Patroba for the woes of the family. She said Patroba had inveigled her into using some money that belonged to the church, in which she was both an elder and the treasurer. Patroba promised her that God was going to repay her abundantly. In short, she was saying that she had no trust in this guy at all anymore, and that was why they had been against my continued relationship with him. But their complaints cut no ice with me.

"Then I was given the opportunity to say what was in my mind. I began by telling the meeting that I was not a happy man, and the cause of my unhappiness was my parents. I said, 'With all due respect, I have come to wonder if these people I have called my parents for thirty-something years are really my parents, or has some truth about my true parents been hidden from me? In all sincerity, I have been thinking my parents passed away when I was young and these guys adopted me as their child.'"

"You said that?!" I asked, incredulous.

"I was also pissed, you know. But it was not a *lapsus linguae,* my friend. It was deliberate. I paused for like a whole squirmy minute to let this statement sink in. I'm like, fuck, if they curse me, let me give them a good reason. Everyone's shocked by this statement of mine. This guy has gone far out . . .

"In no time I heard guys clearing their throats and saw them pinching the bridges of their noses. I had scored a point. I continued with a jeremiad of what I went through at the bush doctors' in the name of being protected from witchcraft. I had everyone's rapt attention, except my parents, who were now at a loss, wondering how the agenda had changed against them. Suddenly they had found themselves on the defensive. I capped my speech by telling them all that if they were to come to me in another thousand years, I would still maintain that their intentions of sending me to the witchdoctors were not good, but a cover-up for the deeper crime of offering my life as a sacrifice. I told them that they did not get along with Patroba because he discovered their secrets, even though by this time I had my own doubts about Patroba.

"Now the questions began for the old folks. They were asked why they had not accompanied me to Lunga-Lunga, knowing very well I was a kid then. They had no answer to that. My dad, who had also been to Lunga-Lunga, was asked if he had undergone the ritual of 'sitting on bills of money,' as I had, and he said he did not. My uncles believed that this ritual was not good. To them it symbolized something like sitting on wealth, progress in life, putting life under me and not putting it in front of me to face. Something was said about my turning my back toward the small hut part of the ritual, and this was equated with my entering some miniature satanic church backwards.

"So Valentine steps in now and says, 'So Charles, you've called us here to tell us you want us to help Ngeti get along with his mother, and it turns out you've been telling him very filthy things, bad things. How do you curse your own son and tell him if you die he will also die? What is that?' Mother was asked how she had removed the charms that my father had admitted were planted by the witchdoctor when he came to the house. We believed those charms were majini. Mom said she and Patroba had prayed over them, after which Patroba said that the Lord had cleansed the homestead of the effects of those charms.

"The meeting was adjourned for another week, and that evening my mother called me and said to me, in Taita language, 'I have never thought of offering anybody as a human sacrifice so I could get wealth, so remove those thoughts from your heart.' But I was so angry. I could not stand what I considered to be this bullshit charade. So I told her, 'There are people in this world who are offering their children as human sacrifice, and you are a human being like them. Therefore, you can also do the same.' And with that retort I stormed out of the kitchen.

"Before the next meeting, I had the opportunity to talk to one of my uncles, who told me that sometime not so long ago my mother had confided to him that she had majini that brought her money. Bingo! Not just for defense! This was fodder for my cannon. My list of *corpus delecti* was getting impressive, Jimmy, so I told him to ask her that question the next time we had the meeting. We wanted her to explain to us what she was feeding her jinnis in return for the money that they brought her. Maybe it was me."

I found Ngeti's story fascinating, but I also strongly believed that he was playing into the hands of his uncles and was surprised that he couldn't see this. "Ngeti! Why did you feel like you were persuading them, and not the other way around? This must have given them so much pleasure, to turn the son of their nemesis against her."

"Maybe they were manipulating me, but you see, there was still my mother's confession, and this egged me on. You know, I had just brought this hidden thing out into the light for the whole world. Anyway, bwana, the next meeting was held a week after the last was adjourned, and there was this new information that we had got from my mother's brother: that is, mother admitting that she had jinnis that brought her money. When the meeting convened again, this uncle of mine asked Mother to tell us where she had acquired her jinnis. When she was asked, she flatly denied that her jinnis were for bringing her monetary benefit. They were for general protection of the homestead and everything in it. But you see, this was still an admission that she kept majini!

"My uncles realized that they were going to seesaw over this claim and decided to move on. They had to give their decision on who they thought was guilty in this case. After some deliberation, it was decided that we should apologize to each other: them for taking me to the witchdoctors, and me for accusing them of being witches. My parents were told to tasa [take liquid— usually homemade beer—into their mouths and spray it out onto the ground or, in this case, a person, to expunge anger and heat from the heart while cleansing the person or object that is being sprayed] over me to show that their hearts were not hot against me. They were to do this with water rather than beer, because mother was involved. And I was to buy my parents honey as a symbol of making their hearts sweet toward me. So my parents did the tasa, saying, 'Ngeti, be opened, to get work, to grow. We want to see you marry and have our grandchildren.'

"But I just stood there feeling this coldness toward them, looking at the whole drama as a pure charade. I did not believe they wished me well in their hearts. These feelings were strengthened by the revelation that Mother, and now I included Dad, had acquired jinnis to enrich themselves at the expense of my success. Before this day, Valentine's wife had told me that a couple of months back some woman had told my mother to her face that she had offered me as a sacrifice to her jinnis. Valentine's wife had her own story to tell me to support the belief that mother was not a nice person. She told me that when her son was working at some hotel in Voi, Mother went to Valentine's wife and told her that her son was going to lose his job. At the time, Mother claimed that the Holy Spirit was revealing this to her, and the reason why the boy was going to lose his job was because of some ancestral curse that was dogging this guy wherever he went. And sure enough, one month after this revelation the guy lost his job. Valentine's wife thought Mother's prophecy was actually a curse. Witchcraft. And later, this guy consulted a bush doctor at the behest of this mother, and he was told that one of Father's sisters—that is, my mother—was behind him losing his job."

"So now you're believing some random 'bush doctor' and the woman your mother punched in the face?" I laughed, and Ngeti laughed too.

"Anyway," he continued, "the meeting ended, but you could tell there was this animosity that was seething inside everyone—especially the old guys, who still had scores from when they were young men."

I had to say that, for all his rebellion against Patroba and his parents, Ngeti didn't seem better off to me at the time. In fact, he seemed a lot worse: he was chain-smoking and boozing, and he had lost a great deal of weight.

And all of his women had left him. I questioned him: "So, Ngeti, how has this turned out for you, accusing your parents of witchcraft? Are things actually better now?"

"Well, to be honest, I got problems, man," Ngeti responded, inhaling smoke. "I'm tired all the time, my mind is confused. I got all this shit that never happened to me before. Like, I get these crazy fucking dreams of toilets and feces almost every night."

"You dream of toilets? That's horrible."

"Yeah, I think it's got something to do with someone trying to put my life in the toilet. You know, people keep majini in their pit latrines. Anyway, it's real upsetting shit. I'm dizzy all the time, being tossed from side to side. I had a very difficult time after confronting these people with this thing!"

"You got sick?"

"I got sick, bwana. I lost a lot of weight and thought I was going to die. It was fucking serious, bwana. After the meeting, we never raised the issues again, but there was this fomenting animosity, which may have been the cause of it. Then one of my mother's brothers died a week later, and maybe it was because of that meeting."

"So what are you going to do now?"

"My plan actually is to buy land in Mombasa and stay away from the Taita Hills completely. My mother's brother, the one who died a week after the confrontation with my folks, he wanted me to inherit land and stay in Taita. Maybe that's why he died. But I tell you, I'm not interested. Anyway, I've told my father a thousand times that I don't plan on inheriting land, and he keeps asking me why. I tell him I'm not interested. Even as I was growing up, I knew I didn't want to inherit. This thing about inheriting, you're waiting for some guy to die! It's not good. So I've always been disabusing myself of this notion. So-and-so is an idiot anyway. If he can get property, so can I."

"But don't you think that pissed off your father?" I asked. "Telling him you don't want his land—isn't the implication that he has no authority over you, and you don't recognize or respect him?"

"Yeah, well, I've always been like that," Ngeti answered. "I've always looked at myself as someone who should alienate himself from these traditional beliefs and practices. I also used to tell my parents, 'If I get married, I don't want my wife hanging around here with you people. You know, I'm not getting married for you people.' I've always been very open about my feelings and my rebellion against these traditional practices. And I wouldn't name my kids after them either, and said so. You know, it's a way of still being dependent on your parents and the past after they're dead. There's this talk among Taita people: someone has such-and-such's name, and it turns out they have taken on all of the characteristics of that person. People say, 'Ah! This guy totally resembles that dead guy!' If he was evil, this guy is evil like his namesake. Somehow, and I'm not sure how, the name contains the characteristics of this fellow. So this naming of someone, there must have been a ritual performed way back when, before we were born, about this naming, because you find these people are born and actually have the characteristics of these guys, and the kid never knew him. See, I want my kids to be their own persons, not to be enslaved to some other guy's characteristics. I don't want my kids later on growing up to curse their kids. Or getting some jinnis to bring them money.

"Anyway, two months after this meeting, I decided to have my own kitchen and start cooking my own food. And this decision was informed by my unwavering conviction that these guys, my parents, were not good people and they were planning to finish me. The only way to accomplish that was through poison. I kept seeing them mixing in some very black stuff in my food, stuff that would finish me very slowly over a couple of months, and this poison would probably give me malaria or typhoid, which was at this time very common in Taita and killing more than 75 percent of its victims."

"What do you mean you 'saw' them?" I asked.

"In dreams," Ngeti responded. "At this time, I was still very saved, so every time I prayed I kept binding and rebuking their demons. This decision to have my own kitchen did not go down well with my old folks. They said it was not okay for me to do this because I did not have a wife, and even if I had a wife, there was a proper way of going about this thing. I did not give a fuck, so I told them I had made up my mind and no amount of talking and explaining on their part was going to make me change it.

"Then, three months after this meeting with the old folks, this guy Patroba died. His death was received with mixed reactions, especially by those who looked at him as a servant of God. To me it was a shock. I had not expected this guy to succumb to a stupid disease like diabetes, let alone die. I recalled a time when my mother told me that this guy was so close to God that he had been told that he would not die but would live almost forever, and one day he would just disappear. The only thing that he would leave behind for his followers as mementos would be his walking stick and a blanket.

"His followers offered many reasons for his death, like that God had decided to remove the guy because people did not take him seriously and

God did not want him to be defiled by this general unbelief of the people. But others said maybe he had pissed God off by moving to Mombasa, because when this guy had begun his preaching work, he used to say that God wanted him to stay in Taita and help his own people. Then there were those who said that this was a test from God to Patroba, that He wanted to prove to the profligates of Taita that this guy was His chosen servant. Those who advanced this theory said that this guy would resurrect on the day that he was to be buried. I kind of believed this last theory because I was still saved at that time, even though I was not seeing any major miracles happening in my own life. This guy's wife told me that a couple of months before this guy died he kept telling her that God was going to give him a test in the month that he died.

"As time went by, I recalled what this guy had told me when he said that my parents were witches. He had expressly warned me against ever confronting them with this information, and if I ever did I would croak. I kept wondering if maybe the old folks had done something to this guy. The more I thought of this possibility, the more I got scared and kept thinking, 'Maybe I'm on the way out, too!'

"Several months later, after I had moved to my new kitchen, my parents brought in the church elders to try and talk me out of this decision. They started off by giving me a story about how they had gone to another home where a guy was cooking his own food and his parents their own. They did not tell me directly that they did not like what I was doing because it contradicted their message of family love, which they kept talking about Sunday in and Sunday out. But I just sat there feeling this seething rage against the whole lot of them. They prayed and said that the Lord was going to cleanse our home of all the medicines that the old folks had got from the bush doctors. They said this was a time for the family to 'make things right with God.'

"After the church elders had gone, a few months passed before the whole church was invited to our home for this home-cleansing crusade, an event that was supposed to be the opposite of what had taken place some twenty years ago when those bush doctors came with their evil paraphernalia to cleanse us and our home. This time the Bible was the modern paraphernalia, which they accompanied with holy hymns and spiritual xenoglossia. This was meant to deport the demons that had been planted in our homestead to hell. Their place was going be taken by the holy angels of the Most High God. This crusade was also meant to restore the fortunes of the family, which by now were nonexistent."

"So now you have the church getting involved in your family politics because you're eating alone?" I asked.

"Yes, they felt I was polluting the area with my insolence. For them, it was like I was a witch, but as for me, I was just trying to take some control over my own life."

I thought about how important eating together is for Taita families, as it is in this act of intimate sharing that one literally opens oneself up to other people and their intentions and feelings. Ngeti's refusal of food expressed anxiety and contempt, and could be interpreted as showing his willingness to do harm to his parents. Now *he* looked like the witch. "That must have been very uncomfortable . . . ," I managed.

"Yes! So I knew it was time for me to leave," Ngeti continued. "Six months after this crusade, I left Taita for Mombasa. In Mombasa I stayed with my brother-in-law, who ran a land and estate business. It was in the month of July. Something happened which I took to indicate that my going to Mombasa was meant to be for good. I received two hundred dollars from you, Jimmy, via Western Union. It had been a long time since I had handled such a big amount of money, and this to me was a genuine miracle, no shit. I continued praying fervently, asking God to deliver me from these shackles that seemed to tie me to the same spot in my life. A cousin of my brother-in-law, who happened to be one of those saved people with a gift of praying for others, told me that she had been praying for me to leave Taita and come to Mombasa. She also told me that this guy Patroba was not a good guy. She said he was a devil worshiper of the highest order."

As Ngeti finished, various feelings and thoughts ran through my head. I felt that Ngeti's frustration with wasting time in the hills had made him lash out against his folks. "Ngeti, I do not believe your mother is bewitching you," I said. "I think the problem is this: you don't feel worthy of your mother's love. You're not satisfied with your position in life and can't believe that your Mother, and your parents, actually have warm feelings for you. And you're angry because you can't believe that, after all this spiritual work, you could easily find yourself stuck in the hills, single and living with your parents, in your mid-thirties. But your situation is not really your fault. What Patroba said made sense to you because he picked up on your worries. And maybe your parents are frustrated with you because you haven't done better than you have." I went on to explain how "witchcraft" is the culmination of certain emotions, and that perhaps these emotions, Ngeti's and his parents', were actually bewitching him. But his parents were not witches—at least not in the Christian sense of evil beings. Maybe in another Taita sense of people whose feelings have gone awry to the point that they have become dangerous. And now Ngeti's had also gone awry.

"Ah, Jimmy, what are you, Freud? Don't bring Freud into something that is an African affair. These are Taita matters. There are people who actually have nothing better to do but try to ruin someone else's life. They enjoy it; it's fun for them. That's what I'm dealing with. This is not about *something else.*"

I knew that, from the point of view of philosophy, Ngeti had a point and that my effort to displace the reality of witchcraft onto emotions might have failed to do justice to the possibility that people were actually trying to bewitch him. This could be read as a dismissal based on Western notions about what is real or not. But when a person is actually accused of witchcraft, Wataita insist upon a discussion of emotional context as the only possible avenue for truth and reconciliation, and this process often leads to equivocation on multiple fronts. I knew Ngeti's mother as a real person, and cared about the both of them, and their relationship. Now I wanted to persuade Ngeti by locating some common point of connection, so I did what I have been doing all along, what you could call my ethnographic method, probably the only methodological technique I know. I revealed something about myself, delving into the murky territory where confession flirts with betrayal, in the hopes of initiating a true, mutually transformative dialogue.

Revelation and testimony are, as all Pentecostal preachers know, exciting and pleasurable acts, which create new forms of intimacy and wash away barriers. Those who enter into this bargain with each other speak a powerful new language. Like the language of divine tongues, it is shared only by them, and when the moment is over, it is hard to believe they ever spoke it, and they're often not sure what it was they actually said.

"Ngeti," I began. "I'm not some straight man who can't possibly imagine being bewitched."

"What's a straight man?"

I explained that a straight man is the rational part of a comedic duo, the voice of an imaginary audience. He's a foil for his friend, the funny mad man, with whom he's partnered in amusing situations. Bud Abbot, Dean Martin, Dan Akroyd ... Anthropologists often play the straight man in ethnographies, even somewhat more "dialogic" ethnographies like this one. I was making the point that I could also appreciate Ngeti's fears about other people using occult means to hold him back.

"What I'm saying is, actually in some ways my situation isn't that much different from yours," I continued. "My father had a wife and family before he married my mother, just like your grandfather did. His first wife was very upset when my dad left her, and I think I remember hearing about a rumor that she had gone to some American 'witchdoctor' so that he would come back to her. I can't remember now. But I did once visit a psychic medium in California who told me that curses from this woman were messing up my life. She said the curse was responsible for my choosing to be an anthropologist, when I was supposed to be a world-class lawyer with ridiculous money," I laughed. "That wasn't an African diviner, mind you. That was a white woman in San Luis Obispo with Catholic crosses and little blue plastic Smurfs on her desk. What she said made sense to me because I knew my father felt guilty his whole life after that divorce and I had, without realizing it, absorbed a lot of that guilt as well, and it made me unhappy and stilted. I only started to feel better when I met the children of my dad's first marriage and we began to put that past behind us, together. My point is that you have to make a conscious decision to try and put aside these differences and genuinely get along, while also explaining openly what is bothering you, without hiding it. Frank discussion is what you need, so nothing festers, because that will just bring more witchcraft . . ."

Ngeti listened patiently, sipped his beer and swallowed. "That's fine for you to say, but unlike you, I actually have to deal with these assholes, because I don't know where else to go," he said. "And you should know that just because witchcraft is meaningful and symbolic doesn't mean it's in people's heads." Then he grudgingly offered, "Maybe we could buy a goat and do a sacrifice. Brew some beer . . ."

"That's right, Ngeti," I said. "We'll all have some fun, and accomplish what you came back here for."

"I probably should start eating with them," Ngeti conceded.

We finished our Tuskers, paid up with the waitress, and started our long walk up the hill.

"And since I'm buying the goat, I'll read the *vula* [entrails] this time," I said. "You know, I think by now I've got it down . . ."

"Why do you still believe in that old-fashioned shit, bwana?" Ngeti laughed aloud and, looking at me in comic disbelief, smacked my shoulder.

EIGHT

_____

Reflections

VICTOR, A FORMER MAI MAI soldier who has now been "reintegrated" into the Congolese army, was sitting outside the door to my room in a small lodge for miners and traders in the town of Bisie, in the Walikale District of North Kivu. While the nonchalant way he carries his AK-47 may suggest otherwise, Victor is a fun, affable Azande guy, who likes to smoke pot to alleviate the inevitable foot and leg pain that comes from hiking long distances in the forest. Victor thinks soldiers—whether Congolese army or not—are the only righteous people in the DR Congo, and he likes to half-jokingly call civilian Congolese "people of lies."

Victor was one of our escorts on the forty-kilometer hike through the rainforest to Bisie, the largest artisanal mining town in the eastern Congo. The small city exploded out of nothing after the price for coltan plummeted following a dramatic tenfold price hike caused by on-line speculation. The sudden drop in prices left thousands of miners and traders stranded in the middle of the forest strapped with loans from their buyers, until word spread about the Mkumu trapper who had found cassiterite at Bisie. Actually, few in the forest at the time knew if the trapper had found coltan, cassiterite, or bauxite, and they certainly had no idea what all of these different things were used for, or that these heavy-material substances, enmired in mud, were the essential bedrocks of the digital age and all of its disembodied virtuality. Nevertheless, the instant town, complete with satellite dishes, soon reached a population of over twenty thousand, though it has never been connected to other towns by roads. Instead, there are two main footpaths that miners, traders, and sex workers must negotiate with their things, often carrying fifty-kilo loads on their heads so they can realize the 100 percent or more markup they'll receive here on everything from beer to chocolate to canned corned beef.

Today, Ngeti and I have been talking to people about a number of differ-ent issues related to the way miners and traders are inserted into digital capi-talism as producers of its raw materials. One issue that came up repeatedly was the use of rape as an instrument of war designed to destroy the family and the means of social production. Bisie has been subject to multiple inva-sions by armed militias of various stripes in recent years, most recently by Sheka, a former coltan middleman turned militia leader. Sheka used the money he made from selling coltan to acquire an armed militia, and his men have forcefully acquired control of Bisie at different times, especially when the prices for the minerals found there have risen. Sheka is one of several figures who have been accused of making rape a means not only of war, but of self-promotion. He uses violence against women to garner the attention of international human rights groups; this in turn creates leverage through which he hopes to acquire a position of permanent influence in the military and government. This strategy of promising the international community to desist from raping women in exchange for a seat at the table has become well known throughout the region, and ordinary soldiers commonly argue that it is most effective, if also horrible. While not the only, or even the main, reason for rape, this practice feeds into a more general strategy, among militias, of developing a connection with the "international community" with respect to something they care about. More often than not, that thing has been miner-als, but in this case it happens to be women's bodies. When the United Nations called DR Congo the "rape capital of the world," their spokespeople surely had no idea that the slogan would became grist for enterprising and ruthless men who were trying to put an end to the unpredictability and inse-curity that characterized their own lives.

As I approached the door to our room, Victor leaned over, grabbed my arm, and whispered, "Ngeti is drunk in there," in Swahili. "He is evolving in reverse." Victor and I have been having spirited discussions about human evolution, an idea that both excites and disturbs him. Victor does not believe that we are descended from apes, and if he did, he might not be able to dine on macaque and chimpanzee, which he thinks of as one of the perks of his occasional visits to the forest. Ngeti and Victor have become fast friends over the last few weeks, and I could tell that the former Mai Mai soldier was a little worried about my companion. Earlier, Ngeti and I had returned from our interviews very worn out and a bit depressed. At one point, Ngeti had even started to cry, declaring, generally, that he hated the way women were treated the world over.

When I opened the door, I found Ngeti passed out on the floor. To his side lay an empty bottle of Amarula, a South African crème liqueur that is by far the most delicious thing to be found in the rainforest. Unfortunately, Amarula costs almost forty dollars a bottle here, and Ngeti seemed to have consumed the entire thing in less than an hour. I was more than a little angry and so bellowed, "Ngeti, what's up?!"

Ngeti pulled himself up from his prostrate position, in tears, and my rage instantly went the way of the Amarula. I asked him what was wrong, and I will always remember his face as he looked up at me, crying, and intoned:

"I'm such a loser, bwana! Nothing I've done has turned out right . . ."

"What do you mean?" I asked.

"My mother was a good woman, bwana! She didn't deserve the treatment I gave her. She was surrounded by horrible people who couldn't understand what she was trying to do. She never harmed me or anyone else. It's me that killed that woman."

"That's not true, Ngeti. Your mother died of diabetes and other health problems."

"No. She died of a broken heart!"

Monica had passed away since my last visit to Kenya, leaving her husband, Charles, alone up in the hills. The guilt surrounding his mother's death still weighed heavily on Ngeti, and his financial situation hadn't improved much. Ngeti spent long stints in the Tsavo desert trying, unsuccessfully, to pull up gemstones from the ground, and he supplemented this work with computer repair and other freelance computer work when he was in Mombasa. But he was regularly delinquent on rent payments, and I had given him most of the things that he owned. At least Ngeti felt blessed by his recent marriage to Jane, a student at the University of Nairobi, and could count this as one major achievement in his life—though he had to continually cement it through more or less regular payments to his wife's in-laws.

It troubled me that Ngeti felt he was responsible for his mother's death, and I believed he was wrong. But I also understood what it was like to suddenly realize that you have been callous or unfair to your parents, only to find that it was too late to do anything about it. I tried to keep things light and helped our conversation to drift back and forth in different directions until Ngeti entered a peaceful sleep. He now seemed to be in a better position to talk about the influence that Patroba and others had exerted on him and the effect that all this had had on his relationship with his family. And so I made up my mind that, when we were done here, we would chat about his present position regarding the past events in his life.

A few months later, I met Ngeti in Mombasa. After a couple of days of catching up, we found ourselves at a hotel bar on the beach south of the city, putting back bottles of Tusker while a Kenyan reggae band played Bob Marley songs, badly. We agreed that our conversation would focus mainly on Patroba and his mother and on the influence they had had on his life. I was also interested in the new social forces that his mother and Patroba epitomized and helped bring into being. I had still not really understood Ngeti's faith in Patroba, whom I had always been suspicious of, and so I wanted to understand what it was that had made him such a compelling figure. In this conversation, Ngeti mostly used Swahili and Kidawida in his recollections of things that other people said to him and in his descriptions of highly localized practices. He used English to interpret events and to explain why he did the things did. Again, I have rendered the entire conversation in English for the sake of clarity.

"That woman is joking!" Ngeti said deploringly as he took a drag of his cigarette and followed a young bikini-clad Kenyan woman with his eyes.

"Why?" I asked.

"She's bringing that tiny ass here and there are Germans! She'll get screwed!" Ngeti explained, reacting more to the reckless sexuality of foreigners than to the woman, although I couldn't help but think that his empathetic feminism had dissipated somewhat since Walikale. "And look at that guy!" he added, referring to a Speedo-clad European senior citizen walking with total disregard for the bodily sensibilities of people in this mostly Swahili Muslim area. "Put on a pair of trousers, motherfucker. That is lack of respect!"

"So, Ngeti," I began, switching on my tape recorder and settling into interview mode. "You no longer think your mother was bewitching you?"

"No," he replied, lighting a Sportsman as he kept an eye out for the waiter. "I don't. I'm not saying she never kept majini, though, but that was her choice. If she did, it was because she knew what kind of motherfuckers she was surrounded by and that being a woman like her was not an easy thing in our society.

"Back then, I was influenced by Patroba, who I thought was my best friend. I'll be honest—I was ready for anything, I was a desperado, and whatever offered hope was a deal for me. So instead of finding solace in drinking, where I didn't find any solace, and instead of smoking bhang and womanizing and all that, which didn't benefit me in any way, I thought that rejecting those things, but at the same time bolstering my acceptance of religion, with its element of fear, was a deal for me. Okay, I needed money. I didn't have any money. Here's a God who promises to be able to bring me money. And it was part of a longer story that went back to my youth. I mean, as a young man I went to a seminary school believing maybe someday I might end up in a pulpit ministering to God's flock, but that didn't happen for reasons that are not really clear to me I believe I am a hedonist by nature. So I accepted whatever was coming to me from this guy with an open mind.

"And at the same time, you know, there was a lot of pressure on my mother's part. That, 'Okay, you need to get your life in order, and I found someone who can work miracles. You can see I had hypertension, eh, but now I'm okay. Your father had been stuck in one place in his work, but now he has been promoted. It's because of this man, Patroba. So the only prerequisite for you to get your life in order is to give your life over to Jesus.'"

"But it seems like almost as soon as you started hanging out with Patroba he starts telling you that your parents have been cursing you," I said.

"Right away!" Ngeti agreed. "It started with my father, almost immediately.

"This is what I think was happening. Patroba knew how to use his own experiences to develop a relationship with others and improve the quality of his life. I came to realize much later that Patroba never had a very good relationship with his own father. He was projecting some of his own shit onto me now. More generally, he had gone through the same process like me, you know, no work no what, and he probably found someone to pray for him like he prayed for me. He got converted. And so he thought, 'Okay, let me try and strike it out on my own'. And at that time there was this wave of Pentecostalism, you know, there was a lot of hypertension, a lot of witchcraft . . ."

In referencing "hypertension," Ngeti was drawing attention to what Wataita consider to be a highly contemporary illness that is at once physical, emotional, and socioeconomic: "hypertension" is brought about by worrying about life and money, as well as by enmity from neighbors. Rhetorically merging witchcraft and hypertension, as Ngeti had done, made sense because the feelings that give birth to hypertension also lead to witchcraft attacks and accusations. Both social disorders are produced by people's moods and emotions, which are ultimately the product of social conditions, especially inequality. According to Wataita, hypertension makes the body "hot" when it should be cool, and hypertension is just a somewhat amped up version of what is now happening to all Taita bodies, as well as to the landscape through deforestation and the privatization of water resources. Each are becoming progressively hotter (a term that, in Kidawida, also implies acceleration) because people have stopped loving one another, which makes for more heat and more "hypertension." In other words, the concept of hypertension, though it comes from Western biomedicine, also reflects and informs broader Taita ideas about what is happening to their world. Pentecostalism, Ngeti argued, emerged as a response to witchcraft and hypertension—it was something new and foreign that people were drawn to, in part, to counteract these new problems.

Ngeti continued, "Yes, this disease of hypertension is brought about by people being unhappy with their lives. And their unhappiness is actually emanating from their neighbors who are not well off, so there is this 'jealousy spirit' that is moving around. So I think that was what happened to Patroba also, because he grew up very poor."

"You grew up in a better situation than him?" I asked.

"Ah, much better! And he was jealous of my mother and my father. And I think maybe he was trying to secretly tear me apart and destroy my connection to my family, the only people I had. Control me and probably kill me, you know. He wanted to fuck me up for reasons that are best known to him. Because when he died, his wife actually went to a witchdoctor to find out what had killed him."

"Hmm," I pondered, reaching to light a cigàrette. Ngeti's story had us both smoking now.

"My God, shield it, there's a lot of wind, you, shield it!" Ngeti coached, dismayed by my inept smoking habits.

He continued, "So his wife went to a witchdoctor to find out why her husband had died and she was told point blank: 'Your husband screwed up with a lot of people's lives. Feeding them lies, turning mother against son, son against father with his lies, because he wanted to eat.'

"See, he wanted to continue with his good life, which he had been denied since he was a child. So this anger and other people's hatred, many people being tired of him and saying, 'This person is not a good person. He's causing people to clash within their families'—all of these people's hearts were hot with their heat. So that heat from people entered into his body up until the point that he wanted to immerse his legs in water. You can only imagine! This guy wanted to put his whole body in water and eat sweet things . . ."

"Interesting."

"Yes, it was diabetes! So people are angry with him, there's anger, there's heat. All those nice, nice things that he had been telling people, which never came to fruition in their lives. This heat is eating him now. Good things he said that the Lord would do for them, sweet things. They haven't yet happened, so now he's craving those sweet things, you see. So the tables have been turned on him. He's craving the sweet things that didn't go to the people as he promised them. Now he's taking them in excess. This guy would drink like ten sodas in one day. He would eat cake like a kid. Like sit and just wallow in cake. And the frosting . . ."

We laughed. I thought it elegant that Ngeti was able to accommodate yet another Western biomedical concept with a distinctly Taita understanding of the effect of emotions on the body. He did so without imagining these different "enactments" of "diabetes" to be incommensurable, even though they were clearly multiple—communicable as a single thing, while also "ontologically" different.[1] The biomedical concept of diabetes relates the illness to the individual who has it: as the outcome of his or her genetic disposition or eating habits, for example. Ngeti's use of the concept of diabetes, though on the surface recognizable to a Western audience, made clear that the disease was the outcome of one's social relationships. Patroba's diabetes mirrored and mimicked his relations with others—it was in fact the abrogated social relationships working themselves out in the body. And this idea of diabetes reflected widespread Taita understandings of illness.

Ngeti went on to tell me about how Patroba taught him that his father, like all old Taita men, hated when their first-borns were males because it meant they would have to pay goats and sheep before they had received bridewealth from the marriage of their daughters. Patroba was the first-born son, and he apparently grew up believing this and developed a bond with Ngeti around this idea. Part of what Patroba and Ngeti were bonding over was their joint suffering in the face of selfish old men who "backwardly" wanted to hold on to their cattle, goats, and money instead of helping their children—and by extension, the future—to develop. Patroba and Ngeti had believed that these old men were stuck in the past and that becoming "saved" would move them both beyond their influence.

"What was Patroba's issue with his father, and what did this have to do with his later life choices?" I asked.

"Patroba's father, and this is back in the 8os, he was in town [Mombasa], and he had gotten himself tangled up with Digo women.[2] So he was not sending money back home, and these guys were literally starving and having a real bad time. The father would come one day, and the next morning he's gone, he has disappeared. So Patroba never really had an opportunity to enjoy his father's presence as the figurehead."

"So how did he get into religion?" I asked.

"Actually, according to him, he got into religion because he was looking for a father! See, one day he had somehow managed to leave Taita to go to his father in Mombasa. So one night he's sleeping in Mombasa and he sees a light in the room and he hears a voice telling him, 'Your father doesn't like you. I am your Father now, but if you want to be a good son, you must suffer, you must preach. Now, I want you to wake up now. And I want you to walk back to Taita. I have a test I want to give you.'

"So the guy wakes up and he walks from Mombasa to Taita, starting at 1 A.M. Meanwhile, his father has come back in the morning after some nights of debauchery with some women. The boy is not there, so he goes to the neighbors' homes and finds no one. Back then there were no cell phones, so he writes a letter to Taita inquiring if Patroba is at home. Two weeks later he gets a letter saying, 'This guy, Patroba, we haven't yet seen him.' Meanwhile, this guy's in the middle of the Tsavo [national park, but also wilderness], walking. Patroba said that it took him a month."

"Why a month?" I asked, knowing that the walk to Taita takes two weeks at most.

And Ngeti explained to me about how Patroba had to stop at Maungu, circling the hill there seven times, once each day, while begging for food. "All the clothes he had are tattered because he's been treading through the forest. You know, he's in the Tsavo half naked. His feet are sodden. And God's appearance to him is sporadic. He can go for a week without hearing anything, then when he's at the point of actually despairing and probably killing himself, he gets a vision. 'Don't give up. I am with you.' So that gave him hope, and I used to think of that when I wanted to give up my prayers, that just when I want to give up most is when something good is going to happen. Anyway, when he arrived in Taita, he found his father, and he told him, 'I left because God told me to leave. He has become my Father now. You are not my father. You have abandoned us. You're in Mombasa. You're sleeping with every kind of a woman. You're not taking care of the family. Now God wants to take care of the family.'

"So from there he started going to church, praying, preaching. And this is about the time when people have a lot of problems, like the witchcraft and the hypertension. Now people hear of a guy walking all the way from Mombasa to Taita. He spiced up his story with meeting elephants, lions, and all of that shit. People loved it!"

"How old was he at this time?"

"Around this time he's probably twenty-nine, and this is the mid-80s, when things were just starting to go really downhill in Kenya, first with coffee prices. People started hearing about this prophet of God performing miracles, and they started doing stuff for him. They work in the shamba, they dig. Now he is taking it easy, the family now is developing while others do the work. So he has achieved something by preaching his gospel."

Patroba was beginning to come across as a more sympathetic figure, perhaps one who even believed in the value of what he was doing. He was responding, in his own way, to a larger problem brought about by the way in which Kenya was inserted into the global capitalist economy as a producer of raw products—mainly coffee. When the price for coffee on the world market fell dramatically in 1986, there were a number of political and economic consequences. To begin with, the Kenyan state used its state marketing boards to try to squeeze more profit out of the coffee growing population. Nonetheless, the government was unable to pay its debts on the loans that it had been more or less compelled to take from donor countries, and the World Bank and IMF, since the 1960s. As mentioned before, this later led to the imposition of World Bank and IMF structural adjustment programs, which would help make formal wage labor a thing of the past while also undermining vaunted social institutions like education, various forms of patron-client-age, and fatherhood. Fathers increasingly came to be seen as leeches on their families, and so Patroba used his intelligence and intuition to reinvent fatherhood, developing a direct connection to a universal and transcendent Father who was also all-powerful and immediate. This Father demanded things from His children, but He always made good, eventually, with love and bounty.

At the same time, Patroba's return home to Taita after an arduous and long journey was a rejection not only of his father but also of the Kenyan city of Mombasa and of the Taita male "tradition" of going there to live for long periods in search of wage labor in order to feed one's family back home. Patroba accentuated this rejection of Mombasa, and the stress and sadness that migrant wage labor imposed on families, by making his religious practice revolve around his home rather than a church. He topped it off by entering into relations of reciprocity that epitomized a threatened Taita essence and past, in which people allegedly shared resources among themselves. Here, his begging for food was especially significant—and loaded.

"But Patroba never had a church?" I asked.

"No. He was a domicile preacher. It's pretty common. There are people who are actually preaching from their homes, and when they do that they call themselves prophets. I'll tell you what has brought this on. Now I will speak with Taita in mind. Most Taitas are Catholics or ACK, the Anglican Church of Kenya. Now, there are people who have heard about these indoor preachers, and they don't want to convert, but they want prayers. So instead of actually going to an evangelical crusade and coming forward for prayers, they would rather do it in private, and still have their affiliation to their mainstream church. It's like you're a Christian but you still go to an mghanga [witchdoctor or healer]. These prophets have become like waghanga, and they're all doing their secret thing where? In the house. Now, you see, therefore, these prophets are competing with bush doctors, who also work in the home and do the same thing these prophets are doing, helping people with physical and social problems. But there is metaphysics here in the sense that they are mixing things up . . ."

"Mixing what up?"

"Mixing up the cosmologies! These prophets, they go to the witchdoctors and they are given talismans to do this work to pull customers."

I was surprised to hear this, because Pentecostals are famous for breaking with the past, so I asked Ngeti, "These Pentecostal prophets are going to the local waghanga?"

"Eh! To receive occult powers! You see, even the pastors now of the mainstream Pentecostal church, like this pastor of the JCC, Jesus Celebration Center—this is a church that began back in the inception of Pentecostalism in Taita. It's where I got saved. That is one of the mainstreams now. They have TV programs. They preach against these domicile prophets like Patroba, who go to waghanga. Meanwhile, domicile prophets are saying, 'Those mainstream churches, those guys, they are going to Nigeria to get some juju to confuse your minds. They remove one problem, you get another. They use the hands-on healing to remove an earache, but they give you a toothache or they give you a nose bleeding, which will happen in one week's time.'"

"Because ultimately they're contracting with demons, and so the cures are false, and not genuine or sustainable?"

"Yes!"

"So the Pentecostals pretend to be breaking with the past, but they are really borrowing from these older practices and framing them differently?" I asked.

"The domicile preachers, now, yes. But the churches, they are totally international. They are getting things from abroad, or from far away, like Nigeria. This is what makes Pentecostalism so powerful, is that it has transmogrified itself, containing the whole world that matters to Taitas in one powerful thing. So it has taken from Taita traditions, but also from places that are farther away."

"It's glocal," I said jokingly, invoking a horrible word that American pundits like Jonathan Friedman have used to describe what happens when something that circulates around the globe merges with something local.[3] The term usually refers to how some icon of global capitalism, like Coke or McDonald's, has become locally meaningful, allegedly without destroying the "culture" that existed before in some specific place. But Ngeti was getting at something more profound: how Africans were crafting innovative responses to the challenges they confronted by drawing from an imagined past and an imagined transnational all at once. There was continuity in this politics of "extraversion," as Jean-François Bayart calls the African practice of creative appropriation and transformation, because it has a very long history.[4] But Pentecostals were also responding to situations that felt qualitatively different and new to them, and in the process they created and innovated constantly.

"Glocal!" Ngeti said approvingly. "Ah, that's a good one. English! English makes you see far! So, for example, take Nigerian movies. They are very popular in Kenya now. There are things in Nigerian movies that people see in Kenya, which got them to convert to Pentecostalism. These movies, many of them were Pentecostal movies. They broadcast these problems about witchcraft and jinnis. And they deal with the domestic problems, like you get married but you don't have children because your mother-in-law is bewitching you. You don't get kids coz your mother-in-law wants to eat your money. These are the real problems that concern people every day."

I was intrigued by the possibility that Ngeti's concerns about his mother might have come from a movie, and so I asked him, "So this idea you had about your mother sacrificing you to get money. Have you seen that in a Nigerian movie?"

"Yes, I've seen a movie where some mother goes to a witchdoctor to confuse her son mentally, so that he can't think, and she woke up in the morning and found money in her purse, or had progress in business, and got elected to some position."

I had also recently seen a Nigerian movie about a wife who had bought her husband a magic stone that she promised would bring him good fortune, but instead it kept him in bondage, as she prospered while he grew sick and destitute.

"So had you seen this movie before and thought about this?" I asked.

"No, I saw it later, but it did strengthen my resolve to believe that my mother was actually using me as a 'stool' for her own good. The Nigerian movies are actually addressing fears that have been there for a long time. What they are doing, they are proving that these things are there, and my proving is in quotes, because nothing has been proven yet . . ."

I began to realize that it wasn't so much that a Pentecostal movie from Nigeria might have planted this idea in Ngeti's head, but that Pentecostal movies reaffirmed people's suspicions that, in this day and age, the most unthinkable things were not only possible, but ordinary. I started to think that one of the reasons Ngeti believed his mother was bewitching him was not that he was "superstitious," whatever that means, but that his attitude toward the world had made him very open-minded. Ngeti realized that to understand the world today you had to be open-minded, because under present conditions of uncertainty it might actually be possible for someone to do the unthinkable—for a mother to bewitch her son for money and power.

Ngeti continued in this vein. "Because you see the world is confusing, man, and these movies explain something about what's happening in the world and make it all very relatable to your real concerns. Anything is possible now. Mud in the Congo makes the iPhone, bwana—I mean, what the fuck?! These guys we saw in the middle of the fucking rainforest digging shit up out of the ground, they're midwifing the iPhone, man. Here you have the lowest thing in the world and the highest, most sophisticated thing in the world all together in this iPhone." He laughed. "And something happens with the price of that shit [coltan], and all hell breaks loose and no one knows what the fuck is causing it. And then those guys in your country pass a law banning minerals from Congo, and it makes things even worse! It's the same here with aid being withdrawn and new NGOs and the International Mothers and Fathers [a local play on the acronym IMF] enforcing constitutional reform and whatnot. The economy is fucked up, the resources have been depleted and are being concentrated with a few individuals who will decide what they do with those resources, and we keep having to pay our debts to people who have stolen from us in the first place, for over a century!

"But you see, most people don't see the bigger picture. They don't throw in politics, they don't throw in the multinationals. They don't understand these things. They say, 'No, this is witchcraft! Someone is bewitching me. Who is bewitching me? Hmmmm. I ran into Jimmy the other day and he looked at me very badly.' This guy now stands up and goes to a witchdoctor because his affairs aren't going well. You look for an immediate excuse here and there because the globe is very complicated, in the sense that politically we don't fucking know what is happening, in short. And in leadership circles, when someone actually comprehends what is happening and starts to rise up and tries to lead people in the smallest way, they say, 'This guy's a witch. He knows those things.'

"And that is what happened in Taita with my mother.

"You want to know my mothers' story?" Ngeti continued. "The story is, my mother has always been vocal. I remember her saying that she had so much brain it was flowing over. She actually said, 'There's enough brain to lend out to those who don't have brains.' She had enough brains to spare!" We laughed. "And that meant, to her, she can take men head on. She believed there were things she could do that men, Taita men, timid as they were in their nature, couldn't do. She transcended that fear.

"So she got into politics, and she started with the church. She'd come up with an idea. Like, okay, there is a Saint Anna. Fine. She'd say, 'Let us form a group, we call it St. Anna.' People would be like, 'This St. Anna, what will it do?' And she would say, 'This St. Anna will buy you rosaries, will get you prayer books. We'll actually dig your shamba. We come together as a group, we merge our energies and come up with one very potent idea to help us in our lives.'

"Your mother wasn't getting the money from somewhere else?' I asked.

"No, it's from within. They share the money with each other to help themselves and the disadvantaged in the society.' So she started that, and she was always the treasurer for these things. Now, there were those who said that, in her cunningness, she could spend this money and no one would know. Because she's the only one who understands the dynamics of this idea. So there was suspicion that came from the power she had. From there she moved on and got into politics, KANU [Kenya African National Union] politics, in the early 80s.

"She was young, only in her twenties, when she started with the church, but she had one quality. She was a very good listener. She would let people taaaaalk. Argue, argue, argue. Then she'd be like, 'Can I speak?'

"'Yes, what do you have to say?'

"'It is this and this and this and this and this.'

"'Ah, that is better. And that is it.'

"Because she knew how the people around her thought. She knew what they wanted. She had that intrinsic ability of leadership. If there was an elected position and she showed any interest, people would be like, 'Okay, fine, you do it.' No one would want to compete against her because they knew they would lose.

"But even then, the reaction from people, not everyone, but many, was, 'That woman is not a good woman.' Men and women both thought this. Even then, they're like, 'Obviously she's gone to get some majini.' Because she used to travel to see my father, who was living in town [Mombasa]. She'd go for holidays, she'd disappear from Taita for like a month, two months. You know, it was like she was accustomed to town, which is where majini come from. And that made many people suspicious. They thought her power to seduce and speak came from these spirits. People would say, 'Oh, she's gone to the witchdoctors.'

"And it didn't help that she was so big. My mother was always big! In fact, when she died, when they were trying to make the coffin, this guy at the morgue was asking, 'Who is this person? She must be a VIP!' She had actually gained weight now that she was on this Water Board thing [a government- and NGO-sponsored project to bring tap water to homes in the area]. And I think that is what intimidated most people. You know, Taita women are tiny, tiny, tiny, and the men are also tiny, tiny. And then there's this colossal woman!"

We laughed loudly together, drinking our beers. "She was very unique," I agreed, chuckling.

Ngeti continued, "Eeh!! Most men used her as an example to their wives: 'Don't you bring habits like that, wife. That woman, that's a man, that one.'"

"They did used to say that . . ." I said.

"Yeah, 'That one is a man, that one.' Because when my mother was pissed off with a man, she'd never blink; just look you in the face, feed you whatever she thought was appropriate, and move away. She was militant all the time.

"But it's interesting that when you die, it's then that people sit down and tell stories about who you really are. Like right now at home, we are very disorganized! When you come home you'll see the rooms aren't clean, a single spoon is just sitting over there. There is no symmetry!" Ngeti laughed.

"It's still just your father alone?" I asked.

"Yes, he cooks food that will last him a week. See, she brought order into our home, and she brought order to politics in Taita. So she progressed until she was chosen to be district chairlady for Wanawake ya Maendeleo, the Development of Women. This began during the time of KANU [the only political party in Kenya until 1993]. This is before she met Patroba. You know, mobilizing women's groups and bringing development: small things, like, each village has to have spoons, cups, plates, and pots for cooking at funerals. Because in Taita a funeral is the glue that holds people together, so she let the politicians know that each village had to have those things. My mother facilitated that idea. And in exchange she campaigned for Mbela back then, mobilizing women to vote.[5] And generally, when people had disagreements with their wives, she was a mediator of sorts.

"And she would mobilize and get information from the grassroots about the political views of people. What is it that the government isn't doing right? How can it bring more development? She would hold seminars, focus groups. And what the church is thinking, because she was a member of several groups in the church. So she'd gather information and convey it to the MPs [members of Parliament]. The idea was that bringing this information would bring development to Taita, because everything depended on having a good relationship with the leadership in those days. She succeeded with these male political figures because she was never afraid to express herself to whoever she was expressing herself to. She had no fear, and that is why people were always putting her in the forefront: 'You can talk to Mbela. You can talk to Mwadoka. You can talk to this other guy. This is what we need them to know, so can you pass this information on.' There are men who couldn't actually talk to Mbela, but my mother would go there and sit down and tell him, 'Listen, this is it. You don't do this and I think we are throwing you somewhere else.' And Mbela would say, 'Okay, I understand.'

"She used to travel a lot back then. She did it for like six years. All of this went on until it reached a point where she was very powerful, but then she screwed herself up when she met Patroba. Patroba was like, 'These political matters, they don't go well with the spirit of God. Politics will dirty you, and God wants you to be a clean person.' And anyway politics was bringing her health problems, she was having hypertension; it was not sitting well with her. So eventually she gave up political life, but not completely. She always had tentacles in the village. She would be chosen by the elders of the village for various committees, long after multipartyism came, actually. She didn't want to go down with KANU [as it became less popular with the onset of multipartyism], so she pulled away from it slowly. But mainly now it was religion: she became a prayer warrior, and prayed for people and their problems. She decided that the solutions to people's problems were not in the secular realm, but in these emotions and in the state of people's souls . . ."

As we talked, I was beginning to understand all of this in a way that I had not before. Ngeti's mother could be thought to be a witch because she transcended (a word Ngeti used often in his description of her) all variety of limitations that were imposed on her, and her society, from outside. She served as a translator, explaining local problems to politicians and others in a way that they could understand. She mediated between husbands and wives, between her village and "the state," between the country and the city. She traveled widely. Later, around the time of her death, she began to mediate between Kenya and the international community, when she worked with international NGOs. In the process, she transcended her own subject position, becoming more "male" than "female," and even more "male" than most men (at least in other people's perception). Even her brains flowed over, escaping the confines of her physical body, which was so big the mortician had a hard time finding a suitable coffin. Most importantly, she transcended her own fear, and everyone else's. At the same time, she embodied the social forces of her era, becoming political at a time when men were increasingly seen as having very little to offer financially and morally.

This capacity to contain different worlds and move between them felicitously was a double-edged sword: it was beneficial and promising, for Monica as much as anyone else, but it was also dangerous, because it challenged the ordinary and constituted a kind of revolution in the making. A potential future, at once frightening and hopeful, resounded in her words and in her actions. The same went for Patroba, who, through his religious practice, communicated the male version of his generation's frustration with the old men who held back development in politics and in the home. His principled reaction to the political, and his embrace of a transcendent religious sphere that eclipsed politics and touched the powerful divine, may have emerged from his position as an unemployed, poor youth, but it found purchase throughout the society. It also became clear to me that someone like Ngeti, who was trying to manage the multiplicities occasioned by globalization in his daily life and practice, was also flirting with witchcraft when he tried to find any way possible to move beyond his confined station.

"So you said there's going to be a celebration at your house for your mother, some kind of Christmas party. What is that about?" I asked, knowing that we were going there in a few days.

"Well, what I'm trying to do in general with my life is move forward now, but I realize that to do this I also have to be more respectful about these things from the past which the Pentecostals told me were demonic. You know, I told you last time that I've always been trying to free myself of these Taita traditions, but all of this Christian stuff that is telling me this tradition is bad—well, that Christianity is also a Taita tradition. So you see, I want to borrow from here and there now, be experimental without judging. After all, I know the *vula* [intestine of an animal, usually a goat, but also the practice of reading these entrails to determine if anyone is angry toward the person or community being divined for, and so if anything is blocking their progress toward a particular goal] is a local thing, fine. But the vula also contains the whole world, as you know, and as you have written in your book. It is all there for people to read, because the goat eats everything and it's all in its belly. That means that you, Jimmy, can be seen in the vula. That America is also there in the intestines of a Taita goat!"

"Nice," I said, then asked: "So what's the plan now?"

"Now listen, when I was in the Tsavo mining, somebody suggested that I go see a diviner. You know, because in Taita we know that when you're dealing with minerals, you're interacting with demons.[6] These are demonic affairs. So I don't want to ignore that demonic aspect of mining. So I went to this old man named Mbatia, near Mworoko in Taita, and I explained to him what I'm doing at the moment, about the mining. I asked Mbatia why I'm not getting any minerals, and he told me to go bring him a male goat. So I bought a goat and I went with it to his house. Then he went looking for herbs, the normal herbs that are used for rainmaking and stuff, and he started to look to see if I will succeed in this endeavor and if my relationship with my environment is okay. When I talk about my environment now, this word has a holistic meaning to it, meaning my health, my family, my relationships with other people. So now, when we're inquiring for information from this goat, we have to ask a specific person. So here I was asking my father's father, who died years ago, because he was head of the paternal lineage.

"So the old man slaughters this goat and he takes out the large intestine, and he begins to read it. He reads it, he reads it, he reads it, and he says, 'Here I see there are people who are dead and they have not been remembered. They died a long time ago. I can see your grandfather, and your maternal grandfather, and I can even see your mother here. I can see your grandfather from whom you are inquiring for this information. And I can see some other people who are related to you.'

"And when I asked Mbatia, 'What are they saying concerning this work I'm doing of digging up rocks?' he told me, 'Here you will not succeed until you have remembered those people who have died.'

"And I asked him, 'How do I remember them?'"

"He said, 'The way I see it here in the vula, they are Catholics. Therefore, go to church, go and have a mass with the priest, and mention each one of them by name. When I look on your mother's side, I can see your mother didn't have anything against you. In fact, your very existence, and your success in life and your brains, means your mother has done a lot of good work.' Because the intestine was filled with shit, which is good, it means the intestine and my life are full in general—abundant. 'But if you don't remember these people, you will just waste whatever money you get. And I see that there's still some bridewealth your father hasn't given for your mother. This, too, is showing up here, and it needs to be paid.'"

"That's interesting," I said. "So a non-Christian Taita diviner says you have to have a Catholic mass to appease ancestral spirits? It shows that these seemingly irreconcilable 'belief systems' are anything but. What else, anything else?"

"I told him that I have some friends and I asked him if they can help me. And at first he said, 'You don't have any friends.' And then he said, 'This vula is saying there are friends but they are not from here.' And he said, 'There is a friend and he's from far away. Not Kenyan. Not Ugandan. Probably an mzungu.' And I told him that I have a friend named Jimmy who's an mzungu. And he agreed."

"Oh yeah? What did he say about me," I asked, interested.

"He said, 'This is a good person. He has a good heart. But it seems that even he has problems, which I can't pretend to know or defend against by passing through you. Maybe if I see the mzungu. But as far as you are concerned, don't rely on the mzungu for this issue of rocks. You give these people a sermon and then return to my place; I have medicine that I'll cut into you. Then your affairs will begin to get better, and they will become clean. But don't expect them to clean up right away. They'll clean up gradually, slowly.'"

Ngeti went on to explain that he had gone home and narrated the events with Mbatia to his dad, who had agreed to immediately pay the remaining cow (which was in fact still owed) to Monica's surviving male kin. Meanwhile, Ngeti arranged for a commemorative mass with the Catholic priest up in Mgange, which they would follow up with a goat roast at the house and a small ceremony in which Ngeti's mother would be declared "head of the household," against all Taita patriarchal tradition. This was apparently Ngeti's addition, and his innovation.

Now our conversation turned to the upcoming Christmas trip to Taita, including preparations for the goat and the chofi, or homemade beer, which we took care of using text messaging from our cell phones. We also decided that, when we returned to Taita, we would visit the old man, Mbatia, with another goat so that he could read the vula for me and open up any pathways that had been blocked in my life. Ngeti thought this was absolutely crucial if he and I were going to continue to collaborate on a book venture, or anything else. After a while, we returned to Ngeti's post-Christmas plans for himself, and he unfolded an idea for a development project, one that poetically reflected his emerging sensibility about his proper place in the world.

Ngeti explained, "You know, bwana, I'm trying hard not to only be concerned about doing things for myself anymore, because this has always led me down a wrong path and gotten me involved with some pretty nefarious motherfuckers. Also, one of my problems has been not taking Taita, and Taita people, seriously. You know, I've always been trying to get out, go do something somewhere else. But I think that maybe it would be better to try to do something good for people back in Taita. Going to Congo made me realize that not everyplace in Africa is the same, as honestly I had always thought. You know, now I feel lucky to be a Kenyan, and a Taita. There are business opportunities in Taita, and you don't need to go to Mombasa, but of course it's better if you have help from outside [internationally]. There is also politics, but first you need to establish yourself with some kind of development project, or in business. Jimmy, you've always talked to people in Taita about solar power, and how it could lead to economic independence for Taita villages and liberate us from these politicians. Right?"

"Yes, Ngeti, that's true, I believe . . ."

"But right now these solar panels are too expensive to do anything big in Taita. But there are NGOs that are interested in this solar thing too, and I am part of a CBO [a registered community-based organization], which can be used to apply for funds. So what we do is to get a donor to give us money to buy one solar panel, and we connect that panel to a business, the profits from which will be used to buy more solar panels and lanterns. So, here is the idea, specifically now. We invest in a solar power panel and use it to run a solar-powered egg incubator, and then we use the profits to buy solar-powered lanterns for Taita schoolchildren. We use M-Pesa [a digital money transfer system] to ensure transparency in the accounts.[7] Right now, there is not a single chicken incubator in the entire Taita Hills! This would be the first. As it is now, poultry farmers have to travel to Mombasa to get chicks, which of course adds to the cost of the chicks and the eggs. And the consumers bear this cost now. The profits will go directly to the kids' solar lanterns, and so ease our dependence on firewood, charcoal, and kerosene now. These lanterns will be given free of charge to the families of school kids in Mgange. And then the rest of the profits we put into a tree nursery. So we are saving trees and also growing trees!"

"Hmmm. If it were successful on a small scale, we could get more funding, maybe from Ford Foundation or the Gates Foundation," I added, growing excited.

"See, and this might help keep unemployed youth in Taita from going to cities in search of work, and also help children at school. Because people have been demoralized from learning because there are no jobs, and then you add to that the pollution from the kerosene lanterns in the homes and the respiratory problems for the adults."

"I think it's a great idea, Ngeti! It's a 'development project' that deals with the family, commerce, and ecology all at once, and it identifies a local solution that is right there and that relies ultimately on the sun."

Later, after our Christmas trip to Taita, on my bus ride back to Nairobi, I would reflect on how this idea expressed, in a new, viable way, the overall strategy that Ngeti had in fact been practicing his whole life. He had moved beyond the older Taita "development" model in which men tried to find work in the city or by modernizing Taita through various large-scale schemes like land consolidation. Rather, Ngeti wanted Taita to connect directly to the power of the sun, but first by developing an unmediated, non-binding connection to a foreign source of wealth. The resulting profit would, ideally, help to generate local commerce while making Taita a nicer place—its ecology greener and its people more cooperative with one another, the way many imagined life to have been in the past.

This strategy of bypassing oppressive and abusive local institutions to improve his life and the life of others had informed Ngeti's early desire to learn English even before he knew a single word of it, back when he had pretended to know the word for a nonexistent herbicide. It had also fueled his conversion to Pentecostalism, as well as his early hopes of obliterating any obstacles to his direct communication with God, especially the Catholic priests and nuns. But this particular idea, this strategy of developing enduring local business and exchange relationships by forging an unmediated connection with exogenous power, was honed in such a way that it seemed to me to be especially likely to generate something positive for himself and his community.

When it grew closer to Christmas, Ngeti and I made our way from Mombasa to the Hills. To start with, we spent time in the Taita administrative headquarters of Wundanyi checking out some of the changes that had taken place since I was last there seven years before. I was particularly impressed by the large new hotel with television sets and hot water, clearly built for the employees of development NGOs, virtually the only Kenyans here who could afford such a place. Later, I helped pick out the goats for the ceremony and the divination, and I took a couple of days to hike all over the hills by myself, catching up with old friends. So many people had died in the last ten years, and the youths that I used to laugh and converse with all had gray hair now. Many of the men still lacked the means to marry and so were technically still youths, but they strained to keep up with the pace of their young men's jobs, such as loading and unloading matatus for passengers. Some of the more enterprising ones had formed youth groups, or CBOs, through which to seek out donors from abroad. There was more electricity now throughout the region, and it was easier to get around on the ubiquitous motorbikes from China, which young men rented from more affluent owners and offered up as a sort of taxi service. A lot of people attributed all of this "movement" to the success of M-Pesa, which had made cash much more available to rural villagers than it had been in the past.

On the night before Christmas, I stayed up late talking to Charles, Ngeti's father, and presented him with a gift: a small, crank-operated radio and flashlight that needed no batteries, probably the number-one daily expense in the hills. Ngeti's sisters came in from Kampala, and more people started to trickle into Ngeti's compound. On Christmas day we drank the chofi that had been delivered the day before, slaughtered and roasted the goat, and held a small service over Monica's grave, which was located at the entrance to the compound. People came and went throughout the day, and Ngeti made preparations for the Catholic mass, which took place after I left. At night, a few of us men went to the packed village bar and danced for hours to reggae and Congolese music. I helped to carry home several of the fallen.

The next day, several of us walked down to Mbatia's place, a couple of miles down the hill, for my divination, with the goat trotting along beside us. We picked up Moses, one of Mbatia's neighbors, who is also skilled at divination, to help with the readings and the blessings. All divinations should have two readers, in case one person makes a mistake. Mbatia arose from his bed of sticks in his mud-and-thatch round house to greet us, and he dragged his aged body into the compound, while his grandchildren went about collecting the medicine-filled gourds that we needed that day. Mbatia prepared the sweet-smelling herbs from the forest, which people say reminds them of the way Taita used to smell when there were still forests everywhere. We rubbed the herbs over the goat and stuffed them in its mouth so that the goat's vula would truthfully communicate the ancestors' words. It didn't seem to matter that the ancestors in this case were born in Hell's Kitchen, New York. Then we took turns smothering the goat "peacefully" with our hands, without bloodshed, so as not to pollute the vula with the goat's "hot" and angry heart. While the young men did the slaughtering, Mbatia and I chatted in Kitaita about life in our respective homes. He told me about what Taita was like when it was a forest, and I told him about the generous return policy for hiking boots at REI.

At various points during the ceremony we performed kutasa, the act of taking chofi into our mouths and spraying it out so that it falls like rain on the target of the ritual. Later, when the large intestine was splayed out on the hide of the goat, Mbatia and his neighbor read the vula, teaching me more about the process along the way. When they were finished, Mbatia looked up at me and said, "When you were young, you fought with your father, and you never apologized. Now he's by himself, and that heat inside him is blocking any blessings that might come to you."

"So what do I need to do?" I asked, a little disappointed by the rather uninspired prognosis.

"You need to ask for his forgiveness and buy him a shirt."

"Just a shirt?" I asked, wondering if the ninety-something-year-old man was being anachronistic, since these days shirts were pretty mundane fare, even in Taita. But he assured me that it was not the price or rarity of the thing that mattered, but the state of my heart when giving the gift, which would rub off on the object and become part of my father's heart when it touched his chest.

I left Taita the next day. It was right after Christmas, and since everybody was trying to get back to home or work, it was hard to get a seat on any bus returning to Nairobi, so I had plenty of time to think. I thought about Mbatia's insistence that I ask my father for forgiveness (no easy task) and how the diagnostic solutions he offered Ngeti and myself were based on emotional considerations, aimed ultimately at establishing personal and social equilibrium. Powerful affective forces, which I might tentatively call "love" and "fear," have fueled all the events that are now depicted in this book, and they seemed to offer a sign about how we could choose to live in the world. Love for Ngeti drove his parents to the witchdoctors, even though it meant public ridicule and even if it guaranteed that the neighborhood rumors about their own witchcraft would have no end. His parents' love and shame goaded Ngeti's father to overcome fear and confront his own father and his wife in the dead of night. Later, Ngeti's love for his mother, and his shame surrounding his own status in life, brought him to Pentecostalism, and admiration for Patroba kept him there. Love and regret caused Ngeti to make amends with his parents, despite initial resistance. And love for Taita was encouraging Ngeti to think about starting his life over there from a new vantage point, and finding a new way to generate "development" by harnessing the power that was already there. Conversely, uncertainty about the reality of love fueled concerns about witchcraft and drove Ngeti to wonder if his parents were actually his parents. And this suspicion in turn led him to want to disconnect from Taita, and to instead develop an affective and imaginative relationship with people outside Taita and Kenya. In all cases, this force I'm calling love dissolved powerful boundaries, whether they were imposed by society, by governmental laws, or by one's own resentful memories. Love allowed people to go traveling.

I also thought about how eclectic and worldly (I almost wrote "catholic") was Ngeti's orientation to truth and knowledge, how accustomed he and other Wataita were to epistemic murk. They constantly moved between different sources of knowledge and ways of knowing, each of which seemed, from the outside, to be ontologically different. They freely translated from one set of codes or genres into another, and deftly incorporated multiple histories, temporalities, and geographies into their talk and practice, without necessarily making these different modes of knowledge equivalent or the same. Ngeti was able to speak English fluently, and to move between Taita and American understandings of things, while still recognizing that there were some experiences that were beyond translation and that he couldn't know or understand. It would be absurd to try and rationalize the affects that are the stuff of witchcraft away, or to imagine that for a thing to be real it must also be seen, felt, or heard. Ngeti not only moved between ways of knowing, but he moved back and forth between certitude and doubt, ultimately coming to the conclusion that he knew very little, and that everything was possible. For him, it made sense to accept the possibility of living ancestors and demons alike, while also maintaining a healthy suspicion along the way—to embrace not knowing and to act accordingly. I thought about how cosmopolitan, for lack of a better word, this approach to the world was, and how, in comparison, I was headed home to a backward place, even if the United States was materially richer (at least for some).

Ngeti and many other Kenyans were working to find ways to develop enduring connections with people they felt to be different in many ways, even if it
was also the case that some Kenyan politicians goaded their constituents to
murder members of "foreign" ethnicities in the run-up to the 2008 elections so
they could retain their seats. Meanwhile, frightened people in my home country were obsessed with building obscenely expensive fences to keep others out,
and as many as one in four Americans believed the nation's first black president
was not a legitimate U.S. citizen. Indeed, the whole world, from Botswana to
India to Saudi Arabia (to say nothing of more well-worn examples, like Texas,
Israel, and South Africa), seemed obsessed with building monumental brick-
and-mortar walls, and even complex matrices of internal walls, in a time of
increasing global connectedness and waning state sovereignty.[8]

At the same time that these ineffective walls were going up, the points of
commonality between different parts of the world were becoming impossible
to ignore. To cite but one obvious example, economic inequality had exploded
in the United States to a level unheard of since the Great Depression, and the
political system was increasingly rigged in favor of elites, a situation that
resembled Kenya and other postcolonial African countries I knew.[9] Moreover,
everything was becoming commodified—meaning that everything could be
bought and sold—and this process threatened the foundations of society and
the possibility of a sustainable future. It was this same commodification of
social relationships and ecology that Ngeti and his family were reacting to in
their witchcraft accusations and counter-witchcraft measures (which is not
to say that ideas about witchcraft are reducible to economic concerns, only
that they do reflect and respond to these concerns). They were in effect worrying about what could, what *did,* happen in a world where everything was
for sale.

Maybe, I thought, such increasingly apparent similarities between "us"
and "them" would help Americans and other people in the Global North to
"evolve" toward Africa—to embrace mobility, dialogue, and radical change
in their lives and politics, a process that Jean and John Comaroff suggest is
already well under way.[10] Maybe Americans and others would recognize
points of connection with people who, like them, didn't "know what the fuck
was going on politically," as Ngeti put it, by focusing on that which unites us
as opposed to that which separates us. Maybe we could take a cue from Ngeti,
whose everyday practice and whole life history embraced a complex global
totality in which meaning could only be established through dialogue. Such
a practice mocks the empty and unsustainable trope of the monolithic wall

that keeps others out, making such walls seem ridiculous and so draining them of their legitimacy and power.

When the bus finally arrived in Nairobi, I made my way to a men's clothing store on Tom Mboya Street and bought a nice peach-colored button-down dress shirt wrapped in cellophane from the Indian shop owner. About a month later, I flew from California to Florida to visit my parents in their assisted living facility. After signing the guest book, I went up the elevator and around the corner to their apartment. The door was open, as always, to allow for the on-site nurses to check in and to distribute "the meds." Debbie, their on-call Jamaican certified nursing assistant, was in the bathroom changing Dad's diapers. I spied, on a fold-out table, her Chinese take-out, which she made pains to hide from the building management so they wouldn't accuse her of pocketing money from my parents' wallets. Mom was on the couch, staring blankly at the Patriots game. She no longer recognized visitors and spoke very little. Eventually, Debbie wheeled Dad into the room, and I sat on the floor in front of him as he strained to see me through eyes plagued by macular degeneration.

"There's nothing to worry about," Debbie assured me. "They get good care, and three times a week I get your mom catfish and hushpuppies, and your dad pulled pork, from Sonny's Barbeque next door, across from the Denny's. They love it. Once in a while we even go to Cracker Barrel. Isn't that right, Roy?"

"If you say so," he managed.

"Does anyone ever call?" I asked. My parents have seven living children between them. It crossed my mind that, if my Kenyan friends could see this, they would find this outsourcing of a parent's care to be cruel, perhaps even unforgivable.

"Your mother's sister calls every week. Sometimes one or two of the other children call."

"Hey, Dad," I said, kneeling in front of his wheelchair. "How are you doing?"

"Not good," he croaked. "They follow my every move. They've planted electrodes in my toes. Every time I move, the electrodes send a message to a computer in the basement." I looked down at his barefoot toes and saw what looked to be a particularly nasty fungal infection.

He continued, "Everyone's a Nurse Ratched. They listen in on everything I'm saying. If they see that I'm going to say anything they don't want the world to know, they send a signal to my brain that changes the way the words come out of my mouth so it sounds like I'm talking nonsense."

Debbie laughed. "Oh, Roy! You have such an imagination. Yesterday he was in Alaska. The day before that we were on the run from the Boston City Police. It's always an adventure, that's for sure."

"I'm sorry, Dad," I said, feeling terrible that he was alone and afraid in this alien, bureaucratic institution. It occurred to me that in his so-called madness, Dad had access to a reality that was especially real, that he was able to see things that others couldn't see, much in the same way as Ngeti had once perceived an invisible realty that was covered over by the polite civility of village life.

"Listen," he continued. "They're running a drug and prostitution outfit and they don't want anyone to know, but I hear them. We're at the center of an international narcotics operation." Given the twenty or so types of potent pharmaceuticals I knew him to be on, this accusation made an awful lot of sense. "They want to control everyone in the country through the food supply. Food distribution. They'll use the poisoned food to turn us all into sheep." Abruptly he stopped and, looking up at me wildly, asked, "Why am I even wasting my time talking to you, when you don't believe anything I say? Just please get me in touch with my contact at the FBI! . . ."

"Dad, I'm so sorry you have to be here. I'm sorry about everything."

"Why?" he asked, the paranoia dropping away. "There's nothing you could have done about it. We all made mistakes along the way. I can't imagine any other way it could have gone. But now you have to help me, because there isn't much time. We have to . . ."

"Well, Dad," I interjected. "I bought you a shirt."

"Oh, look at that shirt, Roy! That's a beautiful shirt!" Debbie chimed in, on cue.

We helped Dad stand up and take off his shirt to reveal his skin, paper-thin from the Warfarin and covered in bruises. The smallest of nicks would produce a small waterfall of pink blood.

But, after a lot of wrestling with Debbie, Dad did manage to put the shirt on, and he smiled. "This is a very nice shirt. Thank you. You didn't have to do that." He was calming down.

"You're welcome, Dad," I choked. Then I reached for my cell phone and texted Moses, the junior diviner, in Taita language.

The text read, "It is finished."

Appendix of Names

PATERNAL KIN

BONIFACE NGETI (1922–94): Ngeti's father's father

ELIZA SAMBA (1925–63): Boniface's first wife, and Ngeti's paternal grandmother

ELIZA "TANZANIA" (b. 1942): Boniface's second wife

CHARLES MWADIME (b. 1942): Ngeti's father (married to Monica Shali)

STANLEY MGHENDI (b. 1945): Charles's brother

VENANT MAGHANGA (1948–2009): Charles's brother

SILVESTER MWAWASI (b. 1959): Charles's brother

GASPARY MWATABU (b. 1963): Charles's brother

ALBERATA (b. 1951): Charles's sister

Ngeti also has three younger sisters, LYN, AMANDA, AND PRAXEDY.

MATERNAL KIN

ANTHONY MAGHANGA (1913–1960s): Ngeti's mother's father (married to Clemence Samba, 1916–?)

MONICA SHALI (1944–2005): Ngeti's mother (married to Charles Mwadime)

DAVID (DAUDI) MAGHANGA (b. 1933): Monica's brother

SALOME MAGHANGA (b. 1936): Monica's sister (married to Fulgence Mwakamba)

FRUMENCE MWASARU ("MVIRINGO") (b. 1939): Monica's brother (married to Magret)

VALENTINE MJOMBA (1941–2005): Monica's brother (married to Veronica, b. 1939)

WILLIAM WACHENJE (1950–2003): Monica's brother

THE PENTECOSTAL FAMILY

PATROBA: Ngeti's Pentecostal mentor and prophet

OLYMPIA: Patroba's wife

WILLIAM: a Pentecostal follower of Patroba, and Ngeti's friend and prospective business partner

MAMA ESTHER AND MRS. MWABILI: deceased women who had once prayed with Patroba, and who introduced Ngeti's mother to Patroba

MTONGOLO: Patroba's wife's father

MERCY: Patroba's youngest daughter

JANE: Patroba's wife's elder sister

NOTES

CHAPTER 1

1. Smith 2011; Smith and Mantz 2006. Although the demand for minerals is important, it is not the main cause of conflict in the Eastern DRC.

2. The Mai Mai are Congolese militias from different parts of the eastern Congo, who emerged in part to resist the invasion of that region by Rwandans and other groups during the Congolese war. In many areas, they also represented and effected a youth revolt against established governmental structures. *Mai* means water in Congolese Swahili; the term Mai Mai refers to their ability to use spritual and material resources from the forest (ancestors, embodied in what Mai Mai refer to as the "leaves") to turn bullets into water.

3. Eggers 2006; Dau and Sweeney 2008.

4. Chernoff 2003, 2008.

5. Ashforth 1999.

6. Griaule 1965; Turner 1967; Shostak 1981.

7. As this book was coming to press, I learned of Binyavanga Wainaina's brilliant memoir focusing on his everyday life growing up as a middle-class Kikuyu during Daniel Arap Moi's presidency (Wainaina 2011). His book, like this one, focuses on people trying to make their way in life and effecting change through their actions. Binyavanga's early life and aspirations, like Ngeti's, were shaped by foreign media, and he felt similarly alienated from his immediate surroundings, which he transcended through books.

8. This phrase comes from Mikhail Bakhtin's essay "The Problem of Speech Genres," in Bakhtin 1986.

9. Wataita like to say that the moist coolness of the hills is reflected in their hearts and dispositions, and that they are more peace-seeking and diplomatic than people who live in the hot plains and in cities made hot by the stress and contention in people's hearts.

10. Ancestors play a major role in much of African life and thought; for an excellent overview and interpretation of African ideas about ancestors and their

relationship to society and social structure, see Kopytoff 1971. In Taita, the idea that people are surrounded by a past that they don't control is embodied most powerfully in Taita's *fighi* forest shrines, which are supposed to protect Wataita but are seen as being currently out of control, sometimes protecting and sometimes causing disease and death to the very people fighi are supposed to protect. Fighi (the word means stopper or cork) are sacred groves composed of ritually treated indigenous forests located at various places in the hills. These fighi once marked the boundaries between neighborhoods and activity zones (separating the fields from the residential areas, for example). People say that the fighi were designed to protect Wataita from outsiders, presenting a kind of magical force field that would prevent an enemy from leaving with social resources like livestock, or that sometimes would simply kill the enemy then and there. These fighi were "made" by ancestors, who in a way programmed them, but these days they do not work in the way they should, because Wataita don't know how to reprogram them, or the fighi resist being reprogrammed. More often than not, they kill the people they should be protecting, because the fighi do not recognize contemporary Wataita, seeing them as alien enemies, or because people are living in places where people did not traditionally live and these new residents are unwittingly violating fighi taboos (Smith 2008). Fighi demonstrate how Wataita feel at once subject to and alienated from the ancestors specifically, and from the past and locality more generally. These days, Taita elders are trying to secure money from international NGOs so they can revitalize the fighi, which they see as a symbol and guarantor of Taita cultural heritage.

11. The term Kidabida, or Kidawida, refers to the language of the hills. Wataita call their language Kidabida, which is actually an emic name for the language. They also use the word Kitaita (the language of the Taita), which is other people's name for this language, as Taita is actually the Swahili word for the people of the Taita Hills, or Wadabida/Wadawida. For clarity's sake, and because this is the word Ngeti uses, I have mostly used Kitaita in this book.

12. This was another thing that was changing in the 1990s: due to "multipartyism," politicians had to court people back home in the rural areas and couldn't always depend on the support of powerful patrons in the way that they did in the 1980s.

13. Monica's religious practice is reminiscent of Michel de Certeau's *The Mystic Fable* (1992), in which he depicted the relationship between medieval and early modern female mystics, who spoke in "tongues," and male-dominated Catholic religious institutions.

14. Ngeti had just helped me to see the central argument that was emerging in my dissertation. For Wataita, "development" didn't have to be synonymous with modernity and capitalism; it could also refer to an imagined social order that was threatened by these forces. And "witchcraft" was as likely to come from outside Kenya in the form of a World Bank structural adjustment program as it was to come from a mother's brother. In fact, these social and economic austerity programs, and other "development" interventions, were sometimes interpreted as plans concocted by an international cabal of devil worshipers, hyperadvanced witches who sacrificed the poor to enrich themselves.

I wrote him an email in response, which was intended to point out certain things Taita and the United States share in common. Part of the email reads,

Thanks, *bwana. Nashukuru sana kwa msaada yako* [I'm grateful for your help]. Your support means a lot. And Taita asses aren't the only ones that are gonna be blasted to oblivion by forces they don't understand. The ice caps are melting and the thawing permafrost is releasing its methane, and when it does I have no doubt my government will respond by trying to extract whatever petroleum is beneath the ice, making all our hearts hotter [this is a reference to Taita ideas about hearts being made hot by contemporary life]. Anyway, say hi to everyone there.

15. In Wundanyi, the government administrative center for Taita District, the first general of postcolonial Christian government elites tore down a fighi forest shrine, a conduit for the power of elders and ancestors, to build a library. In doing so, they hoped to replace an older mechanism for defending Taita's autonomy, through "magic" and ancestor recognition, with education. In the 1950s, the Taita Fighi Union, a political association of educated Taita elites, wrote a manifesto in which they said that "schooling is the fighi of today"—meaning that education would protect Taita communities in the way that elders and, through them, ancestors had done through fighi.

16. Bravman 1998.

17. Fighi are defender shrines that protect geographical areas (see above, n. 9), and *milimu* are lineage shrines that allow household heads to communicate with ancestors.

18. Sahlins 2012.

19. There is a great deal of literature on post-Fordism; two good introductions are Harvey 1991 and Amin 2003. Much of this literature has focused on what Harvey calls the space-time compression brought about by changes in capitalism, and some authors have discussed how these changes in temporality have played out in Africa, including Hoffman (2011), Smith (2011), and Guyer (2007).

20. Kenya's newly independent government agreed to purchase high-quality land from white settlers at inflated prices and borrowed the money to do so from Great Britain.

21. Haugerud 1995.

22. A great deal of current Africanist anthropology is framed by the transformations set in motion by structural adjustment programs and the decreasing ability of states to control their territories, as well as the meaning of "development," under what are sometimes referred to as "neoliberal" or "post-Fordist" conditions. See, for example, Comaroff and Comaroff 2001; Ferguson 2006; Roitman 2005; Smith 2008; Piot 2010; and White 2012.

23. For a related discussion of how African youth consciousness has been shaped by global media and media imagery, see Cole 2010; Weiss 2009; and Shipley 2013.

24. Much of the literature on post–structural adjustment Africa has focused specifically on how Africans work to produce the future in a context defined by extreme crisis and precariousness; see, for example, Ferguson 1999; Weiss 2004; Piot

2010; and Cole 2010. For a somewhat more positive take on how Africans adapt to structural adjustment by drawing on cultural resources to become agents of globalization, see Stoller 2002. Also see Buggenhagen 2012.

25. Much of the literature on post–structural adjustment Africa is also focused on African efforts to determine and fix reality under circumstances of radical flux, for example Jones 2010; Blunt 2004; Weiss 2004; and Newell 2012.

26. Ngeti sees this as an attempt to escape from biological kinship, but Taita kinship relations are, like all kinship relations, ultimately cultural (in Taita, for example, one's father's brother is actually one's father, and this is not just a metaphor but an actual ontological relationship). See, for example, Sahlins 2012.

27. For more on African subjectivities in the context of globalization and neoliberalism, see Werbner 2002 and Makhulu, Buggenhagen, and Jackson 2010. For a somewhat different, and brilliant, discussion of the emergence of a relational subjectivity defined in religious terms, see McIntosh 2009.

28. These contributing conditions of possibility for modern self-formation are numerous, and different theorists from Max Weber to Michel Foucault have emphasized different ones at different times, including Protestantism, capitalism, books of etiquette, state formation and political hierarchy, the French revolution, legal contracts, prisons, psychiatry, and pharmaceuticals, or some combination of these. The basic idea is that over time, and through multiple, mutually reinforcing happenings, "we" came to see ourselves as, and also became, self-regulating "Individuals" of the Promethean variety. Some of the major works that have dealt with this issue in different ways include Weber 2002; Simmel 1972; Elias 2000; Foucault 1995; and Taylor 1992.

29. Macpherson 2011.

30. Williams 1985.

31. An oft-cited example of this is Georg Hegel (2011), who used African nonsubjectivity as a counterfactual baseline for his analysis of a universal World History in which Africa was not included.

32. See, for example, Fortes 1973 and Lienhardt 1985.

33. Comaroff and Comaroff 2012.

34. Harris 1978.

35. On the surface, women were largely excluded from this expansive process of self-becoming through others, instead becoming dependents of men and producers of lineages when they left their homes to marry their husbands. Still, they exercised quite a bit of agency in these homes, and their power became more marked as migrant male workers began spending most of their lives in Mombasa and the women asserted themselves against their senior in-laws over the control of their husbands' wage labor remittances.

36. See Harris 1978.

37. Hoy 2012, 29.

38. Holmes and Marcus 2008; Choy et al. 2009.

39. See, for example, Marcus 2000.

40. Holmes and Marcus 2004.

41. Piot 1999.

CHAPTER 2

1. Appadurai 1996.
2. See Ferguson 1999, chap. 7.
3. To be fair, many of these students had come to believe that there was a "real" historical African culture that had been systematically expropriated from them. Some felt that the tastes, habits, and values with which they had come to identify did not really belong to them, and that their possession of these traits was artificial and destructive. Many hoped to regain their lost heritage in my classes on Africa. To their credit, they were usually pleasantly surprised by what we actually ended up covering—material that tended to focus on the colorful "gray" areas, the interstices between familiarity and difference, in which so much African cultural and political production occurs.
4. See, for example, Mudimbe 1988, 1994; and Appiah 2008.
5. Hegel 2011.
6. Fanon 1967, 17–18.
7. For colonial Kenyan psychological anthropologists of the African mind like J. C. Carothers and Louis Leaky, Africans' knowledge of the European Other combined with their marginalization to produce psychosis that then masqueraded as politics.
8. Ngugi wa Thiongo 1986.
9. Ferguson 2006, 158.
10. I am thinking here of the contemporary fascination with the supposedly "open" communication made possible by digital technology, amply criticized by Evgeny Morozov (2013).
11. Mbembe 2002, 242.
12. Ibid., 258.
13. Deleuze and Guattari 1987, 21.
14. Here I have in mind Gayatri Spivak's influential 1988 essay "Can the Subaltern Speak?" in which she argues that "Other," subaltern practices exceed the representational frameworks of modernist Western thought, and so the subaltern cannot be said to "speak." For a sense of the impact this essay has had on anthropology and postcolonial studies, see Morris 2010.
15. Bakhtin 1986.

CHAPTER 3

1. *Waghanga* roughly translates as healer or doctor, but can also have a negative connotation.
2. *Croissant* is another word Ngeti picked up from the *Oxford English Dictionary,* rather than from the "lived experience" of eating croissants.
3. During the 1890s, Wataita were compelled to work as porters for the railroad, during which time they encountered the infamous "man-eaters of Tsavo," among

other forms of violence. My "butterfly" reference alludes to the fact that Taita seniors, remembering the stories that their elders told them about the coming of whites, sometimes said that the soldiers of the British Imperial East Africa Company resembled butterflies. In a related vein, the nineteenth-century Kikuyu prophet Mugo Kibiru is said to have predicted that his people would be visited by white frogs with butterfly wings, who would rule the land for a period of time before being ousted.

4. In central Kenya, this development project was designed to create a buffer class of cash crop–growing Kikuyu whose sympathies lay with the colonial government. (Kikuyu had formerly been legally prevented from growing cash crops.)

5. For a stunning overview of Kenyan land tenure practices and changes brought about by land tenure reform, see Shipton 2009. Fleuret (1988) has also written about land reform in Taita.

6. Land consolidation also entailed the forced fragmentation of circular villages, composed of up to four generations of brothers and their families, as individual households were relocated to individual plots. The old concentric rings of circular homes orbiting around a single, semipublic space (in Taita, the *baza*) were dissembled, and households found themselves "on their own" in what people sometimes describe as "alien" territory. Some families even talked to me about having found themselves "on Mars." Moreover, sources of community protection and ancestral recognition, like the fighi and ngomenyi, were now located on privately owned land and no longer belonged to the public in the way they had before.

7. For an extended discussion of this model of development, see Scott 1999.

8. Freud 1919.

9. Jean Comaroff, in a class I took with her in graduate school, said that the anthropologist Audrey Richards long ago wrote that "witchcraft is always in the next village." I have never been able to find the quote, but Ngeti's passage here reminds me of it.

10. The Kamba are a large, neighboring ethnic group notorious, among Wataita, for witchcraft.

11. A *kanzu* is a white tunic, associated in Kenya with Swahili Muslims.

12. Smith 2001, 2008.

13. Maji Marefu is a Tanzanian witch-hunter who spent time in Taita when I was there, and who continues to sell his services hunting witches to villages in Kenya. On the Kamba, see n. 10.

14. Mbembe 2001, 108.

15. This woman was proposing taking urban jinn spirits and using them to defend the rural household from what was likely local witchcraft. So they were looking to use a more advanced and commercialized form of witchcraft to defeat inherited knowledge.

16. Because they attract people and things from diverse places, many of whom compete against one another commercially, border towns are considered places of very advanced and exotic witchcraft.

17. This difference would become an issue for interpreters of this ritual later on.

18. Gennep 1960; Turner 1967.

19. He later reworked his theories to include "liminoid" states that extended beyond marked rituals, including the "hippie" movement in the United States.

20. Turner eventually came to believe that communitas, or the dissolution of hierarchy and the production of egalitarian connectedness, was the source of all radical social transformation and historical change. But Turner's writings on ritual in Africa focused almost exclusively on the production of conformity and "continuity" in the face of conflict and "schism." Like virtually every anthropologist of his era, he was more concerned with how people like the Ndembu, ridden with social and ideological conflicts as Turner knew them to be, managed to become good Ndembu.

CHAPTER 4

1. The description of the flying light appears on page 11 of Evans-Pritchard 1976. On page 18, Evans-Pritchard opines, "Witches, as the Azande conceive them, clearly cannot exist." Paul Stoller, in his groundbreaking *In Sorcery's Shadow* (1989), depicts himself, an anthropologist, engaging with this ambivalence most directly. He starts off his fieldwork experience as a positivist social scientist and ends up a shaman, more or less persuaded of the reality of things that are beyond direct empirical perception.

2. More recent literature on the anthropology of witchcraft tends to see witchcraft and counter-witchcraft as ways of apprehending and intervening in political and economic transformations; at the same, witchcraft and counter-witchcraft are not reducible to politics and economics. See, for example, Ashforth 2005; Smith 2008; West 2005; Comaroff and Comaroff 1999; and Niehaus, 2001.

3. This line of reasoning is in keeping with Evans-Pritchard's argument that witchcraft beliefs identify a social explanation for misfortune and are rational for this reason, but recent literature broadens the definition of the social to include larger scales of social belonging, including global capitalism and state-society interactions. See, for example, Geschiere 1997.

4. Ferguson 2006; Geschiere 1997; Comaroff and Comaroff 1999; Smith 2008.

5. West 2007. For similar arguments, see Ashforth 2005; Marshall 2009.

6. Here I also have in mind Evans-Pritchard's *Oracles Witchcraft and Magic among the Azande* (1976), in which he claims that "Azande do not see that their oracles tell them nothing! Their blindness is not due to stupidity; they reason excellently in the idiom of their beliefs, but they cannot reason outside, or against their beliefs because they have no other idiom in which to express their thoughts" (159). The lack of another idiom is clearly not a problem for Ngeti, or his friends.

CHAPTER 5

1. The idea that Africans are modeling or evaluating themselves after their mediated understandings of other parts of the world is a very common theme in Africanist

literature. So, too, is the argument that Africans imagine that economic decline has caused life to become simulacral, or a fake copy of something that exists in a more true form elsewhere. In 1992, Achille Mbembe famously wrote about the performance of postcolonial African politics as "simulacral," in his extremely influential *Public Culture* essay. Anthropologists who have, in one way or another, considered "simulacrality," or the disconnection of signs from referents, as a product of economic decline (including structural adjustment programs) and as a prism for understanding how Africans reflect on their situation include Smith (2008, 2011), Sewell (2009), Blunt (2004), Apter (1999, 2005), Weiss (2009), Stroeken (2005), and Jones (2010).

2. For more on the relationship between Pentecostalism, NGOs, and neoliberalism, see Smith 2008; Piot 2010; and Freeman 2012.

3. Birgit Meyer (1998) discusses Pentecostal ritual as a way of acting on and domesticating globalization.

4. Meyer 1998; see also Marshall 2008.

5. See also Mbembe 2002.

6. Marshall 2009.

7. This theory harmonizes very well with post-Fordist, or neoliberal, philosophy, which privileges the actions of atomized individuals producing the public good over outmoded structures, which obstruct "progress" and which neoliberal interventions erode through deregulation and market reforms.

8. Marshall 2009, 10.

9. As of this writing, South Africa is the only sub-Saharan country with a McDonald's. Many Kenyans (including Ngeti) imagine McDonald's and other fast-food chains to represent the height of Western cuisine and "clean" food *(chakula safi);* in Nairobi, South African fast-food chains offering similar products cater to the demands of that city's growing "middle class." This is another obvious example of how globalization stimulates the imaginations in ways that are at odds with "reality" (meaning, here, the reality of McDonald's).

10. Such as Meyer 1998; Marshall 2009; Guyer 2007; and McGovern, 2012.

11. Meyer 1998.

12. Piot 2010.

13. Marshall 2009; Marx 1975; Benjamin 1968.

14. Marshall 2009, 66.

15. Guyer 2007.

16. Bourdieu 1977.

17. Harvey 1990.

CHAPTER 6

1. Luhrmann 2012.

2. Weiss 1992, 549.

CHAPTER 8

1. Annemarie Mol (1992) discusses, in a very different social context, how multiple diseases, and multiple bodies, are "done" and how these "mutually inclusive" diseases are made to cohere through particular practices and interactions.

2. Wataita often associate Digo women, who live in the hot plains closer to the coast, with witchcraft and intense sexuality.

3. See Besteman and Gusterson 2005.

4. Bayart 1993.

5. Darius Mbela was a hyper-masculine former prize fighter and dockworker who became a notoriously ruthless member of Parliament in the 1980s.

6. Wataita tend to believe that demons live underground; some see ancestors as living closer to the topsoil, but there is often disagreement as to whether ancestors and demons are actually distinct.

7. M-Pesa is run by the cell phone company Safaricom. In this system, money is stored on, and transmitted through, a cell phone, then picked up at a Safaricom kiosk for a fee. In Kenya today, one can go to any market and buy almost anything using the cell phone, without ever exchanging cash.

8. James 2010.

9. In October 2013 the United States came to resemble these countries—one thinks particularly of Zimbabwe—even more profoundly when the government actually shut down because the Congress failed to produce a budget, the one thing it is constitutionally mandated to do.

10. Comaroff and Comaroff 2012.

BIBLIOGRAPHY

Amin, Ash. 1994. *Post-Fordism: A Reader*. Oxford: Blackwell.

Appadurai, Arjun. 1996. *Modernity at Large*. Minneapolis: University of Minnesota Press.

Appiah, Anthony, and the Royal Ontario Museum. 2008. *The Politics of Culture, the Politics of Identity*. Toronto: ICC at the ROM.Apter, Andrew H. 1999. "Africa, Empire, and Anthropology: A Philological Exploration of Anthropology's Heart of Darkness." *Annual Review of Anthropology* 28: 577–598.

———. 2005. *The Pan-African Nation: Oil and the Spectacle of Culture in Nigeria*. Chicago: University of Chicago Press.

Ashforth, Adam. 2000. *Madumo, a Man Bewitched*. Chicago: University of Chicago Press.

———. 2005. *Witchcraft, Violence, and Democracy in South Africa*. Chicago: University of Chicago Press.

Bakhtin, M. M. 1986. *Speech Genres and Other Late Essays*. Translated by Vern M. McGee; edited by Carly Emerson and Michael Holquist. Austin: University of Texas Press.

Bayart, Jean-François. 1993. *The State in Africa: The Politics of the Belly*. London: Longman.

Benjamin, Walter. 1968. "Theses on the Philosophy of History." In *Illuminations*, translated by Harry Zohn; edited and with an introduction by Hannah Arendt. New York: Harcourt, Brace & World.

Besteman, Catherine Lowe, and Hugh Gusterson. 2005. *Why America's Top Pundits Are Wrong: Anthropologists Talk Back*. Berkeley: University of California Press.

Blunt, Robert. 2004. "Satan Is an Imitator: Kenya's Recent Cosmology of Corruption." In *Producing African Futures: Ritual and Reproduction in a Neoliberal Age*, edited by Brad Weiss. Leiden: Brill.

Bourdieu, Pierre. 1977. *Outline of a Theory of Practice*. Cambridge: Cambridge University Press.

Bravman, Bill. 1998. *Making Ethnic Ways: Communities and Their Transformations in Taita, Kenya, 1800–1950*. Portsmouth, N.H.: Heinemann.

Brown, Wendy. 2010. *Walled States, Waning Sovereignty.* New York: Zone Books.

Buggenhagen, Beth A. 2013. *Muslim Families in Global Senegal.* Bloomington: Indiana University Press.

Carithers, Michael, Steven Collins, and Steven Lukes. 1985. *The Category of the Person: Anthropology, Philosophy, History.* Cambridge: Cambridge University Press.

Carothers, John Colin. 1955. *The Psychology of Mau Mau.* Nairobi: Printed by the Govt. printer.

Certeau, Michel de. 1992. *The Mystic Fable.* Vol. 1, *The Sixteenth and Seventeenth Centuries.* Chicago: University of Chicago Press.

Chernoff, John Miller. 2003. *Hustling Is Not Stealing: Stories of an African Bar Girl.* Chicago: University of Chicago Press.

———. 2005. *Exchange Is Not Robbery: More Stories of an African Bar Girl.* Chicago: University of Chicago Press.

Choy, T. K., L. Faier, M. J. Hathaway, M. Inoue, S. Satsuka, and A. Tsing. 2009. "A New Form of Collaboration in Cultural Anthropology: Matsutake Worlds." *American Ethnologist* 36 (2): 380–403.

Cole, Jennifer. 2010. *Sex and Salvation: Imagining the Future in Madagascar.* Chicago: University of Chicago Press.

Comaroff, John L., and Jean Comaroff. 1992. *Ethnography and the Historical Imagination.* Boulder, Colo.: Westview Press.

———, eds. 1999a. *Civil Society and the Political Imagination in Africa: Critical Perspectives.* Chicago: University of Chicago Press.

———. 1999b. *On Personhood: An Anthropological Perspective from Africa.* Chicago: American Bar Foundation.

———, eds. 2001. *Millennial Capitalism and the Culture of Neoliberalism.* Durham, N.C.: Duke University Press.

———. 2012. *Theory from the South; or, How Euro-America Is Evolving toward Africa.* Boulder, Colo.: Paradigm Publishers.

Dau, John Bul, and Michael S. Sweeney. 2007. *God Grew Tired of Us.* Washington, D.C.: National Geographic.

Deleuze, Gilles, and Félix Guattari. 1987. *A Thousand Plateaus.* Minneapolis: University of Minnesota Press.

Eggers, Dave. 2006. *What Is the What: The Autobiography of Valentino Achak Deng—A Novel.* San Francisco: McSweeney's.

Elias, Norbert. 1978. *The Civilizing Process.* New York: Urizen Books.

Evans-Pritchard, E. E., and Eva Gillies. 1976. *Witchcraft, Oracles, and Magic among the Azande.* Oxford: Clarendon Press.

Fanon, Frantz. 1967. *Black Skin, White Masks.* New York: Grove Press.

Ferguson, James. 1999. *Expectations of Modernity: Myths and Meanings of Urban Life on the Zambian Copperbelt.* Berkeley: University of California Press.

———. 2002. "Global Disconnect: Abjection and the Aftermath of Modernism." In *The Anthropology of Globalization: A Reader,* edited by Jonathan Xavier Inda and Renato Rosaldo. Malden, Mass.: Blackwell Publishers.

———. 2006. *Global Shadows: Africa in the Neoliberal World Order.* Durham, N.C.: Duke University Press.

Fortes, Meyer. 1971. *On the Concept of the Person among the Tallensi.* Colloques Internationaux du Centre National de la Recherche Scientifique, no. 544. Paris: CNRS.

Foucault, Michel. 1995. *Discipline and Punish: The Birth of the Prison.* New York: Vintage Books.

Freeman, Dena. 2012. *Pentecostalism and Development: Churches, NGOs, and Social Change in Africa.* Basingstoke, U.K.: Palgrave Macmillan; Jerusalem: Van Leer Jerusalem Institute.

Freud, Sigmund. 2003. *The Uncanny.* Translated by David McLintock, with an introduction by Hugh Haughton. New York: Penguin Books.

Gennep, Arnold van. 1960. *The Rites of Passage.* London: Routledge & Paul.

Geschiere, Peter, and Janet L. Roitman. 1997. *The Modernity of Witchcraft: Politics and the Occult in Postcolonial Africa = Sorcellerie et politique en Afrique: La viande des autres.* Charlottesville: University Press of Virginia.

Gluckman, Herman Max. 1954. *Rituals of Rebellion in South-East Africa.* Manchester: Manchester University Press.

Griaule, Marcel. 1970. *Conversations with Ogotemmêli: An Introduction to Dogon Religious Ideas.* London: Published for the International African Institute by the Oxford University Press.

Guyer, Jane I. 2007. "Prophecy and the Near Future: Thoughts on Macroeconomic, Evangelical, and Punctuated Time." *American Ethnologist* 34 (3): 409–421.

Harris, Grace Gredys. 1978. *Casting Out Anger: Religion among the Taita of Kenya.* Cambridge: Cambridge University Press.

Harvey, David. 1990. *The Condition of Postmodernity: An Enquiry into the Origins of Cultural Change.* Oxford: Blackwell.

Haugerud, Angelique. 1995. *The Culture of Politics in Modern Kenya.* Cambridge: Cambridge University Press.

Hegel, Georg Wilhelm Friedrich. 2011. *Lectures on the Philosophy of World History.* Edited and translated by Robert F. Brown and Peter C. Hodgson. Oxford: Clarendon Press.

Hoffman, Daniel. 2011. "Violence, Just in Time: War and Work in Contemporary West Africa." *Cultural Anthropology* 26 (1): 34–57.

Holmes, Douglas R., and George E. Marcus. 2004. "Cultures of Expertise and the Management of Globalization: Toward the Re-functioning of Ethnography." In *Global Assemblages: Technology, Politics, and Ethics as Anthropological Problems,* ed. Aihwa Ong and Stephen J. Collier. Malden, Mass.: Blackwell Publishers.

———. 2008. "Collaboration Today and the Re-Imagination of the Classic Scene of Fieldwork Encounter." *Collaborative Anthropologies* 1 (1): 81–101.

Hoy, David Couzens. 2012. *The Time of Our Lives: A Critical History of Temporality.* Cambridge, Mass.: MIT Press.

Jones, Jeremy. 2010. "'Nothing Is Straight in Zimbabwe': The Rise of the Kukiya-kiya Economy, 2000–2008." *Journal of Southern African Studies* 36 (2): 285–299.

Kopytoff, Igor. 1971. *Ancestors as Elders in Africa*. Indianapolis: Bobbs-Merrill.

Leakey, L. S. B. 1977. *Defeating Mau Mau*. New York: AMS Press.

Leinhardt, Godfrey. 1985. "Self: Public, Private, Some African Representations." In *The Category of the Person: Anthropology, Philosophy, History*, edited by Michael Carters, Steven Collins, and Steven Lukes. Cambridge: Cambridge University Press.

Luhrmann, T. M. 2012. *When God Talks Back: Understanding the American Evangelical Relationship with God*. New York: Alfred A. Knopf.

Macpherson, C. B. 1962. *The Political Theory of Possessive Individualism: Hobbes to Locke*. Oxford: Clarendon Press.

Makhulu, Anne-Maria, Beth A. Buggenhagen, and Stephen Jackson. 2010. *Hard Work, Hard Times: Global Volatility and African Subjectivities*. Berkeley: University of California Press.

Marcus, George E. 2000. *Para-sites: A Casebook against Cynical Reason*. Chicago: University of Chicago Press.

Marshall, Ruth. 2009. *Political Spiritualities: The Pentecostal Revolution in Nigeria*. Chicago: University of Chicago Press.

Marx, Karl. 1975. *The Eighteenth Brumaire of Louis Bonaparte, with Explanatory Notes*. New York: International Publishers.

Mauss, Marcel. 1954. *The Gift: Forms and Functions of Exchange in Archaic Societies*. Translated by Ian Cunnison, with an introduction by E. E. Evans-Pritchard. London: Cohen & West.

Mbembe, Achille. 1992. "The Banality of Power and the Aesthetics of Vulgarity in the Postcolony." *Public Culture* 4 (2): 1–30.

———. 2001. *On the Postcolony*. Berkeley: University of California Press.

———. 2002. "African Modes of Self Writing." *CODESRIA Bulletin* 2 (1–2).McIntosh, Janet. 2009. *The Edge of Islam: Power, Personhood, and Ethnoreligious Boundaries on the Kenya Coast*. Durham, N.C.: Duke University Press.

Meyer, Birgit. 1997. *Commodities and the Power of Prayer: Pentecostalist Attitudes towards Consumption in Contemporary Ghana*. [The Hague]: WOTRO.

———. 1998. "'Make a Complete Break with the Past': Memory and Post-Colonial Modernity in Ghanaian Pentecostalist Discourse." *Journal of Religion in Africa* 28 (3): 316–349.

Mol, Annemarie. 2002. *The Body Multiple: Ontology in Medical Practice*. Durham, N.C.: Duke University Press.

Morozov, Evgeny. *To Save Everything, Click Here*. New York: Public Affairs, 2013.

Mudimbe, V. Y. 1988. *The Invention of Africa: Gnosis, Philosophy, and the Order of Knowledge*. Bloomington: Indiana University Press.

———. 1994. *The Idea of Africa*. Bloomington: Indiana University Press; London: J. Currey.

Newell, Sasha. 2012. *The Modernity Bluff: Crime, Consumption, and Citizenship in Côte d'Ivoire*. Chicago: University of Chicago Press.

Ngugi wa Thiongo. 1986. *Decolonising the Mind: The Politics of Language in African Literature*. London: J. Currey; Portsmouth, N.H.: Heinemann.

Niehaus, Isak A., Eliazaar Mohlala, and Kally Shokane. 2001. *Witchcraft, Power, and Politics: Exploring the Occult in the South African Lowveld*. London: Pluto Press.

Piot, Charles. 1999. *Remotely Global: Village Modernity in West Africa*. Chicago: University of Chicago Press.

———. 2010. *Nostalgia for the Future: West Africa after the Cold War*. Chicago: University of Chicago Press.

Richards, Audrey. 1935. "A Modern Movement of Witch-finders." *Africa* 8: 448–461.

Ricoeur, Paul. 1992. *Oneself as Another*. Chicago: University of Chicago Press.

Roitman, Janet L. 2005. *Fiscal Disobedience: An Anthropology of Economic Regulation in Central Africa*. Princeton, N.J.: Princeton University Press.

Sahlins, Marshall David. 1988. "Cosmologies of Capitalism: The Trans-Pacific Sector of 'The World System.'" *Proceedings of the British Academy* 74: 1–51.

———. 2013. *What Kinship Is—and Is Not*. Chicago: University of Chicago Press.

Scott, James. 1999. *Seeing Like a State: How Certain Schemes to Improve the Human Condition Have Failed*. New Haven: Yale University Press.

Shipley, Jesse Weaver. 2013. *Living the Hiplife: Celebrity and Entrepreneurship in Ghanaian Popular Music*. Durham, N.C.: Duke University Press.

Shipton, Parker MacDonald. 2009. *Mortgaging the Ancestors: Ideologies of Attachment in Africa*. New Haven, Conn.: Yale University Press.

Shostak, Marjorie. 1990. *Nisa: The Life and Words of a !Kung Woman*. London: Earthscan.

Simmel, Georg. 1971. *On Individuality and Social Forms: Selected Writings*. Chicago: University of Chicago Press.

Smith, James H. 2001. "Of Spirit Possession and Structural Adjustment Programs: Government Downsizing, Education, and Their Enchantments in Neo-liberal Kenya." *Journal of Religion in Africa* 31 (4): 427–456.

———. 2006. "Snake-Driven Development: Culture, Nature, and Religious Conflict in Neoliberal Kenya." *Ethnography* 7 (4): 423–459.

———. 2008. *Bewitching Development: Witchcraft and the Reinvention of Development in Neoliberal Kenya*. Chicago: University of Chicago Press.

———. 2011. "Tantalus in the Digital Age: Coltan Ore, Temporal Dispossession, and 'Movement' in the Eastern Democratic Republic of the Congo." *American Ethnologist* 38 (1): 17–35.

Smith, James H., and Jeffrey W. Mantz. 2006. "Do Cellular Phones Dream of Civil War? The Mystification of Production and the Consequences of Technology Fetishism in the Eastern Congo." In *Inclusion and Exclusion in the Global Arena*, edited by Max H. Kirsch. New York: Routledge.

Spivak, Gayatri. 1988. "Can the Subaltern Speak?" In *Marxism and the Interpretation of Culture*, edited by Cary Nelson and Lawrence Grossberg. Urbana: University of Illinois Press.

Stoller, Paul. 2002. *Money Has No Smell: The Africanization of New York City*. Chicago: University of Chicago Press.

Stoller, Paul, and Cheryl Olkes. 1987. *In Sorcery's Shadow: A Memoir of Apprenticeship among the Songhay of Niger.* Chicago: University of Chicago Press.

Stroeken, Koen. 2005. "Immunizing Strategies: Hip-Hop and Critique in Tanzania." *Africa: Journal of the International African Institute* 75 (4): 488–509.

———. 2008. "Tanzania's 'New Generation': The Power and Tragedy of a Concept." In *Generations in Africa,* edited by Erdmute Alber, Sjaak van der Geest, and Susan R. Whyte. Berlin: LIT Verlag.

Taylor, Charles. 1989. *Sources of the Self: The Making of the Modern Identity.* Cambridge, Mass.: Harvard University Press.

Turner, Victor W. 1967. *The Forest of Symbols: Aspects of Ndembu Ritual.* Ithaca, N.Y.: Cornell University Press.

Wainaina, Binyavanga. 2011. *One Day I Will Write about This Place.* Minneapolis: Gray Wolf Press.

Weber, Max. 2001. *The Protestant Ethic and the Spirit of Capitalism.* Chicago, Ill.: Fitzroy Dearborn.

Weiss, Brad. 1992. "Plastic Teeth Extraction: The Iconography of Haya Gastro-Sexual Affliction." *American Ethnologist* 19: 538–552.

———. 2004. *Producing African Futures: Ritual and Reproduction in a Neoliberal Age.* Leiden: Brill.

———. 2009. *Street Dreams and Hip Hop Barbershops.* Bloomington: Indiana University Press.

Werbner, Richard P. 2002. *Postcolonial Subjectivities in Africa.* London: Zed Books.

West, Harry G. 2005. *Kupilikula: Governance and the Invisible Realm in Mozambique.* Chicago: University of Chicago Press.

———. 2007. *Ethnographic Sorcery.* Chicago: University of Chicago Press.

White, Hylton. 2012. "A Post-Fordist Ethnicity: Insecurity, Authority, and Identity in South Africa." *Anthropological Quarterly* 85 (2): 397–427.

Williams, Raymond. 1985. *Keywords: A Vocabulary of Culture and Society.* New York: Oxford University Press.